D0108727

WOMEN'S LIBERATION
AND THE SUBLIME

Studies in Feminist Philosophy is designed to showcase cutting-edge monographs and collections that display the full range of feminist approaches to philosophy, that push feminist thought in important new directions, and that display the outstanding quality of feminist philosophical thought.

Studies in Feminist Philosophy
Chesire Calhoun, Series Editor

Advisory Board

Harry Brod, Temple University
Claudia Card, University of Wisconsin
Lorraine Code, York University, Toronto
Kimberle Crenshaw, Columbia Law School/UCLA School of Law
Jan Flax, Howard University
Ann Garry, California State University, Los Angeles
Sally Haslanger, Massachusetts Institute of Technology
Alison Jagger, University of Colorado, Boulder
Helen Longino, University of Minnesota
Maria Lugones, SUNY Binghamton
Uma Narayan, Vassar College
James Sterba, University of Notre Dame
Rosemarie Tong, University of North Carolina, Charlotte
Nancy Tuana, Penn State University
Karen Warren, Macalester College
Iris Marion Young, University of Chicago

Published in the series:

Abortion and Social Responsibility: Depolarizing the Debate
Lauri Shrage

Gender in the Mirror: Confounding Imagery
Diana Tietjens Meyers

Autonomy, Gender, Politics
Marilyn Friedman

Setting the Moral Compass: Essays by Women Philosophers
Edited by Chesire Calhoun

Burdened Virtues: Virtue Ethics for Liberatory Struggles
Lisa Tessman

On Female Body Experience: "Throwing Like a Girl" and Other Essays
Iris Marion Young

Visible Identities: Race, Gender, and the Self
Linda Martín Alcoff

Women and Citizenship
Edited by Marilyn Friedman

Women's Liberation and the Sublime: Feminism, Postmodernism, Environment
Bonnie Mann

MGEN
MR 923

WOMEN'S LIBERATION
AND THE SUBLIME

Feminism, Postmodernism,
Environment

Bonnie Mann

BIBLIOTHÈQUES
uOttawa
LIBRARIES

OXFORD
UNIVERSITY PRESS

2006

6292424472

OXFORD
UNIVERSITY PRESS

Oxford University Press, Inc., publishes works that further
Oxford University's objective of excellence
in research, scholarship, and education.

Oxford New York
Auckland   Cape Town   Dar es Salaam   Hong Kong   Karachi
Kuala Lumpur   Madrid   Melbourne   Mexico City   Nairobi
New Delhi   Shanghai   Taipei   Toronto

With offices in
Argentina   Austria   Brazil   Chile   Czech Republic   France   Greece
Guatemala   Hungary   Italy   Japan   Poland   Portugal   Singapore
South Korea   Switzerland   Thailand   Turkey   Ukraine   Vietnam

Copyright © 2006 by Oxford University Press, Inc.

Published by Oxford University Press, Inc.
198 Madison Avenue, New York, New York 10016

www.oup.com

Oxford is a registered trademark of Oxford University Press.

All rights reserved. No part of this publication may be reproduced,
stored in a retrieval system, or transmitted, in any form or by any means,
electronic, mechanical, photocopying, recording, or otherwise,
without prior permission of Oxford University Press.

Library of Congress Cataloging-in-Publication Data
Mann, Bonnie.
Women's liberation and the sublime: feminism, postmodernism, environment/Bonnie Mann.
p. cm.—(Studies in feminist philosophy)
Includes bibliographical references and index.
ISBN-13 978-0-19-518745-8; 978-0-19-518746-5 (pbk.)
ISBN 0-19-518745-8; 0-19-518746-6 (pbk.)
1. Feminist theory.   2. Feminism.   3. Postmodernism.   I. Title.   II. Series.
HQ1190.M34   2006
305.4201—dc22   2006040038

HQ
1190
.M34
2006

1 3 5 7 9 8 6 4 2
Printed in the United States of America
on acid-free paper

To my mother, Donna,

and my father, Arel,

both of whom died too soon.

Preface

Modern men were not thrown back upon the world
but upon themselves. One of the most persistent trends of
modern philosophy since Descartes . . . has been an exclusive
concern with the self, as distinguished from the soul or
person or man in general, an attempt to reduce all
experiences with the world as well as with other human
beings to experiences between man and himself.

—Hannah Arendt

Postmodern hyperspace . . . has finally succeeded in
transcending the capacities of the individual human body to
locate itself, to organize its immediate surroundings
perceptually, and cognitively to map its position in a
mappable external world. It may now be suggested that this
alarming disjunction point between the body and its built
environment . . . can itself stand as the symbol and analogon
of that even sharper dilemma which is the incapacity of our
minds, at least at present, to map the great global
multinational and decentered communicational network in
which we find ourselves caught as individual subjects.

—Fredric Jameson

If the modern predicament stems in large part from
the egocentrism that underlies humanocentrism—often
disguised in the unquestioned meliorism of a technological
existence—the form of a possible solution may well be
ecocentric in character.

—Edward S. Casey

If I were to try to say in a word what motivates me to write a feminist book on the
sublime, I would have to say it's a certain kind of terror. This is not the kind of terror

that is generally associated with that noble aesthetic notion, however. It's a more pedestrian emotion: the mundane, daily fear that grips a woman dependent on her planet for survival, yet unable to stop either her own or anyone else's participation in its destruction. We are, as a species, in the midst of a suicide that neither feminists nor the broader global environmental movements seem able to stop. And when I say "as a species" I ought to note of course that it is those who control the power and the resources who "act"—while the rest of us are condemned, it seems, to "act with" them. In what we call the developed world our lives are structured into such action, our food encased in plastic, our daily routines requiring automobiles, our most human needs, such as bathing and defecating, connected to earth-defiling technologies. Certainly any intelligent extraterrestrial looking in on earth would have to conclude that the humans have lost their minds. Those humans here who belong to cultures where dependence on the earth is a recognized and sacred fact of human existence have long since come to the same conclusion about the rest of us. And those of us who are environmentalists in globally dominant countries have come to that conclusion about the folks who control infinitely more money and power globally than we do. Feminists have noted that those people are almost exclusively men.

In 1958, Hannah Arendt wrote already of "the advent of a new and yet unknown age," marked by an experience she called "world-alienation," characterized by a "twofold flight from the earth into the universe and from the world into the self" (Arendt 1958, 6). Now, the unknown age has a name. Postmodernity is the kind of time and space that we live in, structured by a vast disarray of material and social circumstances, extremes of impoverishment and wealth that defy comprehension, environmental destruction that threatens all of us (but not equally), and the instantaneous networks of communication that are the taken-for-granted backdrop to some lives, while others die of malnutrition and dirty water. In this age, the outer reaches of the universe and the tiniest components of the human genome become increasingly accessible to those who control the machines and the science, while the immediate environment that sustains all of us both socially and physically becomes alien and threatening.

In the centers of global power we are faced with "a growing aestheticization of everyday life in the mass dissemination of signs and images" (Felski 2000, 195). This aestheticization seems to push certain university professors and other intellectuals to take Arendt's twofold flight one step further than she foresaw: both the universe and the self are folded into discourse. World-alienation has taken the form of the self-enclosed universe of the text. Having lost our belief in the referentiality of language, we sacrifice our faith in any relation between words and things. We find ourselves in a world of signs that refer only to other signs, which is our particular predicament and challenge. Now more than ever, thinking our relationship to other persons and to the earth is a matter of survival. Yet, philosophers in the globally dominant United States, feminist philosophers included, seem less capable of thinking these relationships than ever. Anything we might say about the earth or other persons is, we've discovered, already in language. To speak of an "earth" or "nature" that exceeds discourse is to find oneself locked, even so, within discourse. Since the earth, like everything else, has turned into a text, when we try to think our relationship to it, we end up merely rethinking our relationship to ourselves.

Our very real physical and phenomenological experience of world-alienation finds here its theoretical form. We give in to placelessness. As Edward S. Casey writes:

> To say "I have no place to go" is to admit to a desperate circumstance. Yet we witness daily the disturbing spectacle of people with no place to go: refugees from natural catastrophes or strife-torn countries, the homeless on the streets of modern cities, not to mention "stray" animals. In fearing that "the earth is becoming uninhabitable"—a virtual universal lament—we are fearing that the earth will no longer provide adequate places in which to live. The incessant motion of postmodern life in late-capitalist societies at once echoes and exacerbates this fear. (Casey 1993, xiii)

Intellectually, we also find ourselves in desperate circumstances, trapped as we are inside a language that can refer only to itself. Our self-enclosed discursive universe becomes a kind of no place, a world-alienated space without place, and thinking is set adrift from the physical places and intersubjective relationships that give thinkers their moment-by-moment sustenance.

Yet the terror that accompanies our desperation is paired with a kind of frenetic exhilaration and celebrated in the contemporary notion of the "sublime." Sublime experience names precisely that melting away of the real (in both its social and natural forms) that so marks our displacement into the magical world of the text. It takes the place of the old "goods" philosophers pursued and was, beginning in the late 1980s, imported into some versions of feminist theory as a new "ought," in service to which the feminist political project tended to be displaced. I felt compelled to write a book on the notion of the sublime, not because it has been systematically taken up as an explicit rallying point by feminist thinkers of what is somewhat problematically called the postmodern tradition; it hasn't. It is, however, the aesthetic experience of terror/exhilaration that emerges unnamed in important theoretical texts to provide the silent justification for doing away with practically everything else. And it is, I think, a way of naming and describing what it feels like to live dependent on a world we are in the process of destroying; the terror comes from the destruction, and the exhilaration from our power to destroy.

I will argue that the experience of the sublime can and does take different forms, but in its dominant contemporary expression, the sublime is an extreme kind of compensatory experience. In our celebration of it, we too often capitulate to a twofold incapacity to articulate our relationship to the world we inhabit. In the realm of *the political*, we are set adrift from the very structural conditions of our daily lives, unable to comprehend or name the vast global networks of technologies, powers, and players that have changed how we live down to our most intimate experiences of space, time, and meaning; and that link us to other persons and places in egregious ways. In the realm of *necessity*, we are set adrift from the earth itself and become so profoundly forgetful of our moment-by-moment dependence on the planet for sustenance, for breath, water, and food; we actually believe ourselves to be produced by texts. Our sojourn in the world of signs is so paradigmatic of "the postmodern condition," that asking the question of our relationship to other persons across the globe or to the physical planet we inhabit seems naive and nostalgic.

Yet these are precisely the questions that a feminist account of sublime experience will foreground. There are modes of the sublime, I will argue, that emerge in contemporary life and that powerfully expose our relations to other persons and to the natural world. These experiences disrupt masculinist fantasies of independent, sovereign subjects in control of themselves, other people, and the planet. They disrupt the equally masculinist fantasies of subjects produced in a world of signs. They throw us into relation with one another and with the places that we live, and not only that, they *orient us* in the context of those relations. In other words, unlike the modes of the sublime that are implicitly celebrated in key feminist postmodernist texts, these are aesthetic experiences that have a normative force (which is different from claiming that they provide clear-cut prescriptions for action). It is time that feminists take back the experience of the sublime.

If feminists need the experience of the sublime now, it is because the conditions of postmodern life have made a profound disorientation in our relations to others and to the natural world the common experience of everyday life, at least in dominant countries. Fredric Jameson describes our displacement in relation to others when he argues that under the conditions of what we now call globalization, there is a disjunct between phenomenological experience and material conditions. We experience "a growing contradiction between lived experience and structure, or between a phenomenological description of the life of an individual and a more properly structural model of the conditions of existence of that experience" (Jameson 1991, 410). The gap between our experience and its structural truth is a key feature of postmodern life.

> The phenomenological experience of the individual subject . . . becomes limited to a tiny corner of the social world, a fixed camera view of a certain section of London or the countryside or whatever. But the truth of that experience no longer coincides with the place in which it takes place. The truth of that limited daily experience of London lies, rather in India or Jamaica or Hong Kong; it is bound up with the whole colonial system of the British Empire that determines the very quality of the individual's subjective life. Yet those structural coordinates are no longer accessible to immediate lived experience and are often not even conceptualizable for most people. (Jameson 1991, 411)

We are caught in a world where the real workings of systems that are part of our everyday lives, such as this computer I type on now with its Internet capacity and near instant responses to my commands, are experienced as hopelessly incomprehensible by most of us. Of course ultimately, the "structural coordinates" of our experience worry us only because they determine in large part the place occupied by other persons in the systems of relations that make up the truth of our daily lives. It disturbs us that our daily experience is cut off from the structural truths that link us to others because when the phenomenological experience of a person is so constrained, then the world that person is open to will be constrained as well. It will be a "my world" in which others are functionalized, in which some worker, somewhere, made this computer for me, and thus is "present" to me in the form of an invisible functioning, though she has no life or presence in my world as a person.

This kind of fragmentation, or in Jameson's more (updated) Marxist terms, "reification," serves a capitalist world order where it is important to create an insurmountable distance between consumers and the process of production responsible for creating their object world. The "indispensable precondition" for a culture of consumerism is precisely the "effacement of the traces of production" from the commodity.

> Indeed, the point of having your own object world and walls and muffled distance or relative silence all around you, is to forget about all those innumerable others for a while; you don't want to have to think about Third World women every time you pull yourself up to your word processor, or all the other lower-class people with their lower-class lives when you decide to use or consume your other luxury products; it would be like having voices inside your head. (Jameson 1991, 315)

Our forgetfulness of these "others" is structured into the very pace and complexity of postmodern life.

And this forgetfulness is built upon another, symptomatized by our inability to think the earth itself as "the quintessence of the human condition" (Arendt 1958, 2). We live more or less blithely in a suicide/homicide of the species (our own and others), entertained by escape fantasies. As space scientists seriously discuss "terraforming" other planets to make them inhabitable for humans, our own planet is rendered uninhabitable. Such escape fantasies have been one of the defining characteristics of the age of science, as Arendt points out, an age that inaugurated and secularized at its inception the modernist belief that the earth is our prison. Our dependence on the earth was taken to be a kind of curse that could be broken through scientific discovery and technological innovation. Or alternately, it was a kind of developmental stage that the human race was just on the verge of outgrowing. The exhilaration that accompanied the belief in this impending emancipation was only occasionally challenged by the rather understated fear that we would destroy the earth long before we managed to outgrow our dependence on it.

Postmodernity is characterized by the co-existence of this essentially modernist good cheer with a more realistic shrug-your-shoulders nihilism expressed in the often stated belief that since the environment will be destroyed in any case, and no one can stop it, we might as well enjoy the process. If this is a terrifying thought, it is exhilarating as well, a bit like bungee jumping or skydiving.

What we turn away from in both cases is the good sense "to think what we are doing" (Arendt 1958, 5). And though the fantasy of utter emancipation from the earth now seems rather less likely to come true than it did in the wave of scientific optimism that accompanied Arendt's writing in 1958—the Mir space station plummeted into the sea instead of providing the first tourist accommodations in space after all—we seem no more capable of thinking the important political and philosophical questions at the turn of the century than others did nearly fifty years ago. To think these questions, we would need what Arendt called "common sense," that sixth sense that fits our five senses into a common world. In the current environmental crisis, Arendt's insistence on the recognition of a world held in common with others takes on a literalness and an urgency she could not have predicted fifty years ago, even while it seems naively idealistic.

At the same time, we are not surprised that humans have learned to do almost everything. In fact, our common sense seems to be lost to us in direct proportion to the extension of our faith in the technical capacities that augment our own. Now, "we are actually doing what all ages before ours thought to be the exclusive prerogative of divine action" (Arendt 1958, 269). Arendt notes that it is a limited kind of knowledge, or "know-how," that drives these developments. "It could be that we, who are earth-bound creatures and have begun to act as though we were dwellers of the universe, will forever be unable to understand, that is, to think and speak about the things which we are nevertheless able to do," she writes. Know-how and thought have "parted company," leaving us "the helpless slaves, not so much of our machines as of our know-how, thoughtless creatures at the mercy of every gadget which is technically possible, no matter how murderous it is" (1958, 3). We know how to do, without knowing how to stop doing, even if our doing is killing us. Of course, to be accurate we must admit that most of us no more pretend to comprehend the science that can splice the genes of a jellyfish into a moth or send electronic messages around the globe in an instant than we do the mind of god but living with these technologies gives rise to a strange faith. We don't pretend to understand how it is that everything from the proteins of human DNA to a meteor billions of miles away can now be reached by human-made machines. Yet we do have enormous confidence that as "the real" that resists human intervention gives way, "the real" made by human intervention takes its place. In my view the relationship we construct and reconstruct to the natural world in these practices cuts across and thus unites what we distinguish as "modern" and "postmodern" sensibilities.

The melting away of a real that exceeds human making is characteristic of sublime experience in both its modern and postmodern expressions. While the modern posture was to be at least somewhat troubled by our apparent lack of access to the real, in postmodernity we tend to flee into an exuberant affirmation of the irreality of any real that exceeds our creations. Jameson suggests that the sublime experience of the melting away of the real, which predominates in globally dominant countries, is descriptively captured in postmodern philosophies, "where to call for the shedding of any illusion about psychic identity or the centered subject, for the ethical ideal of good molecular 'schizophrenic' living, and for the ruthless abandonment of the mirage of presence may turn out to be a description of the way we live now rather than its rebuke or subversion" (1991, 339). His suggestion that we read our postmodern convictions as descriptive of how we live, rather than as a revolutionary break from the status quo, is remarkably simple, yet evocative. Indeed, it seems to me that in our urgency to explain how the hegemonic West got it all wrong by mistaking its own experiences for universal ontological truths, we tend to unwittingly affirm the habit, continuing to read the subjective experiences of certain folks in certain places as ontological conditions of the world itself. This may seem to be a strange claim in an age when we are taught to read everything as a product of social or textual construction. Yet we mistake our incomprehension in the face of the real that exceeds the text, our incapacity in regard to this excess, for the actual ontological status of anything that surpasses or resists human making. We see a lack of reality as the one remaining real, even essential, property of the real itself. The Kantian claim that we can't know the "thing in itself" is here reversed so that we do indeed know all there is to know about the thing-in-itself; we know that it masks its lack of being in appearances, behind the appearances is an abyss of absence.

Jameson calls for "cognitive mapping," a process of mapping our phenome-nological experience onto the structural realities of a postmodern world. His suggestion affirms the need for both a phenomenology of experience and an ac-count of the material conditions of that experience. This is one important feature of a still-emerging tradition of critical engagement with postmodern theory (Jameson 1991; Eagleton 1996; Harvey 1990). I share a central belief with this emergent tradition: that postmodernism has material conditions. Such notions as "textuality" and "difference" are interpreted in part as "symptoms" (or simply phenomenological descriptions) of experience under conditions of extreme reifi-cation. In other words, "postmodernists" are not wrong; we really do experience ourselves as set adrift in the sign-world of the text or caught up in an endless play of difference, but these experiences themselves are symptomatic of the material conditions that they seem to deny.

These convictions locate this project in the space between phenomenological and materialist philosophies of contemporary life. I necessarily move between these two kinds of description because I understand our phenomenological ex-perience to be situated, neither reducible to nor extractable from the material conditions that shape our daily lives—even though it is most certainly alienated from these conditions—that is, material conditions are as often hidden within as simply expressed in our lived experience.

It often takes a good deal of work to even begin to understand these con-nections. If, for example, postmodern theory is what the double world-alienation we live in looks like in language, then the sense that such theory gives to our lives will not often be on the surface, available for a simple reading. In the realm of the political, we will have to insist on an "outside" to discourse that relocates discourse "inside" a historical time period and its social and political materialities. In the realm of necessity, the task will be to map phenomenological experience onto the reality of our relation to the earth. Our forgetfulness of these relations is extreme and has been deeply sedimented into the ways that we think. Just as our relations to other persons globally structure the daily object worlds we inhabit, our relation to the earth sustains us moment by moment. Yet most of us could not say, on any given day, what forces have altered the air that we are breathing, how our water has been treated and what chemicals it contains, or what happens, even, to the contents of our toilets when we flush them.

That this dual displacement, in the realm of politics and in the realm of necessity, should also find its expression in feminist theory should come as no surprise. Feminists live in postmodern time and inhabit the world we have built no less than other thinkers. In feminist postmodernism, our displacement in the realm of the political is expressed in our *forgetfulness of women*. Our displacement in the realm of necessity is expressed in our *forgetfulness of nature*. As we will see in some detail later, a concern with the deconstruction of metanarratives replaces our concern for women, and the melting away of "women's nature" acts in part as a repressed expression of the melting away of any nature whatsoever. In both cases, we exchange our implacement in the political and natural worlds both through sublime experience and for sublime experience.

This is to say that the feminist alliance with "postmodernism" has given feminist thinkers important ways to talk about the very real experiences that characterize postmodern life, but this talk has often been uncritical. This is a bold claim: what is more critical, after all, than the postmodern drive to deconstruct and disrupt? My point is that, disconnected from concrete projects of social struggle, their relation to the material conditions of postmodernity insufficiently understood, these critical exercises have tended to remain mere technical enterprises. This is to say we have tended to fetishize our technical capacities to deconstruct and disrupt, without sufficient attention to the connection between these experiences and the conditions of postmodern life. Our thinking has consequently become too often alienated from the liberatory projects that are the very heart of feminism.

Because the very conditions of postmodern life are deeply aestheticized, I find that turning our attention to the notion of the sublime can provide some insight into key paradoxes of feminist thinking about epistemology and politics. If the sublime bears a heavily gendered heritage, if it is an experience that negatively characterizes postmodern life and finds uncritical expression in "postmodern" texts, this is not to say that feminists must read it as a monodimensional and unequivocally bad aesthetic category. Instead, a committed feminist engagement with the sublime can help us work our way out of some of the places that feminism (which must always name both a social movement and the intellectual tradition motivated by and connected to it) has been stuck. Not only this, we can reclaim certain experiences of the sublime in the process.

Acknowledgments

Eva Feder Kittay's grace, unfailing goodwill, and support beyond all earthly expectations both returned me to graduate school after a long absence and has seen me through years of writing with exquisite care. Ed Casey took measures beyond what one could either expect or ever explain to encourage this work, including a good number of hours of critical discussion at a café in Berkeley. My thanks to Geraldine Moane, Lorenzo Simpson, Irene Klaver, Kathy Miriam, and Naomi Zack, all of whom read and commented on earlier versions of this manuscript, in whole or in part; and to Beata Stawarska, whose presence to me and my work, both as a colleague and a friend, has been not only fantastically useful but also great fun. All of my colleagues at the University of Oregon have been both a delight to work with and enthusiastic supporters during the revision process. My thanks to the two anonymous reviewers who read an earlier version of the manuscript for Oxford University Press, and whose suggestions have been extremely helpful in the revision process, and to Amy Story for help in formatting the manuscript.

My thanks to Erin, who supported me financially without complaint during the first years of research, who has put up with the piles of books and papers and dirty dishes that appear in odd places whenever I am engaged intensively in writing, and, most important, who has been a source of deep joy in my life. In addition, my thanks to Angel, for her dazzling mind; to Carla, for her extraordinary beauty; to Dee Dee, for her breathtaking wit; to Lizzie, for her remarkable power.

My thanks to Indiana University Press for permission to reprint most of "World Alienation in Feminist Thought: The Sublime Epistemology of Emphatic Anti-Essentialism," which appeared in *Ethics and the Environment* in Winter of 2005; much of the material from this article reappears here in the preface and introduction. My thanks to Rowman and Littlefield for permission to reprint the bulk of two book chapters they had previously published: "Talking Back to Feminist Postmodernism: Toward a New Radical Feminist Interpretation of the Body," which appeared in *Recognition, Responsibility and Rights*, edited by by Robin Fiore and Hilde Lindemann Nelson in 2003; a revised version is included here as chapter 6. "Dependency on Place, Dependency in Place" appeared in *The Subject of Care: Feminist Perspectives on Dependency*, edited by Eva Feder Kittay and Ellen Feder in 2002; a revised version is included here as chapter 7.

Contents

Abbreviations

Works by Judith Butler
ES	*Excitable Speech*
BTM	*Bodies That Matter: On the Discursive Limits of "Sex"*
PL	*Precarious Life: The Powers of Mourning and Violence*
PLP	*The Psychic Life of Power*

All shorter works by Judith Butler and all coauthored works are cited according to the author-date system.

Works by Immanuel Kant
A	*Anthropology from a Pragmatic Point of View*
CJ	*Critique of Judgement*
CPR	*Critique of Pure Reason*
MAR	"Metaphysische Anfangsgründe der Rechtslehre" (the first part of *Metaphysik der Sitten*)
OFBS	*Observations on the Feeling of the Beautiful and Sublime*

Works by Jean-Francois Lyotard
D	*The Differend: Phrases in Dispute*
IE	"Das Interesse des Erhabene"
LAS	*Lessons on the Analytic of the Sublime: Kant's Critique of Judgement*
LR	*The Lyotard Reader*
PC	*The Postmodern Condition: A Report on Knowledge*

Works by Maurice Merleau-Ponty
PhP	*The Phenomenology of Perception*
V/I	*The Visible and the Invisible*

WOMEN'S LIBERATION
AND THE SUBLIME

Introduction

The Linguistic Turn

Sometime in the mid-1980s, feminist thinking in the United States, influenced in part by certain developments in France, gave up its naiveté about language and reality. The linguistic turn came to U.S. American feminism in the midst of the devastating pornography debates. For many thinkers, Lacanian psychoanalysis, Foucauldian genealogy, and Derridean deconstruction offered ways of rethinking the relation between words and things, which was at the very heart of the conflict. These various approaches were lumped together in the United States under the category of "postmodernism," a move that, while extremely annoying to intellectuals from the continent who were scandalized by the sloppiness of such broad strokes, served as convenient shorthand for ways of responding to contemporary controversies that promised something new.[1]

Feminism and Postmodernism: Legend of a Second Marriage

In 1979, Heidi Hartmann wrote "The Unhappy Marriage of Marxism and Feminism: Towards a More Progressive Union" amidst a flurry of publications about what was, by most feminist accounts, an extremely unsatisfactory "union" (Patcheski 1979; Sargent 1981; Weinbaum 1978). The central complaint Hartmann raised was that, "the 'marriage' of marxism and feminism has been like the marriage of

---

1. My own use of the term "postmodern" is, of course, just as controversial. What justifies my own "lumping together" (to use Butler's phrase) of many different kinds of theory under the name "postmodern"? I defend my usage of the term in close dialogue with Butler's contestation of it in chapter 4. For now, the reader might think of the term as naming a kind of fiction, i.e., that mysterious amalgam of theories that we have come to call, in the American context, "postmodern." When I say "postmodern," at least in the current context, I mean that body of thought that has contributed to, or been deployed in the service of, what we might better name the "linguistic turn" in feminist philosophy that occurred in the U.S. context in the mid to late 1980s.

3

husband and wife depicted in English common law: marxism and feminism are one, and that one is marxism" (Hartmann 1979, 424). Indeed, if we were to tell what ensued more in the form of a legend than an "objective" history, we would have to say that this outpouring of dissatisfaction, however hopeful initially for reconciliation, eventually ended in a nasty divorce.

It was at just about this time that contemporary "French philosophy" was undergoing reinvention in America as "postmodernism." Much of U.S. academic feminism became enamored of this new love,[2] and took on, as all passionate lovers do in such relationships, an intense and misguided loyalty. Postmodernism was an outlaw, bad-boy boyfriend with an overgrown adolescent's disregard for conventions and limits, next to whom old man Marx seemed stodgy. This new boyfriend elevated the faculty of desire over that of reason.[3] At a time when reason had been discredited and rational discourse in the form of scientific "knowledge," had been shown to be capable of such untruths, desire seemed to be the more honest human faculty.[4] He promised the triumph of honest desire over manipulative rationality—celebrated the new "truth" of the postmodern worldview, where there is no rational universe to know. Even better, passionate as he was about testing the limits of the real, he could transmute at will into a gay man, or a woman, or even a lesbian, making things more interesting. This finally seemed to clear a space in academia for a lot of folks who hadn't felt welcome. And best of all, this new lover was not often unemployed. Association with him granted not only notoriety as a bad girl and a law breaker but also immanently respectable career opportunities in those institutions that were open to progressive perspectives.[5] The feminism that allied itself with postmodernism went from an unhappy marriage, one marked by a

2. The flurry of publications that established this new relationship took, in its early years, the form of disavowals of the "essentialism" of "cultural feminism" (a new, politically charged term for radical feminism), followed by an articulation of the superior intellectual framework of some progenitor or proponent of postmodern theory. As Teresa de Lauretis wrote at around that time, "Anglo American (feminists) seem for the most part to be engaged in typologizing, defining, and branding various 'feminisms' along an ascending scale of theoretico-political sophistication where 'essentialism' weighs heavy at the lower end" (1994, 2). Some early examples include Alice Echols's 1983 piece in *Powers of Desire: The Politics of Sexuality* entitled "The New Feminism of Yin and Yang" and 1984 article in *Pleasure and Danger: Exploring Female Sexuality* entitled "The Taming of the Id: Feminist Sexual Politics"; and Chris Weedon's 1987 book *Feminist Practice and Poststructuralist Theory*.

3. Or as the editors of *Radically Speaking*, Diane Bell and Renate Klein, put it, "Postmodernism has created a climate in which the rationalist project is being abandoned. Just as women were poised to become part of the world of reason, we have been thrown back onto the troubled world of desire" (1996, xx). Kristin Waters's critique is equally blistering: "Women and persons of color have long been characterized as creatures impelled by animal urges and lacking in rational capacity. For those denied both the attribution of reason and access to the means of developing and reshaping it, the usual realm of their long time ghetto, in this case 'desire,' is repackaged to appear as an appealing goal" (1996, 291).

4. Deleuze and Guatarri's *Anti-Oedipus* in 1972 and Lyotard's *Libidinal Economy* in 1974 were key texts in the elevation of the faculty of desire over the discredited faculty of rationality. For many U.S. feminists based in the academy, instrumental reason has long been a focal point of criticism, and the new "honesty" about the role of desire seemed welcome.

5. The connection between loyalty to postmodernism and academic acceptance has been made by others (Bordo 1993; Schor and Weed 1994; Christian 1996).

constant outpouring of discontent, to a relationship in which effusive devotion was the new tone. In many institutions, feminism began to exchange its barely emergent autonomous base in the academy in favor of this new loyalty.[6] This loyalty was again, as some feminists of color noticed, to a distinctively white, European, and masculine tradition.

It was not only feminism that was assimilated by the new theory. While declaring the end of Marx's grand narratives, postmodernism claimed for itself in one grand gesture the liberation projects of all the marginalized people of the planet. The categories of "difference" or "multiplicity," evoked against the grain of modernism's false universals, themselves became new universalizing terms. Practically anyone who had had anything meaningful to say about anything in the last thirty years became postmodern overnight, many quite against their wills. This new white, European, masculine tradition made it possible to rewrite all those liberation projects, feminism included, on new terms. The most salient and distinctive mark of this rewriting was the transporting of old contradictions out of Marx's messy material universe and into the magic world of the sign.

It was discovered that everything is fiction. Which is true. It was feminism dating back to Beauvoir that taught that women are made not born, meaning of course that men are too. It was antiracist theorists and activists who taught that "white people" are more like something someone made up than a necessary biological thing. But it was an encounter with postmodernism that led many academic feminists to accept the new conceit that such systems of signs have no referents, that is, not only do these things not correspond to something "real" in the sense of enduring and essential and biological, they don't correspond to anything real at all. This includes now real patterns of social, economic, and political power.

What we might learn from this "legend of a second marriage" is that feminism has been, continues to be in some ways, and can be an autonomous political and intellectual movement. While rooted in and drawing on other dominant traditions, feminists need not develop loyalties to these traditions that supersede our commitments to feminist practice. But in the 1980s, what Somer Brodribb called the "Adam's rib approach," the perspective that saw feminism as a part of postmodernism, became widespread (Brodribb 1992, xxv). Craig Owens's essay entitled "The Discourse of Others: Feminists and Postmodernism" was an early and stunning example.

> The absence of discussion of sexual difference in writings about postmodernism, as well as the fact that few women have engaged in the modernism/postmodernism debate, suggests that postmodernism may be another masculine invention engineered to exclude women. I would like to propose, however, that women's insistence on difference and incommensurability may not only be compatible with, but also an instance of postmodern thought. (Owens 1983, 61–62)

---

6. A concern for the lost autonomy/identity of feminism is central to feminist criticism of the feminist/postmodernist alliance; see Brodribb 1992; Benhabib 1995; Bell and Klein 1996; Ahmed 1998; and Daly 1998.

Brodribb's fear was that the annexation of feminism as an instance of post-modernism would erode the specificity of feminist theory and practice. An outpouring of just this concern can be traced among thinkers from a number of traditions. Critical theorist Seyla Benhabib, for example, argued that "The post-modernist position(s) thought through to their conclusions may eliminate not only the specificity of feminist theory but place in question the very emancipatory ideals of the women's movement altogether" (Benhabib 1995, 20). Radical feminist metaphysician Mary Daly recounted how "a light bulb switched on in my head when I read a text by a 'postmodern feminist theorist' expressing her fear of the 'conceptual sloppiness' that she perceived in Feminist thinking. She contrasted this with the 'intellectual rigor' she believed could be found in male-authored postmodern theory. Aha! Those old patriarchally embedded feelings of women's intellectual inferiority were at work" (Daly 1998, 138). Marxist feminist Teresa Ebert worried that "not only has postmodernism—at least in its dominant ludic forms—erased the issues of labor and production, it has called into question the concepts grounding feminism: from identity, difference, and the category of woman/women to the very nature of politics and the real" (Ebert 1996, 129). And culture critic Teresa de Lauretis cautioned, "feminist theory is not of a lower grade than that which some call 'male theory,' but different in kind" (de Lauretis 1994, 11).

In spite of these diverse interventions, the alliance between feminism and postmodernism in the U.S. American academy birthed a new, and powerfully influential, form of feminist epistemology. The early feminist practice of sorting through and unmasking appearances to get to the real underneath was discredited as "essentialist."[7] Feminist standpoint epistemology was one attempt to respond to this accusation by using social location as a "standpoint" from which at least local and situated knowledge could be articulated.[8] But even this and other social constructionist approaches were eventually criticized in some postmodern accounts as essentialist.[9] The reigning epistemology in feminist postmodernism came to be that of the simulacrum. Here "the real" played a part only as that which

7. Mary Daly's classic formulation of feminist epistemology as a journey from the foreground world of deceptive patriarchal appearances to the background realm of "Wild Reality," first appeared in print in 1978. Another formulation was published in 1989 with MacKinnon's treatise on the practice of feminist consciousness raising; here "Consciousness raising is a face-to-face social experience that strikes at the fabric of meaning of social relations between and among women and men by calling their givenness into question and reconstituting their meaning in a transformed and critical way" (1989, 95). Though very different in starting points and assumptions, both of these accounts involve a sorting through of the givenness of patriarchal relations and the emergence of another (deeper) meaning.

8. For a good account of the history of and debates about feminist standpoint epistemology see *Feminist Epistemologies*, edited by Linda Alcoff and Elizabeth Potter, especially "Rethinking Standpoint Epistemology: What Is Strong Objectivity?" by Sandra Harding and "Marginality and Epistemic Privilege," by Bat-Ami Bar On.

9. Cressida Heyes argues in her book, *Line Drawings*, that feminist anti-essentialism is today focused on essentialist moments within social constructionist arguments (2000). More on this below.

dissolved into the appearances themselves. Behind the appearances, if there had been such a place, would have been sheer absence.[10]

As these developments were taking place in the academy, I was moving back and forth between graduate school in philosophy and years of direct service work in the battered women's movement. As the category of experience collapsed in theory and we discovered that the temporal relation between language and identity, politics, and morality had been misunderstood (we naively believed language to be an expression of these, emerging after them in time, rather than the ground of their very constitution), I took crisis line calls from women who, it seemed, needed to be convinced that their experience was real and could be expressed or obscured, but never simply constituted, in language. Yet the new theories were compelling in their capacity to unsettle categories of experience and thought that militated against a feminist response to domestic violence as well.

These developments in feminist epistemology sparked my interest in the aesthetic category of the sublime. I became fascinated, as did so many of my generation, with the work of Judith Butler in particular. Butler is a crucial figure in the developments I am describing, not because she is clearly and simply representative of them, but because her work is, in my view, the best and most important work in what is problematically classed as "feminist postmodernism" in the U.S. context. Her thinking has had an impact nationally and internationally that is unparalleled for a U.S. American feminist working out of the continental tradition. She is one of the few feminist intellectuals whose work has spilled out of philosophy and literary criticism into other disciplines, and indeed out of the academy and into queer politics. Though she herself disavows any connection to what we call "postmodernism," it is her work that is most universally associated with the term, not only in the U.S. feminist context but much more broadly as well, partly because she has produced an enormous body of work that addresses many of the most difficult and important questions in feminist thinking. Her recent work, I will argue, departs significantly from some of the most important commitments of her early work, and in a direction that disrupts the very experience of the sublime that the early work implicitly celebrated and produced. This work provides footing for a different feminist account of the sublime, one that discloses rather than severs relations (see chapter 7).

Though the aesthetic category of the sublime is not a theme that Butler explicitly takes up, the sublime is at work in her early writings. These texts turn on the abyss of absence at the heart of the real, though there are important moments of ambiguity that can be read in other directions. Her critiques of Lacan and Žižek, for

10. Soja's brief rendition of Baudrillard's "4 epistemes" is useful here. The first, where appearances mirror reality, gives way to the second, where appearances are thought to be deceptive and must be sorted through to get to the real underneath (this is the "counter-epistemology" of critical theory and practice according to Soja, and this was early second-wave feminist epistemology as well). "Baudrillard's third phase, wherein the image masks the growing absence of a basic reality as a prime referential, can be interpreted as the inaugural moment of contemporary postmodernity and the first step toward the denouement of his fourth phase, when all images become their own pure simulacra, bearing no relation to any reality whatsoever" (Soja 1989, 120).

example, involve the deconstruction of their notions of "lack" to uncover the pre-discursively fixed real (the threat of castration) that is smuggled in under the sign of absence. Butler excavates an even deeper abyss at the heart of "the rock of the real" (*BTM* 1993, 187–222). I found Butler's technical capacity to deconstruct and disrupt to be both exciting and frightening in its completeness, and I found as well that these deconstructions and disruptions created their own kind of experience. This was an aestheticized experience that was embraced by many as the new purpose for feminist thinking (see chapter 4). When I ask what it was that was aestheticized in certain texts, it seemed to be the dual displacement I discussed in the preface. Arendt's double world-alienation is mimetically replayed through the deconstructive excesses of the text. The terror and exhilaration that ensue mark these experiences as sublime. It seemed to me that in many passages the sublime experience of world-alienation was taking the place of the old project of women's liberation.

"Women's Liberation" is, in fact, too nostalgic and naive a term to be mentioned without a good deal of embarrassment, but I have chosen to use it anyway. I find that it grates significantly enough against the grain of contemporary feminist linguistic conventions to be annoying, and my hope is that it will itself serve the purpose of disruption. This term is called for, as well, because there is a promise of a particularly postmodern freedom—that achieved through sublime experience—which serves to displace/replace the old notions of changes in social, political, and economic structure that would have defined "liberation" as formerly understood. When I use the term "Women's Liberation" I mean it to recuperate the liberatory impulse of feminist thinking, but not through a simple return to earlier times. My sense is that a revitalization of feminist liberatory practice may be enabled by our engagement with the very work that has most undermined our sense of a clear feminist project.

It is my position that feminism and feminists went through a period of "disciplining" in which postmodern feminist theory played an important part, one that is still with us to a significant degree.[11] We were disciplined into a particular kind of thinking, and at the same time, whole areas of inquiry were disciplined out of "good feminist scholarship." The shutting out was something that happened actively and often took the form of an unexamined suspicion that entire areas of inquiry were "essentialist," where "essentialist" was understood to be the opposing term to the "oughts" of postmodernism (difference, plurality, multiplicity, the local; or alternately, gaps, lack, or catachresis). "Essentialism" functioned for a time hegemonically, and still tends to function as a sort of scarlet letter, alerting all around to the moral danger of association with those who wear it.

I want to make it very clear that I am not blaming Butler for this. No single thinker can have such power, and Butler's own philosophy of agency should have convinced us of that by now. Her work becomes part of certain tendencies that are much broader and much more complex, though it also exceeds these tendencies in important ways. The "disciplining" of feminism I describe is a complex

---

11. The term "disciplining feminism" was first used as a critical reproach to postmodernism, to my knowledge, by feminist philosopher Kathy Miriam (1998).

social/intellectual process where words like "essentialist" get their power and meaning in much the way Butler argues that words get power and meaning: through an accumulated history of use and misuse in which all of us find ourselves immersed.

It seems to me that the question of essentialism is most adequately understood as the question of *freedom* as it has come to expression in the context of feminist thought. This explains why discussions of it have been so volatile, yet we rarely make this connection explicit, or explicit enough. Advocating essentialism (explicitly or implicitly) has been key to the process of justifying women's subordination historically, while defeating it still seems to be the key to all of our projects of liberation. Yet I will argue that we misunderstand the question of freedom when we equate freedom with the defeat of essentialism, and domination with its continued power; not only that, we reaffirm the oppositional association of necessity with nature and freedom with culture that is so deeply entrenched in the Euro-masculinist traditions of both modernism and postmodernism—and which has been complicit in such harm to women and the natural world. While it may seem that all that can be said about essentialism in feminism has long since been said, if the question of essentialism is really the question of freedom, and if this is the central question and project of feminism itself, then we are unlikely to ever finish with the question of essentialism because feminist thinking will always be thinking the question of freedom.

Emphatic Anti-Essentialism Disciplines Feminism

> It is extremely important that people think a little bit more critically about what they are saying when they are talking about essences, and I have probably been as guilty or more guilty than anybody else in not thinking quite clearly enough. —Judith Butler in Cheah and Grose, 1998

If there was one thing that marked the initial alliance between feminism and postmodernism, it was its emphatic anti-essentialism. This was the "essential" mark of the feminist rapprochement with postmodernism in the academy, in fact. In this context, the accusation "essentialist!" came to exercise a disciplinary force among feminists, while attempts at critical intervention were unable to unseat the anti-essentialist orthodoxy.[12] The philosophical and political stakes that made the question of essentialism such a charged one remained largely unaddressed.[13]

---

12. One of the earliest attempts that I know of to grapple critically with this situation was Diana Fuss's 1989 *Essentially Speaking: Feminism, Nature, and Difference*. This was followed by the 1994 anthology, *The Essential Difference*, edited by Naomi Schor and Elizabeth Weed. For a more recent and very thoughtful history of the essentialism debates, analysis of what is at stake, and proposal for a Wittgensteinian way out, see Cressida Heyes, *Line Drawings: Defining Women Through Feminist Practice*.

13. Reflecting on the philosophical stakes of the term is precisely what Butler urges in the interview from which the 1998 epigraph at the beginning of this section is taken. This is a sign, I think, that by 1998 things had begun to improve somewhat, though emphatic anti-essentialism still has a strong influence in feminist thinking today (Judith Butler in Cheah and Grose, 1998).

The term served, rather, to "mark" something as antithetical to postmodernism, or the other way around, feminist postmodernism saw itself as the antithesis of essentialism.

I use the descriptive term "emphatic" to differentiate postmodern disavowals of essentialism from earlier feminist and antiracist disavowals dating back to Beauvoir and early antiracist theorists. Early accounts stressed that the wrong sorts of essentializing notions were applied to women or various races, but neither defined essentialism so broadly as in later accounts nor disregarded it on principle.[14] The developments that led to the emphatic anti-essentialism that became hegemonic for feminist theory have a complex and troubled history.

On the one hand, the recognition of, the positive loss of innocence about, "instrumental rationality" and its "universal" perspective in the pursuit of "truth" was key.[15] That rationality[16] had proved itself to be capable of such untruths, and that these untruths had served various institutions of political power was a new "truth" that accompanied much of critical philosophy after the Second World War. The relationship between scientific inquiry and political power was called into question, with the role of rationality in creating essentializing definitions of whole categories of people in the forefront. A new consciousness emerged about the lethal and particular connections between scientific reason and power. These connections threw the purported universality of scientific endeavor into critical question. The pursuit of truth in and of itself was not necessarily questioned initially, though rationality proved to be neither a privileged vehicle of access to it, nor politically neutral, nor universal in the sense it claimed itself to be.

On the other hand, the "problem of truth" was reworked by new philosophies in a way that threw the whole pursuit of truth into even deeper question. Foucault's famous or infamous claim that "there is no outside to power" infused a flurry of new thinking on issues of language, reference, and reality. These new theories reworked old philosophical problems, cohering around a central suspicion: not only had reason missed the boat in being wrong about what it identified as the truth, it had itself constituted "truth" in ways that are contingent on power rather than some privileged access to an extradiscursive reality.

That these issues entered feminist theory with a vengeance is no surprise. Feminist thinkers had contributed a great deal to debunking essentialist and universalizing claims about what women are, starting with Beauvoir's manifestolike proclamation that women are made not born. The essentialism that was disputed was primarily a biological essentialism that deployed accounts of women's hormones, anatomy, and physiology (especially in terms of menstruation and reproduction) to justify the political and social domination of women by men. Feminists set out to tell the truth about

14. Cressida Heyes uses the term "principled anti-essentialism" to differentiate today's broad strokes anti-essentialism from the specific critiques that earlier feminists employed (2000).

15. Evidence of this development is widespread. From Husserl's *Crisis* to Arendt's notion of "world-alienation" to Berman's *Reenchantment* to more recent feminist work, most important that of Susan Bordo.

16. Throughout this section, I am referring to "rationality" in its reductive, instrumental form. This is not to be construed as a rejection of reason understood in a fuller sense.

women, against what were recognized as essentializing fictions. At the same time, feminist resistance itself used language that essentialized women in another way. This later discovery came first from women of color and lesbians who criticized the falsely inclusive use of the category of "woman" much as other feminists had criticized the falsely inclusive categories of "mankind" or "human."[17] Monique Wittig's own manifesto, "Lesbians are not women," (Wittig 1992, 32) functioned as an ironic addition to Beauvoir's earlier claims.[18] These developments were sparked by concrete issues of power in movement organizations and politics. In the late 1980s and '90s, however, the problem of essentialism became one that was theorized more and more in the academy.

Many academic feminists pitted postmodern theory against older activist-based feminist theory and found the latter wanting.[19] Particularly, feminist theory in its "radical feminist"[20] form was found to be essentialist. "Essentialist!" took on

17. See for example, Anzaldúa's and Moraga's, *This Bridge Called My Back* Moraga writes, "Lesbian separatist utopia? No thank you, sisters. I can't prepare myself a revolutionary packet that makes no sense when I leave the white suburbs of Watertown, Massachusetts and take the T-line back to Roxbury" (1981, xiii). See also "A Black Feminist Statement: the Combahee River Collective," in the same volume, and Angela Davis, *Women, Race, and Class*. These early critical works did not question the category of woman per se but rather separatist politics and the power of white women to define feminism that amounted to a false inclusion of "other" women in what seemed to them to be a white, middle-class, heterosexual category. Elizabeth Spelman took up these critiques in her *Inessential Woman: Problems of Exclusion in Feminist Thought* in 1988. She wrote against "a tendency in dominant Western feminist thought to posit an essential 'womanness' that all women have and share in common despite the racial, class, religious, ethnic, and cultural differences among us," and set out to "show that the notion of a generic 'woman' functions in feminist thought much the same way the notion of generic 'man' has functioned in Western philosophy: it obscures the heterogeneity of women" (1988, ix).

18. "What is woman? Panic, general alarm for an active defense. Frankly, it is a problem that the lesbians do not have because of a change of perspective, and it would be incorrect to say that lesbians associate, make love, live with women, for 'woman' has meaning only in heterosexual systems of thought and heterosexual economic systems. Lesbians are not women" (Wittig 1992, 32).

19. Sawicki 1988 writes explicitly, "I . . . want to contribute to the movement beyond polarized debate, specifically by further developing the theoretical and practical implications of a *more adequate* sexual politics in the work of Michel Foucault," in *Feminism and Foucault* (emphasis added). In the U.S. American academy, those feminists accused regularly and almost ritualistically of essentialism in its most reviled form included Adrienne Rich, Robin Morgan, Andrea Dworkin, Catharine MacKinnon, and feminists who affirmed an ontological connection between women and nature, such as Mary Daly and Susan Griffin. This list, give or take a few names, appeared in article after article and functioned as a kind of warning to other feminists. Association with "essentialism" would mean association with this group of feminists whom academics believed to be discredited to the point of disgrace. Even now, papers at feminist conferences sometimes include offhand remarks about Catharine MacKinnon, whose monumental academic success seems to have made her the inheritor of the spite formerly directed at the list of women above. Her name is too often thrown out as the "marker" for essentialist, i.e., bad feminism. Catharine MacKinnon, an emphatic social constructionist if ever there was one, occupies this position in what can only be called a wildly ironic twist of the anti-essentialist logic. Not incidentally, all of these women are associated with 1970s and '80s feminist activism, politicized lesbianism, separatism, and/or anti-pornography work—feminist positions that have thrown the norms of heterosexuality deeply into question. As Schor claims, this may be one of the keys to unlocking the political stakes of what I call emphatic anti-essentialism, and its vehemence.

20. This is also when the term "cultural feminist" was created to stand in for the self-definition "radical feminist" by those opposed to radical feminist positions.

almost battle-cry status in academic feminist circles, and the accusation became one that both shamed and discredited. Efforts to critically intervene in this situation were passionate and cut across a wide spectrum of feminist thinkers. Yet these efforts have not effectively stemmed the tide of an anti-essentialist orthodoxy that doesn't sufficiently question its own convictions. I quote a number of such efforts from diverse thinkers in feminism:

> Has essentialism received a bad rap? Few other words in the vocabulary of contemporary critical theory are so persistently maligned, so little interrogated, and so predictably summoned as a term of infallible critique . . . as an expression of disapprobation and disparagement. (Fuss 1989, xi)
>
> All too often . . . the opponents of essentialism use the word polemically as a term of abuse and with a certain air of superiority, as if they were in the know about some new and decisive discovery that removes the need for argument. (Nussbaum 1992, 205)
>
> Assessing where we are now, it seems to me that feminism stands less in danger of totalizing tendencies of feminists than of an increasingly paralyzing anxiety over falling (from what grace?) into ethnocentrism or "essentialism." . . . We need to consider the degree to which this serves, not the empowerment of diverse cultural voices and styles but the academic hegemony (particularly in philosophy and literary studies) of detached, metatheoretical discourse. (Bordo 1993, 225)
>
> The term essentialism covers a range of metacritical meanings and strategic uses that go the very short distance from convenient label to buzz word. Many who, like myself, have been involved with feminist critical theory for some time and who did use the term, initially, as a serious critical concept, have grown impatient with this word — essentialism — time and again repeated with its reductive ring, its self righteous tone of superiority, its contempt for "them" — those guilty of it. (de Lauretis 1994, 1)
>
> What revisionism, not to say essentialism, was to Marxism-Leninism, essentialism is to feminism: the prime idiom of intellectual terrorism and the privileged instrument of political orthodoxy. . . . The word essentialism has been endowed within the context of feminism with the power to reduce to silence, to excommunicate, to consign to oblivion. Essentialism in modern-day feminism is anathema. (Schor and Weed 1994, 42)
>
> What I am very suspicious of is how anti-essentialism, really more than essentialism, is allowing women to call names and congratulate themselves. (Spivak 1994, 71)
>
> Only knowledge of the male body and male thought is considered essential, the female is unessential, the female is essentialist. (Brodribb 1996, 300)
>
> "Essentialism" is the nemesis of "post-modernist" feminism. It is its chief target of attack, and yet the critique of "essentialism" relies on the very framework post-modernism is at such pains to reject. The meaning of "essentialism" depends on a master narrative of truth. "Essentialism" is to be avoided because it is false, and it is judged to be false from a position which is outside all positions, on criteria which would be everywhere and always the same. (Thompson 1996, 334)
>
> "Essentialist" — that ultimate sin which seems to confer an express ticket to hell. (Klein 1996, 348)
>
> It is a concept of essentialism so often directed against anyone who believes in or suggests political action that some feminists and other activists have come to believe that the word is just a way of saying that political action is vulgar. (Jeffreys 1996, 372)

Some insist that the word women is "essentialist" and should be replaced by constructs such as "persons gendered as feminine." Of course, women who live and breathe in the (real) world outside the walls of academentia might not guess that this bizarre construct refers to them. . . . But postmodern theorists need not bother their heads about the (real) world, since for them it does not exist. (Daly 1998, 134–35)

Essentialism is presented as a concern, a feature of bad feminist theory, any one of a multitude of sins, "lingering" even where it was supposed to have been eradicated. . . . Yet the pejorative use and broad interpretation of essentialism makes it difficult to detect what is to be avoided, or even if essentialism, in some form or another, can ever be avoided. Many feminist commentators use "essentialist" as one of a string of critical adjectives directed at other feminist work, yet in order to make that accusation stick, they frequently attribute forms of essentialism to their opponents that are not obviously philosophically unjustified or politically dangerous. . . . Unless we are clear about what essentialism is and is not, and what is wrong with it, the pejorative adjective essentialist simply wastes theoretical time and energy and obscures a myriad of methodological and political issues within feminist theory that are worthy of more differentiated critique. (Heyes 2000, 20–21)

Despite these critical voices, the term "essentialist" continues to have a disciplinary function among feminist thinkers in many places in the academy, albeit a less hegemonic one.[21] It still tends to shut down thinking rather than inspire careful scholarship.[22] We might understand the term "essentialist!" to have become yet another kind of performative speech act, a kind of interpellating speech. I borrow my terms here from Judith Butler's adaptation of Althusser but deploy them in an unusual direction.

In Althusser's notion of interpellation, it is the police who initiate the call or address by which a subject becomes socially constituted. There is the policeman, the one who not only represents the law but whose address "Hey you!" has the effect of binding the law to the one who is hailed. This "one" who appears not to be in a condition of trespass prior to the call (for whom the call establishes a given practice as a trespass) is not fully a social subject, is not fully subjectivated, for he or she is not yet reprimanded. The reprimand does not merely repress or control the subject, but forms a crucial part of the juridical and social formation of the subject. The call is formative, if not performative, precisely because it initiates the individual into the subjected status of the subject. (*BTM* 1993, 121)

Butler claims that the doctor's exclamation, "It's a girl!" is the first interpellating speech act that begins the process of "girling the girl" (7–8). The accusatory "essentialist!" still has the power to function in many contexts with a kind of self-legitimating authority, to

---

21. Two thinkers who have recently moved beyond a criticism of anti-essentialism to advocate a rethinking of essentialism itself are Linda Alcoff, in *Visible Identities: Race, Gender and the Self* (2005), and Naomi Zack, in *Inclusive Feminism: A Third Wave Theory of Women's Commonality* (2005), albeit from very different perspectives.

22. See Jane Roland Martin 1994 for an account of the "chilly research climate" created by the accusation of essentialism.

"essentialize the essentialist," whose work need not be carefully read or responded to once this accusation has functioned to dismiss it as "bad feminism."[23]

Equivocation between various kinds of essentialism has been key to what Naomi Schor referred to in 1994 as "the policing of feminism by the shock troops of anti-essentialism" (Schor and Weed 1994, viii). Schor distinguished four separate critiques that targeted four different kinds of essentialism. The first she called the liberationist critique and credited to Beauvoir and the journal *Questions Feministes*,[24] who first argued that "femininity is a cultural construct" and must be sharply distinguished from the anatomical and hormonal qualities that define a woman as female (43). The second was the linguistic critique, which Schor credited to Lacan and those influenced by his work, who criticized the essentialist as "a naive realist who refuses to acknowledge that the loss of the referent is the condition of man's entry into language" (44). The third was the philosophical critique, which she credited to Derrida and feminist Derrideans, who saw essentialism as "complicitous with Western metaphysics," particularly with notions of ontology (44). The fourth was the feminist critique, which came from within the feminist movement, targeted the false universalism of concepts such as "woman," and displaced "woman-as-different-from-man by the notion of internally differentiated and historically instantiated women" (45). To update Schor's important distinctions, we would need to add yet a fifth critique of essentialism within the U.S. context, this one targeted to marxism or other perspectives primarily concerned with the structural determinants of social power, such as the economy. The social contructionist critique views the emphasis on the power of social structures to determine human possibilities as an "ontologizing" of these structures, that is, the creation of a kind of human nature in a social register. Here the relative intransigence of social structures functions as a kind of "second nature" that is considered to be essentialist as well.[25]

---

23. Naomi Schor argues that "definitions are by definition, as it were, essentialist," and claims that anti-essentialists have essentialized essentialism by creating a context in which all sorts of essentialism are treated as equally heinous. She argues that the first task is to "de-essentialize essentialism" (1994, 43). Diana Fuss argues similarly that "there is no essence to essentialism . . . (historically, philosophically and politically) we can speak only of essentialisms" (1989, xii).

24. Schor and the contributors to this volume are engaged in large part with the essentialism debates in France, though relating their insights to the situation in the United States. My sense is that these two debates need to be carefully distinguished. In France, radical materialist feminists like Monique Wittig and Christine Delphy have not been accused of essentialism as a primary strategy to discredit them, whereas in the United States, radical feminists with similar political agendas have been the targets of this accusation. A reconsideration of essentialism in the French context would need to take into consideration very different political and intellectual terrain than the United States.

25. Schor predicted this development in 1994, when discussing the "movement" of various kinds of thought, such as existentialism, originally opposed to essentialism, across the divide of what is defined as essentialist. She wrote, "This remapping is instructive, for it may be that in the future what now seems most radically disjoined, say essentialism and constructionism, will be conjoined and opposed to a third term as yet unknown but whose time will come" (1994, viii). It is perhaps no surprise that by 2000, Cressida Heyes noted that "recent feminist anti-essentialist critique . . . has mainly been directed at essentializing moments within social constructionist discourses" (2000, 33).

To push Schor's analysis further, it is important to consider what was disciplined out of feminist theory when the scope of "essentialism" widened, and what feminist theorists were disciplined into. If "good" feminist theory was not essentialist, good feminist theorists had to engage in either highly localized empirical studies of particular groups of women or discourse theory. To be sure, many feminist thinkers resisted these constraints and continued to work in areas that had been radically called into question, but there is no doubt that feminist thinking as a whole was quite dramatically impacted by rigid new guidelines for "good feminist thinking." Whole areas of inquiry, that roughly corresponded to the five critiques outlined above, were discredited. The first and most obvious of these areas was that of biology, since biological essentialism, the idea that female biology determined women's destiny, had long been a central and legitimate target of feminist protest.[26] Further, the dissolution of the referentiality of language had the effect of disciplining out the use of categories like "woman" and "feminist." Here we see that Schor's "feminist critique" became a kind of subpoint to the linguistic critique, since definitions of key terms to feminist practice were seen to exercise a kind of definitional intrusion and exclusion at the same time, both forcing a definition on those included in the notion and excluding some who would have liked to have been included (Spelman 1988). Any such effort at defining terms relied on an outmoded faith in the relation between words and things, a "naive realism" that refused to accept that there wasn't some "real thing" called a woman or a feminist that was referred to by the signs "woman" or "feminist."[27] In addition, phenomenological notions of ontology, and the philosophical practices which seemed to require them, were disciplined out as well since such notions had fallen into broad disrepute, and feminists had noted how they had been used to abnegate full human status for women in Western metaphysics.[28] Finally, the notion of relatively intransigent social structures, more recently caught up in the sweep of emphatic anti-essentialism, is in danger of being disciplined out of feminist inquiry. If women's difference from men is asserted, even as a function of social structures of domination and subordination,

---

26. Feminists who have seemed to base their theoretical or political work on women's capacity for motherhood or nurturance, or women's physical or biological characteristics, are the particular targets of this critique. Feminists as diverse as Carol Gilligan, Luce Irigaray, and Maria Mies have all been accused of this kind of essentialism.

27. In its postmodern, and in some formulations "postfeminist," form, this development centers on an affirmation of gender "performativity" where such cultural phenomena as drag are taken to expose the lie of gender/sex in its more pedestrian forms. Again, the work of Judith Butler is central to this development, but it has come to be widely accepted.

28. Feminist ontology or feminist metaphysics, kinds of philosophical inquiry that were most effectively short-circuited by the "essentialist!" accusatory, now seem to be contradictions in terms. Heyes argues, in fact, that "metaphysical essentialism . . . formally understood, . . . is not manifested in the work of any contemporary feminist theorists and is not at stake when feminists accuse each other of 'essentialism' " (2000, 22). This argument is both overhasty and obfuscating since feminist philosophies of religion, some ecofeminist work, much spiritually based work of indigenous feminists, feminist phenomenology, etc., affirm metaphysical essentialism in some way.

this seems to "freeze" women in the position of victim and deny women's agency.[29]

It is impossible to deny that the concerns motivating feminist anti-essentialism, even in its emphatic form, are deep and serious, nor that feminist thinkers learned a lot of important lessons through these critiques. Real movement-based political struggles over exclusion and inclusion fueled the anti-essentialist fire. Yet emphatic anti-essentialism has served much less as a political corrective to inequalities of power between women, which remain remarkably unchanged, than as an intellectual policing tool. Susan Bordo argues more broadly that:

> the programmatic appropriation of poststructuralist insight . . . is, in shifting the focus of crucial feminist concerns about the representation of cultural diversity from practical contexts to questions of adequate theory, highly problematic for feminism. Not only are we thus diverted from attending to the professional and institutional mechanisms through which the politics of exclusion operate most powerfully in intellectual communities, but we also deprive ourselves of still vital analytical tools for critique of those communities and the hierarchical dualistic power structures that sustain them. (Bordo 1993, 218)

Our preoccupation with the questions of inclusion and exclusion in theory may have served more to repress the practical realities of material differences in resources and power than to encourage intervention in them. The theoretical version

---

29. This accusation has most often been leveled at the work, both political and intellectual, of Andrea Dworkin and Catharine MacKinnon, whose anti-pornography activism and theory is called "essentialist!" in spite of MacKinnon's almost dogmatic social constructionism. MacKinnon was one of the first American feminists to question the sex/gender distinction from a social constructionist perspective (of course Monique Wittig was an important predecessor in this regard). As early as 1987, MacKinnon was making gender the primary of the two terms:

> On the first day that matters, dominance was achieved, probably by force. By the second day division along the same lines had to be relatively firmly in place. On the third day, if not sooner [sexual] differences were demarcated, together with social systems to exaggerate them in perception and in fact, because the systematically differential delivery of benefits and deprivations required making no mistake about who was who. Comparatively speaking, man has been resting ever since. (1987, 40)

And two years later, "the molding, direction, and expression of sexuality organizes society into two sexes: women and men. This division underlies the totality of social relations. Sexuality is the social process through which social relations of gender are created" (1989, 3). MacKinnon argued that *both* the sex and gender distinctions were socially created through the social construction of sexuality as heterosexuality. "To limit efforts to end gender inequality at the point where biology or sexuality is encountered, termed differences, without realizing that these exist in law or society only in terms of their specifically sexist social meanings, amounts to conceding that gender inequality may be challenged so long as the central epistemological pillars of gender as a system of power are permitted to remain standing" (1989, 233). In refusing a naturalized, pre-social, "sex difference," MacKinnon has more in common philosophically with Judith Butler than with biologically based essentialism, yet one has the impression that her work has rarely been read since she gained a reputation as the quintessential "essentialist!"

of the practical question of inclusion and exclusion has involved a translation: in theory exclusion/inclusion is rewritten as the philosophical question of the one and the many. This translation allows us to focus our attention on *concepts* deployed in general or universal ways rather than on employment opportunities or promotion and tenure policies. This is not to deny that the practical and philosophical can and should be intimately connected, but descriptively considered in this instance, they have long since parted company.

In addition to repressing the practical concerns that we credit with giving rise to the theoretical concerns in the first place, we have neglected other philosophical questions that are equally implicated in the essentialism debates. Opening up these questions may also open up some of the impasses we've run up against. One of these neglected questions is that of freedom and necessity.[30] In fact, we might say that this question is a hidden or repressed question in the essentialism debates, even as its centrality seems obvious. Any sort of "essentialism" claims a kind of necessity. The first feminist criticism of "essentialism" was in reaction to the consignment of women to the realm of necessity. Women claimed political freedoms over and against the antifeminist insistence on the immutable and exclusive relation of women to this realm, as opposed to the political.

If anti-essentialism no longer exerts the near hegemonic control that it did at one time, it is still a powerful disciplinary force in feminist thinking. Critics of anti-essentialism in its emphatic form have yet to take the question of essentialism up as a question of freedom. Yet surely it is the possibility of freedom that we care about, rather than essentialism per se. Here, I shift the terms of the discussion so that the tension between freedom and necessity becomes the key to understanding the stakes of the feminist flight from essentialism.

From the One and the Many to Necessity and Freedom

Both anti-essentialist feminists and their critics have addressed the problem of essentialism primarily as a problem of the one and the many. The debate was framed in this way, starting with early protests by women of color and lesbians, and was perhaps most explicitly articulated in Elizabeth Spelman's 1988 book, *Inessential Woman: Problems of Exclusion in Feminist Thought*. This book, motivated by and engaged with feminist antiracist commitments, was a watershed for anti-essentialism and raised many questions that were fairly new for feminism in the late 1980s.

In a chapter entitled "Woman: The One and the Many," Spelman analyzes the way categorization obscures particularity. "If there is an essential womanness that all women have and have always had, then we needn't know anything about any woman in particular. For the details of her situation and her experience are

---

30. My thanks to Eva Kittay for pushing me to explore the shift I was making in my work from the philosophical question of the one and the many to that of necessity and freedom (conversation, November, 2000).

irrelevant to her being a woman. . . . All those particulars become inessential to her being and our understanding of her being a woman. And so she also becomes inessential in the sense that she is not needed in order to produce the 'story of woman'" (Spelman 1988, 158). It is the important political problem of exclusion and inclusion, the problem of who gets to "tell the story" of woman, in feminism, that motivates Spelman's work. The tendency to generalize from one's own experience to all women, she points out, collapses the particularities of different women into a false unity. "For essentialism invites me to take what I understand to be true of me, 'as a woman' for some golden nugget of womanness all women have as women; and it makes the participation of other women inessential to the production of the story. How lovely: the many turn out to be one, and the one that they are is me" (159). Structural differences in power make it more than likely that the one who has the power to define women, by falsely universalizing her own particular experience, will be white, heterosexual, and middle class.

This contribution to early anti-essentialist discussions helped to set off a flurry of concern over essentialism in U.S. American feminism. Interestingly, the philosophical framework Spelman provides for the discussion has hardly been questioned by those on either side of the debate since. Anti-essentialism has developed into an assault on the methodological necessity of *generalizing* about women, based on the connection (assumed to be inevitable) between such generalizing and exclusion. Efforts to articulate women's condition or status in any general way, it is argued, are always inadequate to women's differences from one another, and always involve the imposition of those general categories feminists with more social and economic power deem most important. The only way to avoid the abuse of power is to make sure that the many predominate over the one, that particularity is elevated to a status over and above the general.

Critics of anti-essentialism have tended to define the problem in much the same way as anti-essentialist feminists, as a problem of the one and the many. Both Susan Bordo (1993) and Cressida Heyes (2000) argue the necessity of generalizing, and the disjuncture between generalization and essentialism, in their critiques of anti-essentialism. Bordo notes that "nothing in the early feminist critique of gender theory . . . declared the theoretical impossibility of discovering common ground among diverse groups of people or insisted that the abstraction of gender coherencies across cultural difference is bound to lapse into a pernicious universalization" (Bordo 1993, 221). She links this new "gender skepticism" to a shift from practical political questions of exclusion and inclusion to an academic quest for a kind of theory purified of essentialism. Yet as Bordo points out, such purity is elusive: "If generalization is only permitted in the absence of multiple inflections or interpretive possibilities, then cultural generalization of any sort—about race, about class, about historical eras—is ruled out. What remains is a universe composed entirely of counterexamples" (239). Heyes, similarly, argues that "there is an important and obvious distinction . . . between generalizations and universals" (Heyes 2000, 56). Accusations of essentialism often function to conflate these two. It would be more useful for feminists to come to an understanding of how to generalize, or how carefully to generalize, rather than to simply accuse one another of doing so under the code word "essentialist!"

These discussions, focused as they are on the philosophical problem of the one and the many, have been and continue to be an important part of the feminist debate over essentialism. Yet the question of necessity and freedom, certainly as politically charged and practically complex as that of the one and the many, is equally implicated in the discussion. How might approaching the issue of essentialism through this question change the terms of the discussion?

First, looking at essentialism as a question of necessity and freedom reframes the debate so that "bad" essentialism, equated with exclusion, and "good" anti-essentialism, equated with inclusion, can be evaluated through another lens. The exclusive focus on inclusion and exclusion has tended to preclude feminist inquiry into the realm of necessity where essentialism, after all, has its home. But to consider what is necessary for human life, what might be "essential" to human life, need not be a practice of exclusion in the sense of separating those who are in from those who are out.[31] This framework can open inquiry into common conditions. In fact, it links the essentialism debate to the broader environmental issues that tend to be disciplined out in emphatic anti-essentialist feminism. Because we are, in fact, and necessarily, creatures that are bound to place through our dependence on the immediate environment for sustenance; the question of necessity can tie the essentialism debate back into a concern with the places we inhabit.

Second, this approach can provide insight into the positive motivation driving the "disciplining out" of biology, ontology, intransigent social structures, and the referentiality of language, which seems to be a fear of anything that would reattach women to the realm of necessity. Elizabeth Grosz suggests this when she writes of masculinist theory: "In claiming that women's current social roles and positions are the effects of their essence, nature, biology, or universal social position, these theories are guilty of rendering such roles and positions unalterable and *necessary* and thus of providing them with a powerful political justification" (Grosz 1994, 85; emphasis added). Given that in the dominant Western philosophical tradition, the realm of necessity has been intimately bound up with the feminine, the feminist flight from this realm is understandable. The realm of necessity has also been that which must be overcome in order to philosophize at all, from Plato to Marx to Shulamith Firestone, emancipation from this realm is the precondition for a life that is fully human.[32] Overcoming necessity has meant a masculinist

---

31. Though of course it can be. Martha Nussbaum's defense of Aristotelian essentialism provides an example of why essentialism needs the light of continued scrutiny. In her efforts to provide an account of "certain central defining features" that characterize human life, Nussbaum admitted that certain "offspring of two human parents" who are profoundly disabled would not fit into this definition and would be outside the purview of her moral argument about what a society owes to the majority who do fall under the definition of human (1992, 228). My approach is not to *define* what is human, but to *describe* a human condition of dependence on the planet. I find Eva Kittay's approach to social/political/ethical questions through an acknowledgment of dependence (1999) much more fitting for feminist politics than Nussbaum's, at least on this point. See chapter 7.

32. Hannah Arendt traces this history in *The Human Condition*. The term *vita activa* was the term by which a life of contemplation could be distinguished from a life of necessity. The *vita activa*, "excluded everybody who involuntarily or voluntarily, for his whole life or temporarily, had lost the free

transcendence of the feminine and has defined both "freedom" and humanity in the Euro-masculine tradition. Consequently, women's attachment to the realm of necessity has justified all manner of male supremacy. The feminist flight from essentialism is to be understood in the context of this history.

Third, attending to the problem of freedom and necessity allows us to see how certain modernist commitments are carried over uncritically into the postmodern. The definition of freedom as freedom-from-necessity is one such commitment. In postmodern theories, emancipation from necessity as nature is translated into emancipation from necessity as discursive determinacy. While discursive determinacy is necessity in its postmodern form, freedom is translated into discursive contingency. A kind of deconstructive affirmative action makes this new freedom available to all subjects, but the masculinist structure of freedom as emancipation from the realm of necessity tends to be carried over from modernism. In postmodern feminist accounts, an emphatically anti-essentialist feminist epistemology, where a sublime melting of determinacy into discursive contingency takes center stage, sets women free from any realm of necessity by doing away with that realm entirely in favor of discourse. By attending to the question of necessity and freedom, we can attend to how this modernist commitment crosses the border of the postmodern.

Fourth, framing the question in this way links it explicitly to the notion of the sublime. A sustained examination of sublime experience is important now because the question of necessity and freedom is the very question that works itself out through the sublime, starting with Kant. If the sublime has become an experience that is not only celebrated by but also constituted in textual practices after the linguistic turn, and if what is at stake in these practices is a certain aesthetic experience of freedom, then we begin to understand something important about the linguistic turn itself. In a world in which practices of freedom are reduced to consumer choice, while the structures that shape our daily experiences escape our comprehension and thus control, in which feminist victories in law and policy are being steadily rolled back, while we are bombarded by images and messages that offer us never dreamed of opportunities for aestheticized self-fashioning, it makes a good deal of sense that we turn to the realm of the aesthetic as an appropriate site for freedom. Yet the needed response is not simply a rejection of the aesthetic in favor of the political, indeed these two realms are far too intertwined for that, but a careful examination of the politics of aesthetic notions like the sublime which might begin to make sense of what is lost when certain kinds of sublime experience are uncritically celebrated.

---

disposition of his movements and activities," it included only ways of life that "were concerned with the 'beautiful,' that is, with things neither necessary nor merely useful" (1958, 12–13). Thus, Arendt argues that the debasement of the earth and elevation of the subject makes a continuous line from the Greeks to the present, material necessity and freedom have been seen as contradictory, and freedom from the realm of necessity has always been seen as a good. Maria Mies and Vandana Shiva apply this same insight in their ecofeminist work and argue for a feminist understanding of freedom as sharply distinguished from emancipation from necessity (Mies and Shiva 1993).

Feminists have only just begun to study the notion of the sublime in the context of an engagement with the philosophical tradition in aesthetics. This engagement both affirms the importance of aesthetic experience and threatens to destabilize all of its established categories. The gendered history of the beautiful and the sublime, and the sexualized nature of their historical distinction, are of particular concern to feminists, since what is at stake in aesthetic experience has so often been expressed in gendered and misogynist terms. Feminism stands, and must stand, in a critical relation vis-à-vis the philosophical tradition in aesthetics, and especially vis-à-vis masculinist narratives of the sublime, at least at the outset.

1

Feminism and the Sublime

Feminism and Aesthetics

After the linguistic turn, life becomes art. The boundary between the two is one of those boundaries associated with modernity that postmodernism seems determined to tear down. Feminists have had an uneasy relationship with these developments, and for good reason. Rita Felski argues that one of the things that is promising for a feminist engagement with the "postmodern problematic" is precisely the dissolution of this opposition (2000, 195),[1] while Amy Newman reminds us that "at least historically aestheticist thinking has been a vehicle for blatantly masculinist ideologies privileging a certain kind of aesthetic experience, that arising within male corporeality," and suggests that postmodern aestheticism may be no different (1990, 21).

A number of feminist thinkers see the philosophical study of aesthetics in general as having a natural affinity with feminism because both aesthetics and feminism have been relatively marginalized in dominant philosophical discourse (Brand and Korsmeyer 1995). Feminists, it is argued, can make good use of this tradition, because it has always been grappling with the questions of particularity and plurality, which are also central to feminism. Hilde Hein notes that feminists tend to find ourselves at odds with unitary theories, favoring instead the many over the one, and aesthetics does this too. It can be "a model for feminist theory," she

---

1. Felski thinks the affinity between aesthetics and feminism is best served when feminists take a more postmodern approach to aesthetics than that found in early feminist advocacy of "women's art." "Gender and the aesthetic are intertwined in a manner quite unlike conventional feminist aesthetics. Art is not subordinated to a feminist demand for a fixed and coherent female identity. Rather, art is the place where identity fails, where the fictions of separate, unitary and complementary male and female selves are revealed as fictions" (2000, 184). This is, of course, extremely hopeful thinking, but it is also an important articulation of the aspirations that make the realm of the aesthetic so important for contemporary feminism.

argues, because it "thrives on the inconstancy and inconsistency of its domain" (Hein and Korsmeyer 1993, 8). The aesthetic is constantly working in the paradox of individual experiences and universal, or at least general, aesthetic judgments—just like feminism works in the space between private experience and the general claims it must make to be effective politically.

Yet the philosophical tradition in aesthetics has a long and burdened history of egregious gender commitments that feminists cannot ignore. If the aesthetic has been a privileged site for the self-constitution of the Euro-masculine[2] subject in the West, then it has also been a privileged site for women's exclusion and subordination. A flurry of new writing on women's art and women artists took on these problems in the context of the production, consumption, and study of art beginning in the 1970s (Hess and Nochlin 1972; Tufts 1974; Chicago 1975; Lippard 1976; Petersen and Wilson 1976; Sutherland and Nochlin 1976; Honig 1978; Greer 1979; Munro 1979). It took feminists a good deal longer to begin to address the philosophical study of the aesthetic, which overlaps with but is not reducible to the study of art. It wasn't until the very late 1980s and early 1990s that feminists in the United States began to take on the philosophical tradition in aesthetics. Feminist engagement with this tradition is consistent in its criticism on several points. It is criticized for its masculinism, for adhering to the same sort of false universalism that plagues philosophy in general, for claiming that aesthetic judgments are disinterested, and for relying on the notion of "genius" and a distinction between "high" and "low" art, both of which tend to legitimize the kinds of hierarchy that feminists generally oppose.

Feminist criticism of the masculinism of aesthetic philosophy has taken a number of forms. Korsmeyer suggests that the problem of masculinism in aesthetics is not a simple one since "there are several modes of 'gendering' to be found in concepts in aesthetics, including a practical mode that is evident when there are actual barriers erected.... There is a conceptual mode that frames the way we think.... And there is a mode that exerts power over desire and fantasy that probably is most evident in fashion and personal choice" (Korsmeyer 2004, 4). Feminists have criticized the ways in which women's art and women artists are concretely excluded from "legitimate" or "great" art; they have raised the issue of "whether and how the gender of the artists—as well as their other socially marked identities—are to count as properties of works of art and to be recognized as aesthetically relevant" (Brand and Korsmeyer 1995, 16) thus challenging the notion of the generic aesthetic subject; they have traced the history of the relation between certain aesthetic notions

2. I use the term "Euro-masculine" as a political term that tries to efficiently enfold both the racialized and gendered aspects of this identity. Such attempts are always imperfect, and this term no less than any other. I mean neither to apply this term to all white men of European descent nor to exclude some others, including white women, completely. The term is meant to name an identity based on conquest and domination, conquest of the persons in the colonies and domination of women—any particular person's identification with this term would depend on multiple factors: their relative share in Euro-masculinist power, in the resources looted from the colonies, in the privileges of masculinity, and even their own political commitments.

and gender hierarchy; and perhaps most significantly have begun to analyze what Korsmeyer calls "deep gender." "At the deepest level of gender significance lie entire conceptual frameworks that are founded on presumptions whose connection with gendered ways of thinking is by no means immediately evident. Here gender resonance is slant and opaque, and explicit references to masculinity and femininity are likely to be altogether absent" (2004, 3).

These challenges to the masculinism of traditional aesthetics entail a consistent rejection of its claims to universality. The hope that judgments of taste might be universally valid or belong to a generic, universal subject is dashed against the rock of feminist and postmodernist criticism in a number of ways. A feminist theory of art maintains that "art is not produced in a rarified atmosphere that transcends gender-identification" (Lauter 1990, 98) that "removes the perceiver from his or her particular and contingent situation" (Brand and Korsmeyer 1995, 16). A feminist philosophy of the aesthetic insists that "the universal subject is historically situated (masculine, patriarchal, imperialistic)" (Brand and Korsmeyer 1995, 7) and assumes "that images, representations, and crafted expression of ideas are important not only for their beauty, virtuosity, or intrinsic value, but also because they are indicators of social position and power" (Korsmeyer 2004, 1).

Far from being removed from the realm of interest, then, "art and aesthetic taste are powerful framers of self-image, social identity, and public values" (Korsmeyer 2004, 1). Our aesthetic values are "attached to grossly material things, like health and money and the houses we live in" (Lauter 1990, 102). They are also attached to and expressive of deeply gendered interests. The feminist theory of the male gaze has played a significant role in bringing this latter point to light (Brand and Korsmeyer 1995, 15–16). Gendered power is manifest in the way that vision is structured in and by art and other forms of cultural production.

> Perhaps nowhere is the ideology of extreme disinterested contemplation more questionable than when applied to paintings of female nudes, with which one feminist scholar virtually defines the modern fine art of painting. Aesthetic ideologies that would remove art from its relations with the world disguise its ability to inscribe and to reinforce power relations. With visual art, those relations are manifest in vision itself: the way it is depicted in a work and the way it is induced and directed in the observer outside the work. (Korsmeyer 2004, 51)

The feminist critique acknowledges "the cultural authority of art to perpetuate power relations" (Korsmeyer 2004, 57); it rejects the notion of a disinterested perceiver and emphasizes instead "the affective value of art," and "the ways art has always served political systems" (Lauter 1990, 100). Of course this emphasis on the politics of art will be one reason for discrediting feminist aesthetics as itself plagued by interests that subvert the aesthetic (Battersby 1990, 89).

Notions of "genius" and "high" and "low" art that have been important in the Western tradition have been criticized precisely in terms of the kinds of power they tend to legitimize. Linda Nochlin's groundbreaking 1971 essay, "Why Have Their Been No Great Women Artists?" raised the question of how notions of genius or fine art are built around the exclusion of works by women (1971). Brand and Korsmeyer note that "the concept of fine or high art, along with the notion of artistic genius, is exclusionary both historically and conceptually" (1995, 8). Feminist aesthetics works against such notions by refusing to identify art as something that is strictly separate from the useful, decorative, or otherwise functional (Lauter 1990, 98–99) and by valorizing art that "remains embedded in the everyday," where "beauty and its ontological intensity . . . are not withdrawn, leaving the mundane workaday world all the more profane and providing aesthetic illumination only for an elite" (Donovan 1993, 53–54). Feminists have noted that notions of masculine genius, while drawing on or appropriating traditionally feminine characteristics, still serve to exclude actual women from the category of "great artists" (Korsmeyer 2004, 13; Battersby 1990).

If life becomes art after the linguistic turn, then the masculinist tradition in aesthetics assures that, for feminists, it will be a troubled life. On the one hand, when we approach the realm of the aesthetic at its deepest, we enter into questions that are central for feminist thinking and practice. Our troubled relation to this realm is also our chance to make feminist sense out of experiences of embodied perception, spatiality, and temporality. On the other hand, it is simply not possible to ignore the extreme misogyny of the traditions we engage when we engage these questions.

The modernist tradition in aesthetics gendered aesthetic experience most explicitly by dichotomizing the notions of the beautiful and the sublime. By the time of the publication of Edmund Burke's 1759 *Philosophical Enquiry into the Origin of Our Ideas of the Sublime and Beautiful*, the two aesthetic notions were deeply entangled with the norms of idealized European femininity and masculinity. It is in Kant's 1764 *Observations on the Feeling of the Beautiful and Sublime*, a work which both draws heavily on Burke's essay and reworks its general themes in a less physiologically engaged direction, that the full expression of the gendered entanglements of the two notions is realized (see chapter 2). If the emerging body of feminist work in aesthetics has tended to articulate its criticisms of the masculinist tradition in the form of responses to Kantian aesthetics,[3] this is appropriate for several reasons. Kant's work on the beautiful and the sublime holds an extremely important place in the dominant canon and is commonly held to draw

---

3. Mary Devereaux writes "In point of fact, feminist critiques of philosophical aesthetics have focused almost exclusively on a single, [narrow], target: Kant and the tradition of neo-Kantian formalism. . . . Indeed, it would be no great exaggeration to say that critiques of 'Kant and formalism' have largely come to define what is meant by feminist aesthetics" (2003, 657). Devereaux's concern with this narrow focus, while an important one, also acknowledges that feminists are responding to Kant because Kant has been important in mainstream developments in philosophical aesthetics. Jeremy Gilbert-Rolfe argues in "Kant's Ghost Among Others" that Kant needs to be retained in contemporary aesthetics as what is to be rejected or surpassed. "Kant's role in contemporary art is to be ritually exorcised. To say that capitalism is not Marxist and the post-modern is not Kantian is to define both through recourse to what they are not" (2000, 107). My argument is that very significant elements of Kantian aesthetics are carried over into postmodern treatments of the sublime, so that such a definition over and against Kant fails. Important exceptions to this feminist tendency to focus on the Kantian sublime include Amy Newman, who focuses on Nietzsche and Heidegger (1990), and Paul Mattick, who works more with Burke and Rousseau than with Kant and attributes a "female sublime" to Mary Wollstonecraft (1995).

together and express most eloquently a number of central concerns in modern aesthetics.[4] His version of sublime experience is the one that Lyotard, whose work on the sublime is largely responsible for contemporary interest in the category, finds so compelling. Kant's early book on aesthetics includes a chapter on women's proper relation to aesthetic experience, which is also a normative treatise on gender relations, and a chapter on aesthetics and national character that makes more or less explicit the racialization of sublime experience. In Kant's later work in aesthetic philosophy, gender goes largely, not completely, underground—here feminists have found evidence of what Korsmeyer refers to as "deep gender" in the relation between humans and nature and between the faculties of imagination, understanding and reason.

Though the focus of my work here is on the notion of the sublime, it is not possible to discuss the sublime in depth without some attention to its foil: beauty. In fact, beauty will make a number of appearances throughout these pages and will become particularly important toward the end in my discussion of the liberatory and the natural experiences of the sublime. A few brief remarks on the notion of beauty and feminist engagement with it here will, I hope, help set the stage for those appearances by beginning to trace the complex relationship of the notions of the beautiful and the sublime.

Feminism and Beauty

It is in the philosophical contemplation of beauty that women become most radically interchangeable with English gardens and landscape paintings. Certainly women often find ourselves in the position of the object in philosophical texts, but nowhere so clearly and consistently as when the topic is the aesthetic experience of the beautiful. Here women, nature, and art all occasion the experience for men, and in a way that points to a labyrinthine relationship between the three.

Though the association of beauty with the feminine of the human species is an ancient one, evident in many times and places both inside and outside the Western tradition, it is in Western modernism that beauty is assigned to the white European woman as a normative life-project. In Kant's early work in aesthetics, beauty is the feminine life-task that is opposed to the masculine pursuit of contemplation. Paradoxically, the fair sex simply *is by nature* the sex that busies itself with making itself and its domestic environs beautiful, and yet *it needs forceful reminding* that this is its proper sphere, and contemplation is to be left to the men. When women do pursue a life of thinking, as Kant famously remarks, they "might as well grow beards," might as well, that is, cover their beautiful faces with ugly masculine hair. Beautiful appearance is a casualty of deep thought.

---

4. Most important, how to understand aesthetic experiences as deeply subjective yet capable of generating universal judgments, aesthetic experience as disinterested, how to draw the distinction between beauty and the sublime, and how aesthetic experience contributes to man's sense of his place in relation to the world of nature.

Of course the association of the feminine and beauty does not take place first in a philosophical text but in the larger cultural milieu. Modernity and postmodernity as time periods hardly differ in their cultural assignation of the project of beauty to women (and we need only look to the images that saturate our present culture for evidence), though they do differ in their notions of what feminine beauty is. They are consistent in assigning women the *task* of appearance. This is to say, women are to inhabit the same space of appearance other objects do, but for women, as opposed to daisy-strewn meadows, a great deal of work is involved. The stakes are high: how we inhabit this space, how beautifully we appear, is understood to determine a great deal about our individual experiences of power, value, family, love, and acceptance. No wonder that Mary Wollstonecraft worried that denying women the opportunity to develop their faculties of reason leaves them in a state of slavery, not to men exactly, but to the (devalued) world of sense. "Taught from infancy that beauty is woman's sceptre, the mind shapes itself to the body, and roaming round its gilt cage, only seeks to adorn its prison" (1986, 57). No wonder that one of the earliest protests of second-wave feminism in the United States was the 1968 storming of the Miss America pageant in Atlantic City. Feminists recognized early on that women's status as subjects of thinking, action, or history would never be secured as long as our very agency was tightly harnessed to the project of turning ourselves into beautiful objects, that is, as long as a woman's culturally defined success as a woman was more or less determined by her success at the task of appearance.

Even as modernity made beauty the project for certain (European, affluent) women, it understood the pursuit of beauty to be an apparently frivolous one from the perspective that mattered on a grander scale, that of European men. I say "apparently" because the beauty embodied and created by European women was deeply implicated in the central structures of Euro-masculine identity at the time, not the least of which was the temporal structure that distinguished the "civilized" man or woman from the savage (see chapter 2). Yet beauty is seen to be the pursuit of an essentially frivolous creature, one incapable of a life governed by reason, and incapable of living well without masculine guidance.

If there is one thing that clearly distinguishes the contemporary era from the modern, it is that in postmodernity everything becomes appearance, which is to say everything becomes frivolous. This means, of course, that frivolity becomes very serious indeed. So while beauty remains the central and primary cultural task of women in postmodernity, the saturation of culture with images of beautiful women and women striving for beauty, messages about the power that comes with feminine beauty, the specter of the failure of feminine beauty, and the mass marketing of technologies of beauty are undeniable; so is the fact that, more and more, beauty becomes the task of men as well.

If Kant is important to feminists now, it is because the world of appearance is the world that we inhabit with a vengeance under conditions of postmodernity, and it was Kant who assigned knowledge to the world of appearance where beauty is also at home. Though he considered women and their pursuit of beauty to be as necessary, yet entertainingly frivolous, as other thinkers of his time, he also (and paradoxically) made the realm of appearance into a very serious place. This is why Hannah Arendt proceeded to look for Kant's political philosophy in his aesthetics (1992).

For Arendt, the *Critique of Judgement*, especially its discussion of aesthetic judgments of the beautiful, is the key text in Kant's mostly unwritten political philosophy because it is concerned with the faculty that concerns itself with particulars (reflective judgment), yet is utterly bound to a communicable and public sociability that Arendt believes Kant understands to be "the very origin, not the goal, of man's humanity" (1992, 74). Kant's important discovery is that there is "something nonsubjective in what seems to be the most private and subjective sense," that is, intersubjectivity, which makes it possible to overcome egoism (67). Arendt's favorite passage of the third *Critique* is clearly section 40: "Taste as a kind of *sensus communis*." Kant explains: "By the name *sensus communis* is to be understood the idea of a *public* sense, i.e. a critical faculty which in its reflective act takes account (a priori) of the mode of representation of everyone else, in order, as it were, to weigh its judgment with the collective reason of mankind" (*CJ*, 294). This means that the very enabling basis for my judgments of taste is other people, as these judgments must be both communicable and public; I am taken out of myself by such judgments into an intersubjective field held together by common sense (see chapter 8). If judgments of taste are disinterested, as Kant so famously claimed, then for Arendt, this simply means that in such judgments we are working from a kind of enlarged mentality that entails "putting ourselves in the position of everyone else" (*CJ*, 294) and not from self-interest.

In reflective judgment the particular is not subsumed under the general, sacrificing thereby its particularity, but becomes a kind of participant in the general through exemplary validity—as when a beautiful work of art becomes the example we point to to explain what we mean when we say that something is beautiful. Here the particular and the general (Arendt translates *Allgemeines* as "general" rather than "universal") are linked, so that the usual escape from particularity does not take place. Particularity is retained in the general.

What is true of judgments of taste, Arendt points out, is also true of the political. The political inhabits the realm of appearance and depends on communicability and publicity. The particulars (events, people, governments, nations) are always much more important to the political than the general, yet they provide pathways to the general, especially when certain particulars are taken up and narrated by the spectator-public as exemplary, that is, as having or pointing to meaning that is generally significant. Although political actions or events often involve a great deal of self-interest, they are necessarily judged, historically speaking, from a position that takes humanity, not self-interest, into account.

If experiences of the beautiful remind us of the intersubjective world we share with others, they also remind us that we belong to nature. For Kant, beauty is experienced when an encounter with nature (or woman or art) sets the imagination and understanding into a state of harmonious play, where the freedom of the imagination and the rules of the understanding coincide without conflict. It is because nature appears to us to be purposive, that is, our faculties of imagination and understanding must attribute something like design to nature, that such encounters set our faculties into free, harmonious relation with one another. After all, we also experience ourselves as purposive in Kant's sense, as creatures of organization and design, as creatures who make sense in and of ourselves. Beauty in nature makes it possible for us to experience ourselves and nature as in a relationship of belonging because we experience the beauty of nature as also making sense, and without reference to any function—beauty makes sense like we do, all by itself.

It is important to wonder a bit about Kant's narrative of harmony with nature in the context of his discussion of judgments of taste, and not only because this account is in such contrast to the relationship with nature that emerges in his account of the sublime. The delight that the subject experiences upon encountering an apparently purposive nature seems to imply that there is something surprising about the coherence of our experience of ourselves and nature. The subject who is delighted by the beauty of nature has already understood nature to be alien, has already known the things in themselves to be utterly inaccessible. This is the point that Hartmut and Gernot Böhme take up in great detail in their book on Kant's relation to nature, *Das Andere der Vernunft*. Following Schiller, they note that "The longing for nature is the expression of the loss of homeland, of context. . . . Nature is discovered first against the background of its loss. The separation makes nature visible as the Other. Man has to move away from himself in order to find nature" (1983, 30).[5] Indeed, Kant's Copernican turn hinges on the distinction between the thing in itself and the world of appearance, on both a separation between and a distance between the two. By the time he writes the third *Critique*, the loss of nature is already well established. And even as a certain longing for and reconciliation with nature plays itself out in the aesthetic experience of the beautiful, man's fundamental rupture with nature is replayed in its most violent and dramatic form in his account of the sublime.

Feminism and the Sublime

Nowhere has the misogyny of the Western tradition in aesthetics been more explicit than in philosophical discussions of sublime experience, yet the experience of the sublime has come to quintessentially characterize the postmodern. Jean-Francois Lyotard's recuperation of the notion of the sublime from Kantian aesthetics initiated an extraordinary revival of interest in this seemingly outdated notion. Christine Pries, whose book *Das Erhabene: Zwischen Grenzerfahrung und Grossenwahn* (*The Sublime: Between Border Experience and Madness*) is part of this revival, writes, "the Renaissance of the Sublime is even more astounding, since this concept, which can look back over a long tradition in German philosophy, was so forgotten in the course of the twentieth century, that today hardly anyone really knows what it means" (1989, 1).[6]

---

5. My translation. The original text reads as follows, "Die Sehnsucht nach der Natur ist der Ausdruck des Verlustes von Heimat, von Zusammenhang . . . die Natur gerade erst auf der Hintergrunde ihres Verlustes endeckt wird. Die Trennung macht sie als das Andere Sichtbar. Man muss sich von sich selbst wegbewegun, um die Natur zu finden."

6. My translation. The original text reads as follows: "Die Renaissance des Erhabenen ist um so erstaunlicher, als dieser Begriff, der in der deutschen Philosophie auf eine lange Tradition zuruckblicken kann, im Laufe des 20. Jahrhunderts so sehr in Vergessenheit geraten ist, dass heute kaum noch jemand weiss, was er eigentlich bedeutet."

Perhaps the sublime owes its renewed popularity to the fact that it is, in its postmodern form, precisely that experience through which the border between life and art is torn down. Here it is helpful to look briefly at Fredric Jameson's reading of the postmodern sublime.[7] Jameson understands the sublime as that which names precisely the intensity of experience produced when the real is dissolved into the postmodern text. He describes the sculptures of Duane Hanson to illustrate this point. Hanson's life-size polyester sculptures are on first glimpse lifelike. They are displayed in "real" settings. His "museum Guard," for example, is actually placed in the position a museum guard might occupy, and "Tourists II," two stereotypically touristlike sculptures, are placed in a museum staring uncomprehendingly but importantly at a work of art. These images have a "peculiar function," Jameson notes, which "lies in what Sartre would have called the derealization of the whole surrounding world of everyday reality" (1991, 19). They are intended to be mistaken for the real thing. The experience created by making and then realizing this mistake is one of sublime intensity.

> Your moment of doubt and hesitation as to the breath and warmth of these polyester figures, in other words, tends to return upon the real human beings moving about you in the museum and to transform them also for the briefest instant into so many dead and flesh-colored simulacra in their own right. The world thereby momentarily loses its depth and threatens to become a glossy skin, a stereoscopic illusion, a rush of filmic images without density. But is this now a terrifying or exhilarating experience? (Jameson 1991, 19)

It is both, of course, and it is precisely this terror-exhilaration that characterizes the sublime experience of the dissolution of the boundary between art and life. This boundary isn't dissolved by a mutual reunification of the two sides, however, but by the rather violent annexation of one by the other. *It is life that is subsumed by art.* While art remains art, artifice, design, life loses its character as a dense reality entangled with necessity at every turn and is pulled into the realm of cultural production.

No wonder that in one of the inaugural volumes in feminist aesthetic philosophy (as opposed to art history or criticism), the 1990 special issue of *Hypatia*, Amy Newman worries that this revival of aesthetic experience as "a kind of visceral, sensuous rush" (1990, 22) means that "in effect, subjective intensity of experience substitutes for political action" (23). When life is subsumed by art, so is politics. "Through the dissolution of the distinction between artist and political activist, the intellectual and the person on the street, the transformation of society becomes a textual, visual, or auditory reality (and thus the mode of immediacy advocated is at

---

7. Jameson's account is based on critical readings of explicit and implicit notions of the sublime in the work of Lyotard and Baudrillard. See especially Lyotard's classic "What is Postmodernism," in *The Postmodern Condition* (1984), and Baudrillard's, "The Ecstasy of Communication," in *The Anti-Aesthetic: Essays on Postmodern Culture.* See also Slavoj Žižek, *The Sublime Object of Ideology* (1989, 201–7). In more philosophical terms, "the sublime" is an intensity of experience that occurs at the moment of the death of ontology. It is, in other words, the moment when we are "in the midst of the Thing-in-Itself" (Žižek 1989, 205) and find, essentially, that there's nothing there.

the same time a dissociative mode of being)" (23). Newman is concerned with the masculinism of sublime experience and how it crosses the border between the modern and the postmodern.

This is my concern as well. When we trace this crossing, we find that some of the specific ways that the experience of the sublime is gendered and racialized are to be found on both sides of the boundary between the modern and the post-modern. If contemporary interest in the sublime has to do with a kind of aes-theticized self-fashioning and self-understanding, then it is not surprising to find that the first flurry of interest in the experience of the sublime had to do with Euro-masculine self-constitution and self-understanding as well.

This has certainly been the claim of the sublime's feminist critics, starting with Irigaray's powerful essay on the Kantian sublime "Paradox a Priori." This essay—the first explicitly feminist essay on the topic that I am aware of—was published in French in 1974 but not translated into English until 1985. In the ensuing two decades, English-speaking feminists have produced a smattering of self-standing essays and shorter treatments in larger works on aesthetics critical of the sublime as it is articulated in the dominant tradition (Newman 1990; Battersby 1990, 1995; Wiseman 1993; Kneller 1993, 1994; Mattick 1995; Gould 1995; Hall 1997; Klinger 1997). A few others have attempted to recuperate the notion of the sublime to understand aspects of women's embodiment, aesthetic experience, or art (Freeman 1995; Lintott 2003; Korsmeyer 2004). This is to say that while male philosophers have been explicitly writing about sublime experience for well over three hundred years, women seem to have entered this discussion only when feminist interest in the sublime emerged explicitly three decades ago! To notice this is, of course, a different thing than to claim that women do not either experience the sublime or produce art that turns on the experience.

Here I turn to the Kantian sublime out of an interest in how the sublime functions as a mode of Euro-masculine self-constitution and how we might un-derstand, in detail, what this means and how it works. Just what kind of subject is being constituted in the experience of the sublime in its modernist/Kantian ren-dition? What are its modes of self-constitution, meaning, what exactly does it do to itself when it constitutes itself? How are its relationships to others implicated in and entangled with its practices of self-constitution? What will this tell us about the modes of self-constitution that are at work in the postmodern version of sublime experience?

In taking up these questions, I both join the conversation that Irigaray started with her 1974 essay and carry it forward in a slightly different direction. Other work has taken up the gendering of the notions of the sublime and beautiful, of the imagination and reason, first pointing out that the notions are gendered, and then looking at the implications of this gendering for either Kantian aesthetics as a whole or for other aspects of Kant's philosophy. I want to look at how gender works in the constitution of a particular form of Euro-masculine identity that is built on the ground of two paradoxes, both of which are gestured toward but not developed in detail in Irigaray's early essay. The first I will call the *paradox of space*. It seems to me that the Euro-masculine subject that emerges in sublime experience is trying to work through a deep confusion about *where* others are in relation to himself.

The boundary between inside and outside that is so important to this subject, is also unimaginably flexible, and external others often reappear on the inside of the subject. The "resolution," or better said, repression of this spatial paradox rests on a deeply gendered structure of spatial relations. The second paradox is the *paradox of time*. The Euro-masculine subject that emerges in sublime experience has trouble knowing where he is *in time* in relation to others. He is continually pushing others who are present with him now back in time so that they come to occupy a temporal point in his own past. The repression of this paradox rests on a deeply racialized structure of temporal relations. These particular structures are important to us today, not only because they are still with us but also because they seem to be under reconstruction in postmodernity, though today the gendering and racializing goes even further underground, becomes "deep gender" and "deep race," and is easy to mistake for something else, even liberation. If Kant provides us with a particularly rich set of texts for tracing the movement of the two paradoxes that are the focus of my reading, this is not to say that we couldn't also find them in other texts of the time period. Neither is it to say that Kant's work is to be reductively identified with the structures we unearth here, as noted above, something quite different, though related, goes on in Kant's discussion of the beautiful (to mention only one example). Yet it is also important not to treat the paradoxes at work in Kant's account of sublime experience as somehow marginal or tangential to either Kantian philosophy or Western modernism as a whole. These are defining structures for a kind of identity that is European, masculine, and triumphant at the turn of the nineteenth century, just as the deep structures of postmodernity are defining, without being seamless or hegemonic in the absolute sense, for us today.

2

The Kantian Sublime

A Story in Two Paradoxes

It sometimes happens that the sun causes the earth to shake underfoot, and people fear being knocked over, or thrown sickeningly downward into the pit, or even flying off into the void. To reestablish the balance that has been so dangerously disturbed, the philosopher decides that from now on nature overall will be put under the control of the human spirit and her origins will be based on her necessary obedience to the law. So the ground will now rest upon a transcendental ceiling that is propped up by the forms and rules of representation and is thus unshakable. To build this construction, man was, of course, obliged to draw on reserves still in the realm of nature; a detour through the outer world was of course indispensable; the "I" had to relate to "things" before it could be conscious of itself. But this initial period of cooperative creation is forgotten in an arrogant claim to sovereign discretion over everything. (203–4)

—Luce Irigaray

Hannah Arendt worried that modern man's "attempt to reduce all experiences with the world as well as with other human beings to experiences between man and himself" (1958, 254) would eventually succeed and that this very success would constitute a massive human failure. Today we see this worry come to life, as human activity reorders both the climate and the genetic makeup of living creatures so that when we look at the weather or at the farmer's corn field we see only a monstrous version of ourselves. Philosophers in what we call the West have been at the forefront of the tradition that keeps transforming relationships to others into relations between man and himself. Feminists have been at the forefront of challenging this tradition and of sorting out in detail how the fiction of a sovereign and autonomous masculine subject is maintained.

In her essay on Kant's third *Critique*, Irigaray finds that relationships to Others in Kant's aesthetics are provisional relationships, entered into only as a way of bringing about the "union between [man] and himself." In sublime experience, an encounter with a powerful and overwhelming nature becomes a mere detour on the path to a securely sovereign subject. Kant's use of the "outer world" of things, even as he securely locks away the things-in-themselves from knowledge, means for Irigaray that *"the paradox of a kind of symmetry has been evaded. One kind of difference,* inverted in the mirror, will never be analyzed" (1985, 210). It is the reworking of this kind of difference (between humans and nature, men and women) into a mere occasion for man's knowledge of himself that is the very foundation of Euro-masculinist subjectivity.

In the process of this reworking, Irigaray maintains, sexual difference is primary. In Kantian aesthetics as in the broader masculine tradition, "woman will constitute the imaginary sub-basement that shores up the mine, will act as man's guiding thread in his various relationships with the many faces of the sensible world" (1985, 212). This "imaginary sub-basement" shores up the mine out of which the resources to produce the phantom we know as the free, autonomous, and sovereign Euro-masculine subject are continually prospected.[1]

It is not surprising that relationships to Others should be central to Kant's notion of the sublime since it was developed in a historical and cultural context in which the nature of European man's relationships to the natural world, to women, and to the peoples of the colonies was passionately contested. While the Euro-masculine subject's entanglement in relationships of dependency and power with these others is the key factor in his movement toward the possibility of freedom, autonomy, and sovereignty (since the very possibility of such noble things rests on the material benefits he reaps from these relationships), his dependency on these Others must also be "forgotten" in order to secure his fantasy of independence. As we will see, the process of forgetting puts enormous strain on the subject that results.

An intellectual battle over the human relation to the natural world raged around Kant and was expressed most poignantly in Kant's ongoing debate with his former student Herder over the status of the *Aufklärung* (Enlightenment) in relation to the *Stürm und Drang* (Storm and Stress) philosophers and poets who, it seemed to Kant, threatened the absolute ascendancy of the human subject as distinct from nature (Zammito 1992). While the *Stürm und Drang* intellectuals "stressed wonder and awe" in relation to nature "and even developed complex psychological accounts of the experience, they first of all found the ground for such an experience in the objects of nature" (227). Kant will find the ground for these experiences in man himself. The sublime will be one key site of Kant's insistence that a misplaced reverence for the natural world be replaced by an appropriate reverence for human reason.

---

1. Other critics agree. Böhme and Böhme argue that "the rise and triumph of reason is at once the history of the overthrow of nature in the female and the feminine in nature: a conquest that is first made possible through the strict separation of the heavily armoured masculine subject from woman and nature" (Böhme and Böhme 1983, 20; my translation).

Kant displayed a great deal of passion in relation to the raging debate over the social position of women as well. Theodor Gottlieb von Hippel, Kant's contemporary, became the mayor of Königsberg and was an ardent feminist who believed passionately in women's equality (Schröder 1997). The social and legal position of women was still clearly subservient to men at the time, and women were excluded from university education in Germany, including Kant's university (Schott 1997, 323). In Kant's own social commentary on women, he builds one argument for women's subordination by reference to their legal status at the time. Women were *unmündig*, that is, not legally considered adults.[2] But at the same time, the "ideas of universal human freedom and equality" that characterized the Enlightenment were ready tools for those arguing for equal education for women, or for women's equality to men more generally (Klinger 1997, 195). Of Kant's feminist contemporaries, certainly the most well-known was Mary Wollstonecraft, whose *Vindication of the Rights of Woman* caused a stir among the educated classes of Europe in the early 1790s. This pamphlet is a response to "Rousseau, and most of the male writers who have followed his steps, [who] have warmly inculcated that the whole tendency of female education ought to be directed to one point:—to render them pleasing" (Wollstonecraft 1986, 49). She refers further to the shrewd observations of "one German writer"—and appears to be referring to Kant and his *Observations* by the content of this and a number of other remarks (59). But whether or not either Kant or Wollstonecraft were aware of one another at all speaks less to the point here than the general milieu in which both writers worked, one in which universalist Enlightenment arguments in favor of democratically organized societies based on human reason and autonomy were in contradiction with social realities—not the least of which was the reality of women's subordination to men—and were being taken up and used by feminists in favor of women's emancipation. In the face of these challenges, "the majority of Enlightenment philosophers," writes Cornelia Klinger, "made every endeavor to find new foundations for gender difference in order to legitimate the status quo of gender hierarchy" (Klinger 1997, 195). Kant was no exception, his own efforts have been seen by feminist critics as oriented toward finding new ways to "shore up older versions of masculinity" (Battersby 1995).

These debates in Europe were themselves contextualized by the increasing globalization brought about by European imperialism. Kant lived and worked at a time when European identity had been made and remade through global conquest. Reports of colonizing activity on every continent had been flowing back to Europe for three hundred years, a constant stream of information about who and what a European was, in contrast to "savages," "barbarians," and "Caribs." In spite of this three-hundred-year history, the identity that was being forged for Europeans was still in the process of construction, in good part through the proliferation of European travel narratives describing visits to exotic and faraway lands and encounters with non-European others. A new European identity unified the various

---

2. In his "Metaphysische Anfangsgründe der Rechtslehre."

peoples of Europe for the first time as "white." This designation was based on distance (spatial and temporal) from the "primitive" and "savage," notions which were themselves entangled with distinctions of gender. European "ladies" owed their relatively privileged status both to the flow of resources from the colonies to Europe[3] and to the discursive distinction that distance from the "savage" afforded.

The turn of the century then, as now, was marked by a preoccupation with relationships of Otherness, both internal and external to Europe. In establishing his difference from these Others the Euro-masculine subject also established himself. The very possibility of erecting a convincing edifice of freedom, autonomy, and sovereignty rested on what he did with these Others. Kant wrote his *Observations* and, more than two decades later, his "Analytic of the Sublime" in the midst of these debates. He tried to sort through the confusions that characterized the Euro-masculine relation to Others, both as a philosopher and as one of the founders of the new field of anthropology, which crystallized an epistemology of the primitive and civilized that would be key to European self-constitution. These confusions are sometimes explicit: is nature inside the subject or outside the subject? But they need not be articulated as such, instead they may bubble just beneath the surface of the explicit concerns that mark the philosophical texts.

We might understand these confusions as swirling around two general sets of paradoxes, which I am choosing to call the *paradox of space* and the *paradox of time* (though many other names for each might have been chosen). In the first instance we are considering these sorts of questions: Where are the Others of the Euro-masculine subject in relation to him? Inside or outside? What kind of space or place does this subject inhabit? Is a woman a part of a man? If so then how is it that a man is not partly a woman? How is this subject's spatial self-constitution built around his spatial relations to nature and women? In the second instance we are considering questions of time and sequence: What kind of time does this subject inhabit? What kind of time inhabits him? Where are others in this subject's time? Are racialized others that I encounter encountered in my time? How is temporal self-constitution built around temporal relations to racialized others?

The Paradox of Space

> The principal object is that man should become more perfect as a man, and the woman as a wife. —Immanuel Kant

> In matrimonial life the united pair should, as it were, constitute a single moral person, which is animated and governed by the understanding of the man and the taste of the wife. —Immanuel Kant

---

3. As Eduardo Galeano writes in his well-known *Open Veins of Latin America: Five Centuries of the Pillage of a Continent*, "Latin America is the region of open veins. Everything from the discovery until our times, has always been transmuted into European—or later United States—capital, and as such has accumulated in distant centers of power.... *Our defeat was always implicit in the victory of others; our wealth has always generated our poverty by nourishing the prosperity of others*" (1973, 12).

Kant was preoccupied with the problem of freedom. How can a creature of nature, subject to the natural laws of mechanical causality, be free? How can an animal with a body be a moral agent? Which is to say, how can a creature of nature not be a creature of nature at all? The first task was to radically differentiate humans from nature, to forge a boundary between the world of appearances where human beings also appear to one another (and where the laws of nature govern all occurrences) and the world of morality in which human beings are rational and free agents responsible for discovering the principles of reason. But if the phenomenal realm, the realm of necessity, and the noumenal realm, the realm of freedom, are separated by such an impenetrable frontier, how is it that anything we might do as moral agents makes any difference in the world we actually inhabit?

> Between the realm of the natural concept, as the sensible, and the realm of the concept of freedom, as the supersensible, there is a great gulf fixed, so that it is not possible to pass from the former to the latter (by means of the theoretical employment of reason), just as if they were so many separate worlds, the first of which is powerless to exercise influence on the second: still the latter is *meant* to influence the former—that is to say, the concept of freedom is meant to actualize in the sensible world the end proposed by its laws. (*CJ* 1928, 14)

Providing a pathway between these two realms that keeps reason purified of sense is Kant's great challenge in the third *Critique*.

Kant will work through the question of necessity and freedom in part by translating it into the question of the one and the many. The basic form of this latter question concerns the relation between humans and nature. We can begin by asking the question this way: if nature is part of the human, how can it be that this part is not a part of the whole in any determinative sense? If humans are, even partly, natural creatures, how is it that this natural part doesn't ruin the freedom of the whole? In fact, by taking a look around, we realize that it does ruin the freedom of the whole person all the time. The closer we are to a situation in which we are just meeting our basic bodily needs for survival—that is, acquiring food and paying the rent or mortgage that keeps a roof over our heads—the less free we are to determine how we spend our time for a good part of the day. If we are responsible for meeting the basic bodily needs of others, often children, we are even less free to choose to not go to work or to make an ethical decision that will make the boss mad and get us fired. Women in many parts of the world spend a great deal of their time going long distances to get potable water and carrying it home—not in the least free not to go one day, even if they are sick or just sick and tired of carrying water. Of course this is not, with the exception of the ethical decision example, the kind of freedom Kant had in mind, exactly. The point here is simply that there is a closely lived conflict between bodily needs and freedom that is at the root of Kant's dilemma.

In order to secure the moral autonomy of the subject (Irigaray calls it an "amoral autonomy," and Böhme and Böhme call the subject who imagines this autonomy for himself the "armoured subject"), Kant has to imagine a strange relation between the part and the whole. The ideal model is close at hand. Women are both legally and culturally understood to be parts of a whole, of a "single moral person" in Kant's words, by virtue of their marriage to an individual man. Yet even as the woman is part of the man, the man is paradoxically not understood to be part woman, and this is just the special relation of part to whole that Kant needs. The assimilation of the woman into the very subjective life of her husband is a primary mode of women's subordination to men, as feminists have noted since Wollstonecraft. It is in fact one of the important ways that domination works when it is gendered. The desire for the freedom that accrues to an autonomous, armoured agent can work itself out through a fantasy of the assimilation of woman to man's inner life.[4]

Here I trace several moments of the Euro-masculine subject's fantasy of freedom by reading three separate texts as part of the same fantastic story. In Kant's *Observations*, European women, who are granted a weak sort of subjectivity in their "capacity" as perceivers of the beautiful, see this subjectivity give way to their much more primary role as beautiful objects of masculine contemplation. The feminine is assimilated to the phenomenal object world in the *Observations*, and the object is assimilated to the very workings of the masculine subject's faculties in Kant's critical work. The movement of *Verinnerlichung* (internalization) results in the phantasmatic expansion of the powers of the subject. Yet for the story to be complete, the now internal Others must be brought under proper control. One climactic moment of Kant's drama of freedom is recounted in the "Analytic of the Sublime," where internal violence establishes the dominance of the masculine over the feminine at the same time that it catapults the subject out of his dependence on nature and into a fantasy of his own freedom.

The Observations

Kant's first treatise on the subject of women's proper place and education is also his first treatise on aesthetics.[5] Of the two aesthetic feelings, Kant tells us, the sublime is the higher[6] and the province of the man who is not "subject to the inconstancy of external things" (*OFBS* 1960, 65). In the natural world, those things that evoke a sense of eternity, the infinite, and grandeur are sublime; those that evoke a sense of inconstancy, multiplicity, and delicacy are beautiful:

4. This claim is closely related to Robin Schott's claim regarding Kant that the "desire to detach the self from contingency and embodiment is itself an effect of particular gender relations, is itself an expression of the flight of masculinity from the temporal, embodied, uncertain realm of phenomenal existence" (Schott 1997, 321).

5. Rousseau's influence is apparent. Klinger notes, "Kant differs from Rousseau in translating the normative conceptions of polarized gender roles that the two thinkers share into the language of aesthetics. The gender difference is expressed in aesthetic terms, and vice versa: gender difference is inscribed in aesthetic categories" (Klinger 1997, 194).

6. In this first treatise, Kant distinguishes three kinds of sublime: the terrifying, the noble, and the splendid sublime. These in turn become part of his characterization of peoples of different nations. These distinctions aren't a significant part of section 3, however, Kant's treatise on women and men. Neither does he maintain these distinctions in the third *Critique*, where the sublime is undifferentiated.

Tall oaks and lonely shadows in a sacred grove are sublime; flower beds, low hedges and trees trimmed in figures are beautiful. Night is sublime, day is beautiful Temperaments that possess a feeling for the sublime are drawn gradually, by the quiet stillness of a summer evening as the shimmering light of the stars breaks through the brown shadows of night and the lonely moon rises into view, into high feelings of friendship, of disdain for the world, of eternity. The shining day stimulates busy fervor and a feeling of gaiety. The sublime moves, the beautiful charms. (*OFBS* 1960, 47)

In human character, anger, bold revenge, resolute audacity, true virtue, "subduing one's passions through principles" (57), and the "stern duty of justice" are sublime. Deceit, vanity, tenderheartedness, complaisance, gaiety, and action from "good hearted impulses" (74) are beautiful. Distinct affective responses are provoked by these differences; "sublime attributes stimulate esteem, but beautiful ones, love" (51).

Kant discusses both sexual difference and national difference in the *Observations*. As Zammito noted, "there is ... an anthropological and moral purpose behind the little essay, far more than an aesthetic one" (1992, 32). A twenty-page section of his seventy-page treatise, entitled "Of the Distinction of the Beautiful and Sublime in the Interrelations of the Two Sexes," is devoted to drawing the connections between aesthetic categories and sexual difference. Just as he begins the entire treatise distinguishing between the feelings of the beautiful and the sublime, he begins this section distinguishing between the "fair sex" and the "noble sex." The following passage, which is perhaps the most well-known, appears about three pages into this section of Kant's essay.

Deep meditations and long sustained reflection are noble but difficult, and do not well befit a person in which unconstrained charms should show nothing else than a beautiful nature. Laborious learning or painful pondering, even if a woman should greatly succeed in it, destroy the merits that are proper to her sex, and because of their rarity they can make of her an object of cold admiration; but at the same time they will weaken the charms with which she exercises her great power over the other sex. A woman who has a head full of Greek, like Mme Dacier [who translated the *Iliad*, *Odyssey*, and other Greek and Latin classics into French], or carries on fundamental controversies about mechanics, like the Marquise de Chatelet [whose essay on the nature of fire won the French Academy of Science prize in 1738],[7] might as well even have a beard; for perhaps that would express more obviously the mien of profundity for which she strives. The beautiful understanding selects for its objects everything closely related to the finer feeling, and relinquishes to the diligent, fundamental, and deep understanding abstract speculations of branches of knowledge useful but dry. A woman therefore will learn no geometry; of the principle of sufficient reason or the monads she will know only so much as is needed to perceive the salt in a satire which the insipid grubs of our sex have censured. The fair can leave Descartes his vortices to whirl forever without troubling themselves about them. (*OFBS* 1960, 78–79)

7. See Goldthwait's notes (*OFSB* 1960, 121).

When Kant writes on gender, and let us be clear that his theme is gender among the "well-bred" classes of Europe, he seems at first to give a descriptive account. Yet his work is full of "shoulds" and "oughts" to such an extent that it undermines the descriptive mode and in fact amounts to an implicit admission that, in terms of gender, things are far from what they should be. One gets the distinct impression, in fact, that Kant is writing in order to shore something up, that he is using his wit, sarcasm, and considerable rhetorical talent against the tide of other perspectives.

He draws on a deep framework of associations of the feminine with particularity, multiplicity, and passivity and of the masculine with universality, unity, and activity—all common gender associations, and common themes in modernist aesthetics. In fact, the aesthetic notions of the sublime and beautiful, entangled as they are in structures of deep gender, will allow Kant to rework the central paradox of Enlightenment gender relations, that is, the subject status of those who were, legally and socially, more often regarded as objects. We might call the confusion between women's subject and object status a "productive" confusion because it is through this confusion that Kant's notion of gender is produced in the text.[8]

It is helpful here to link these reflections to Kant's explicit reference to women as *gegenstände* (things) in his "Metaphysische Anfangsgründe der Rechtslehre" (the first part of *Metaphysik der Sitten*), written at the end of Kant's career in 1797. Here Kant created a category to encompass the slippage between subject and object when he described women as *verdingliche Menschen* ("thinglike people") (Schröder 1997, 285). Man's relation to woman is one of acquisition (*Erwerbung*) (MAR 1959, 91). Acquisition is further defined as *wenn ich mache das etwas mein werde* (when I make something mine) or *etwas in meine Gewalt bringe* (bring something under my power) (MAR 1959). The relation between women and men most closely resembles the *Verhältnis des Besitzers zu einem Gegenstand* (relation of an owner to an object) (190). Here women have a kind of "minimum personhood" in that they cannot be bought and sold (Schröder 1997, 287), but men have a *persönlichen Recht* (personal right) (MAR 1959, 189) to use such a person, once acquired, *als eine Sache* (as a thing) (MAR 1959, 190–92). There are three justifications for this state of things:

8. Korsmeyer notes in relation to Hume:

in this philosophy gendered concepts like the standard of taste are a symptom of ideas of femaleness that oscillate in their proximity to and distance from the paradigmatic human. Thus it is not correct to say that women are ignored by Hume's philosophy, such that his conclusions apply only to males, indeed, only to eighteenth-century, genteel, male Europeans. It is clear that women are not only intentionally included within the scope of his ideas of human nature, but also that in some respects female presence is accommodated as easily as male. On the other hand *and* at the same time, the concept of human nature proceeds from a point of view that shifts women from the position of participating subjects to that of objects to be considered in philosophical deliberations about "human nature," so frequently arrived at by a combination of introspection and social analysis. (1995, 63)

A similar ambivalence is at work here.

the first is a divine justification—God intended it so; the second a natural one—women of whatever age are considered to be *unmündig* (immature) and never become full adults[9]; and the third is a legal justification—the law has always considered women to be *verdingliche Menschen*. A "thinglike person" is a strange construction indeed since what marks a person for Kant is certainly its very difference from a thing. Yet this is a concept capable of holding together an explosive paradox—the same paradox that was indeed exploding in the political and social upheaval over gender dominance in the Enlightenment.

Kant's struggle with this paradox is already at work in the *Observations*. While he clearly believes that women are able to "greatly succeed" at higher learning, for example, he writes, "I hardly believe the fair sex is capable of principles" (*OFBS* 1960, 81). Though Kant sets out to discuss women's "strong inborn feeling for all that is beautiful, elegant, and decorated" (77), as if women are to be treated as knowers in his work, in the very next sentence we find that "even in childhood they like to be dressed up, and take pleasure when they are adorned" (77). Women, who possess a beautiful understanding, nevertheless find their primary role is to appear as beautiful objects. "A woman is embarrassed little that she does not possess certain high insights, that she is timid, and not fit for serious employments, and so forth; she is beautiful and captivates, and that is enough" (93). In fact, though women are seen to possess "taste," and men "understanding," this different and unequal subjectivity is far less the topic of Kant's essay then men's judgment of women as beautiful objects. "Certain specific traits lie especially in the personality of this sex which distinguish it clearly from ours and chiefly result in making her *known* by the mark of the beautiful" (76; my emphasis).

Here a woman is the sort of being who is both subject and object, but in a certain sense this does not differentiate her from men, whose phenomenal existence as appearing objects and noumenal existence as moral agents so occupied Kant. The difference is that women's subjectivity is permanently occupied with appearance, is devoted to appearance, and thus, is permanently compromised by her status as an object. Her subjectivity is *in service* to her primary role as an appearing object.

The Observations *and the First* Critique

Interrogating this confusion leads directly to connections between Kant's social criticism and his epistemology. There are striking similarities between Kant's

---

9. There is clearly both an evolutionary and developmental temporality operating in Kant's social commentary since the subordination of women is justified, in part, by their failure ever to reach adult status. Men are considered to be permanently "older" than women. The temporality of the first *Critique* involves the evolutionary maturity of reason, for only mature reason is capable of true autonomy, of severing nature's "leading strings." The entire project of the first *Critique* is undertaken as a project fitting "the matured judgment of the age, which refuses to be any longer put off with illusory knowledge (*CPR* 1965, 9, Axi) and is considered not merely intellectually but developmentally superior to other approaches.

Observations and his first *Critique* in terms of what I am calling the "productive confusion" between subject and object. Here we see that the dynamics of assimilation are at work both in the way women slip almost through slight of hand from subjects to objects in Kant's social commentary and in the epistemological relation between the knowing subject and the phenomenal world.

The *Observations*, written in 1763, and the first *Critique*, written in 1781, are separated by eighteen very important years for Kant. Yet a great deal unites them. In both books, there is a critique, a carving out of appropriate regions, a delineating of areas of right. In the *Critique of Pure Reason*, of course, this carving out is extremely technical and involves the question of how the subject knows its object and what kind of object it knows. In the *Observations*, the proper scope and relation of two aesthetic feelings are delineated in a more lighthearted way, along with their proper objects. In section 3 of the *Observations*, Kant continues this critical enterprise by carving out regions appropriate to women and men: what female subjects have as their proper objects and what male subjects have as theirs.

Though far from the transcendental (universal and necessary) a priori claims of the *Critiques*, Kant prefigures the subjectivism or mentalism of his critical work in this early esssay. In the *Observations*, Kant argues that "the various feelings of enjoyment or of displeasure rest not so much upon the nature of the external things that arouse them as upon each person's own disposition to be moved by these to pleasure or pain" (OFBS 1960, 45). After listing the objects that arouse the feelings of the sublime and beautiful respectively, Kant remarks, "In order that the former impressions could occur to us in due strength, we must have a *feeling of the sublime*, and in order to enjoy the latter well, a *feeling of the beautiful*" (OFBS 1960, 47). Objects arouse (*erregen*) and occasion (*veranlassen*) these feelings, rather than (more actively) causing them (*verursachen*). The power of the world of sense experience is reduced here to that of a mere catalyst.

In the first *Critique*, the power of the subject over the object of appearance is what constitutes Kant's famous Copernican turn. In keeping with the Western scientific conceit inherited from Francis Bacon, Kant writes, "a light broke upon all students of nature. They learned that reason has insight only into that which it produces after a plan of its own, and that it must not allow itself to be kept, as it were, on nature's leading strings, but must itself show the way with principles of judgement based upon fixed laws, constraining nature to give answer to questions of reason's own determining" (CPR 1965, 20, Bxiii). The attitude with which a student of nature approaches learning is of utmost importance to Kant.

> Reason, holding in one hand its principles...and in the other hand the experiment which it has devised in conformity with these principles, must approach nature in order to be taught by it. It must not, however, do so in the character of a pupil who listens to everything that the teacher chooses to say, but of an appointed judge who compels the witnesses to answer questions which he himself has formulated. Reason...must adopt as its guide...what it has itself put into nature. (CPR 1965, 20 Bxiii)

The images of a passive pupil awed by a powerful teacher, or a passive child pulled about on the leading strings of a powerful mother, provide a background of possible ridicule to properly socialize the masculine subject. In these passages, reason is a husband who is urged to wear the pants in the family, to compel the submission of wife/nature by force—or a young man who is kept in check by a leading string, literally tied to his mother, urged to cut the humiliating ties and be off on his own.

This masculine independence is not to be assured through the subject acting on an external Other, however, but through the assimilation of the object into the very interior world of the subject. In the *Critique of Pure Reason*, Kant's revolutionary move is to establish the transcendental subject himself as the "necessary condition of the possibility of all representations." In a passage that has been foundational for much of philosophy since Kant, he writes:

> Hitherto it has been assumed that all our knowledge must conform to objects. But all attempts to extend our knowledge of objects by establishing something in regards to them a priori, by means of concepts, have on this assumption ended in failure. We must therefore make trial whether we may not have more success in the task of metaphysics if we suppose that objects must conform to our knowledge. This would agree better with what is desired, namely, that it should be possible to have knowledge of objects a priori, determining something in regard to them prior to their being given. (CPR 1965, 22, Bxvi)

Kant sets out to establish the conditions under which the object thus given submits to the subject. Three characteristics of the Kantian object contribute to its assimilation: first, it has the mode of *givenness*, that is, I encounter the object as *available* to my mental faculties. Second, it is *constituted* as an object by the subject, that is, my encounter with the object requires that it first be *fashioned* by my mental faculties. Third, this constitution is also an overcoming of the object's multiplicity, which is *synthesized*; it becomes a unitary phenomenal object at all through the internal form-giving powers of the subject. The conditions under which the object submits to the subject, then, involve the expansion of the interior universe of the subject to include the phenomenal object.

The position of the object here is paralleled in important ways by the position of women in the *Observations*. There, women slip quickly from their role as perceivers of the beautiful into a mode of *givenness* to man. In the first lines of a treatise that is marking out the capacities particular to the two sexes as knowers, Kant talks immediately of women *as known*. Kant grants women the capacity for feeling the beautiful; at the same time he conflates this sensibility with the definition of her as a beautiful object for man to such an extent that even her feelings of the beautiful become part of what arouses and occasions a positive judgment in the male knower. Beauty as it pertains to women is less a capacity than a *mode of givenness* to masculine perception.

The theme of "constitution" also crosses over from Kant's social commentary in the *Observations* to his epistemology in the first *Critique*. Kant is extremely clear that, for women, failure to remain in the role of a beautiful object, in the mode of givenness to men, results in failure to be a woman at all. Anne Dacier and the Marquise de Chatelet are not real women for Kant. They might as well grow beards. As Kant writes in the *Observations*, foreshadowing the first *Critique*, "As it is our purpose to judge concerning feelings, it cannot be unpleasant *to bring under concepts*, if possible, the difference of the impression that the form and features of the fair sex make on the masculine" (*OFBS* 1960, 86, emphasis added). He goes on to distinguish merely "pretty" women from truly "beautiful" ones. But the intellectual woman cannot be brought under the concept of "woman" at all, and such women, if not growing beards, are certainly either prudes or Amazons (94). Though Kant has not yet developed his technical account of the subsumption of objects under concepts whereby the intelligibility of the object is constituted by the subject, we find that he performs this very subsumption here by himself deciding which women are intelligible as women and which ones are not. With the transcendental turn in the first *Critique*, the intelligibility of the phenomenal object is not a property of the object itself but an active contribution of the subject. For Kant of the *Observations*, women are the sorts of objects that appear in the perceptual world of the male viewer/knower, whose judgment renders them intelligible as women (or not).

The theme of multiplicity and unity also crosses the boundary between social commentary and epistemology. In Kant's epistemology, the multiplicity of the object is tamed by the unity of the transcendental subject. In the *Observations*, "multiplicity is beautiful" (*OFBS* 1960, 67), and beauty is at home in the multiplicitous world of sense experience (81). The sublime is unity, especially in its noble variation. A man who possesses a feeling for the sublime "orders his sensations under principles. They are so much the less subject to inconstancy and change" (64). Masculine unity is what sets to work in marriage since "in matrimonial life the united pair should, as it were, constitute a single moral person" (95)—the single moral person that they constitute is, of course, following the legal tradition at the time, the husband. Just as in the first *Critique*, the unification or "marriage" of the subject and object is grounded on the transcendental unity of the subject; in the *Observations* the association of beauty with sensation and the sublime with principles makes the bearer of the feeling of the sublime the bearer of unity as well. In precritical social commentary and postcritical epistemology, it is the Euro-masculine subject that stands for unity.

What women share with Kant's phenomenal object is, then, a mode of givenness, constitution by the Euro-masculine subject, and a wild multiplicity that must be tamed by he who "holds principles in his hand." These are the characteristics that allow for the domination of the woman/object through its assimilation into the very inner life of the autonomous and sovereign masculine subject.

The Drama of Gender in the Third Critique

Cornelia Klinger's critical work on the Kantian distinction between the beautiful and sublime draws on Kant's *Observations* to expose the gendered structure of these categories in the third *Critique*. As she shows, the gendered dichotomy in the third *Critique* has gone underground but still exposes itself in the more subtle distinction of "immersion in nature v. distance from nature" (Klinger 1997, 196) and in more subtly gendered language. In Korsmeyer's terms, it becomes "deep gender."

Both the experience of the sublime and the experience of the beautiful are feelings that arise when independent faculties are set into relation with one another. Judgment of the beautiful involves a harmonious connection between imagination and understanding. Judgment of the sublime involves the conflict-ridden relation of imagination and reason.

> The two faculties, understanding and reason, are not only different in character but also the relations in which they enter with imagination are of completely different kinds. The relation of imagination and understanding is a harmonious one; a feeling of the beautiful arises when our understanding is in harmony with nature, when the form of a natural object is corresponding to our rational capacity and conveys to us the impression of a meaningful whole or totality. . . . By contrast, the relation of imagination and reason is based on conflict and therefore is accompanied by a feeling of "displeasure." . . . Conflict, disharmony, struggle, and violence are the predominant features of the sublime and yet, there is also a strange kind of attraction, a "negative pleasure" connected to it. (Klinger 1997, 197)

The strange pleasure in the sublime comes with the subject's experience of the infinite superiority of reason over the imagination, which is still tainted by sense, thus connected to nature. It is a feeling of reason's independence from and dominion over nature (Klinger 1997, 198). The imagination in the third *Critique* plays very much the role of the woman as possessor of a beautiful understanding in the *Observations*. Imagination is still connected to the matter of sense experience, to the multiplicitous; it is gendered feminine. Reason is autonomous from sense experience, thus from nature, and is gendered masculine.

Klinger continues with readings of Lyotard on Kant, further exposing not only the gender hierarchy in the text but the violence as well. Lyotard's extraordinary and seemingly exultant narrative on the Kantian sublime, which he refers to as "a family story" centers on a scene in which father (reason) rapes mother (imagination):

> The sublime is the child of an unhappy encounter, that of the Idea with form. Unhappy because this Idea is unable to make concessions. The law (the father) is so authoritarian, so unconditional, and the regard the law requires so exclusive that he, the father, will do nothing to obtain consent, even through a delicious rivalry with the imagination. He requires the imagination's "retraction." . . . He fertilizes the virgin who has devoted herself to forms,[10] without regard for her favor. He demands regard only for himself, to the law and its realization. He has no need for a beautiful nature. He desperately needs an imagination that is violated, exceeded, exhausted. She will die in giving birth to the sublime. She will think she is dying. (*LAS* 1991, 180)

---

10. To avoid confusion, on my reading, this reference to "forms" has to do with the forms of intuition, space and time—these are the kinds of form for which the Idea has no use. Even though space and time are form-giving powers of the subject, they are too close to sense experience to be "pure" of it—and thus are tainted with the status of the passive object.

The "primal scene" between reason and the imagination is both gendered and violent. The feminine is assimilated into the faculties of the masculine subject, and there she is raped and brought to her knees.

Whereas the feeling for the beautiful is occasioned by nature tamed, the sublime feeling arises on the occasion of a confrontation with nature at its wildest and most formless. What most approximates the sublime in nature—what most approximates the infinite in both magnitude and might—allows the Kantian subject to experience his own might and magnitude. The sublime originates in a feeling of "astonishment mounting almost to terror, the awe and thrill of devout feeling, that takes hold of one when gazing upon the prospect of mountains ascending to heaven, deep ravines and torrents raging there" (*CJ* 1928, 269). Nature as chaos, disorder, and danger occasions the experience of the sublime, "bold, overhanging, . . . threatening thunderclouds piled up in the vault of heaven, borne along with flashes and peals, volcanoes in all their violence of destruction, hurricanes leaving desolation in their track, the boundless ocean rising with rebellious force, the high waterfall of some mighty river" (261).

While the experience of beauty in nature is harmonious and calls the subject back into relation with the natural world from which he has been alienated, the experience of the sublime is a call to war. Reason demands that the imagination provide for him a representation of the magnitude (the mathematical sublime) and might (the dynamical sublime) of nature, which threatens his sovereignty, and striving to fulfill this demand in an act of comprehension, the imagination is broken (*CJ* 1928, 254). The sheer magnitude of nature "in its wildest and most irregular disorder and desolation" (246) brings the imagination to the limits of an excess that is "like an abyss in which it fears to lose itself" (258). The imagination cowers before the might of nature, forced as she is to recognize her physical helplessness in the face of such power (262).

But the imagination's very failure becomes the rational subject's success, since reason *can* comprehend the might and magnitude with which it is confronted. The Kantian subject uses what most approximates the sublime in nature as a mirror, which allows him to experience his own might and magnitude as sublime.[11] At the moment of the imagination's defeat, the subject's destiny flashes out on the border between the nameable and the unnameable. "Therefore the feeling of the sublime in nature is respect for our own vocation, which we attribute to an Object of nature by a certain subreption (substitution of a respect for the Object of nature in place of one for the idea of humanity in our own self—the Subject);

11. In Terry Eagleton's reading of the "Kantian imaginary," he uses the "mirror stage" of Lacan to read Kant's own mirror, "The Kantian subject of aesthetic judgement, who misperceives as a quality of the object what is in fact a pleasurable coordination of its own powers, and who constitutes in a mechanistic world a figure of idealized unity, resembles the infantile narcissist of the Lacanian mirror stage, whose misperceptions Louis Althusser has taught us to regard as an indispensable structure of all ideology" (1996, 87). Kant corrects the "misperception" of the object, so that we now understand the Euro-masculine subject's contemplation of the sublime object as pleasurable insofar as in and through this contemplation the subject *feels* his destiny.

and this feeling renders, as it were, intuitable the supremacy of our cognitive faculties on the rational side over the greatest faculty of sensibility" (*CJ* 1928, 258). The expansion of the subject continues: in the *Observations* the man's very subjective life expands to include the woman he marries, in the first *Critique* it expands again to include the entire phenomenal world, and here the very might and magnitude of nature become properties of the inner life of the rational subject. By recognizing the "subreption" that has occurred, the subject reclaims these powers for himself.

The true subreption occurs, of course, when Kant cuts the subject loose from the natural world and reverses the order of dependence so that the world is dependent on the autonomous subject. It is a fantasy that is built on a violent rupture in the relation of reason to the imagination. The sublimity of the ideas of reason is first felt in that moment when imagination is broken. Yet at this very moment he discovers himself in the mirror, that is, discovers that the true owner of this magnificent capacity for violence is the rational part of the subject himself. It is reason, not nature, that breaks the imagination. Violating the imagination ruptures the subject's relationship to that part of himself still tied to sense experience, thus to the natural world, and gives rise to a heady experience of independence (*CJ* 1928, 260, 262). This salvific violence, gendered through and through, allows the subject to experience his vocation or destiny, that is, his freedom. In fact, "it is ... for us a law (of reason), which goes to make us what we are, that we should esteem as small in comparison with ideas of reason everything which for us is great in nature as an object of sense; and that which makes us alive to the feeling of this supersensible side of our being harmonizes with that law" (*CJ* 1928, 258).

But if imagination is truly a faculty of the subject, how is it that the subject himself is not broken in the process? What allows for the subject's triumph through a narrative of violation of part of the subject himself? What sort of a thing can be part of a person, but not in a determinative sense? What kind of an internal "part" is no part at all? Just as in the marriage relation in Kant's social commentary, the wife is subsumed into the identity of the husband, who does not become partly feminine in the process—the strange "unity" of the subject that emerges here depends on a gendered model of unity where the part collapses into a whole that remains untainted by it. Were it not for this device, the subject of sublime experience would be a wounded subject, not a triumphant one.

For Kant, sublime feeling is really a kind of knowing that is not cognitive. It is through this feeling that the subject achieves access to his own destiny, something that reason and understanding cannot provide on their own. The feeling is experienced when displeasure and its related emotions—horror, terror, regret—are violently transcended and turn into their opposites: pleasure, awe, triumph, excitement. The sublime feeling is not any of these, but is precisely the border and the movement between them. This feeling does not just confirm the subject's destiny, it is the emotive allusion to the thing itself, to the unpresentable real thing. What does it feel like? Like excitement (*CJ* 1928, 246), like "a vibration" (258), like a "pitch of feeling" (246), like a "check to the vital forces followed by a discharge" (245). Indeed, the sublime is Kant's one glorious ejaculatory moment.

The Paradox of Time

The subject stands for unity in Kant, while multiplicity is on the side of the object. Yet Lyotard's fascination with the Kantian sublime has everything to do with an irrecoverable moment of multiplicity he believes he has found there.

> The analysis of the beautiful allows hope for the idea of nature, grounded on the subject as the unity of the faculties and on a legitimization of the agreement of the real object with the authentic determination of the subject. The Analytic of the Sublime smashes into the matter to which this double construction is dedicated like a meteor, and seems, even though it is a "mere appendix" to put an end to this hope.[12] (*IE* 1989a, 91)

This meteor shatters the unitary subject, on Lyotard's reading, and leaves it without hope of recovery.

The revival of interest in the Kantian sublime has to do with our current fascination with plurality, which is celebrated in much of postmodern theory as, in and of itself, liberatory. As Christine Pries puts it:

> The feeling of the sublime is plural, and that is *in itself* plural. This means, it isn't only plural because it has taken on the most varied forms at various times, that are all present in "our" concept of the sublime, but rather it is also plural in itself, split, and *irreducible*. The sublime lets itself be simplified into a unified and specific feeling only through violence. Therefore,—in contrast to the unified beautiful—is the Sublime fitting for the fundamental plurality and complexity of our times. More, it even explicitly demands this plurality through its internal incommensurability. Only when one takes into consideration the conflict between the Imagination and Reason in the sublime does one come upon the crux of this feeling. Plurality and critique cohere closely. The sublime is therefore a deeply critical feeling.[13] (Pries 1989, 25)

12. My translation. The German reads as follows:

Die Analyse des Schönen lässt auf eine Begründung des Subjeckts als Einheit der Vermögen und auf eine Legitimation der Übereinstimmung der realen Gegenstände mit der authentischen Bestimmung dieses Subjekts, die Naturidee, hoffen. Wie ein Meteor schlägt die Analytik des Erhabenen in das Werk ein, das dieser doppelten Erbauung gewidmet ist, und scheint, auch wenn sie nur ein "blosser Anhang" ist, diesen Hoffnungen ein Ende zu setzen.

13. My translation. The German text reads as follows:

Das Gefühl des Erhabenen ist plural, und zwar *in sich*. Das heiss, es ist nicht nur plural, weil es zu unterschiedlichen Zeiten die unterschiedlichsten Formen angenommen hat, die alle noch in "unserem" Begriff des Erhabenen präsent sind, sondern es ist auch in sich plural, gespalten, und zwar *irreduzibel*. Das Erhabene lässt sich nur mit Gewalt zu einem einheitlichen und eindeutigen Gefühl vereinfachen. Dadurch wird es—eher als das einheitliche Schöne—der grundlegenden Pluralität und Komplexität der heutigen Zeit gerecht. Ja, es fordert diese Pluralität durch seine interne Inkommensurabilität sogar

For postmodernists working against the grain of modernist metanarratives, the sublime seems to be a fitting notion for our times since sublime fragmentation gives the lie to a determinate, fixed, or unitary identity.

In the context of the feminist turn to emphatic anti-essentialism, this is important because fragmentation and multiplicity are how subjects perform their anti-essentialism. Particularly in discussions of gender, a multiply identifying subject (a subject in drag is the classic example) is seen as the subject of resistance. But our postmodern faith in plurality depends on the myth of a dichotomized relation between unity and multiplicity. I will argue here that they are far more intertwined, even in the Kantian sublime, than we have recognized. And far from being in itself a cause for celebration, the fragmentation of the subject is key in its construction of the "Others" of Euro-masculine identity as subordinate. The "fixing" of a sovereign identity is not tied to a unitary subject in some simple way, as some postmodernist theorists have imagined. Instead, a fragmented subject is, at least in some cases, one whose multiple identifications are part of the very way identity gets "fixed." The implications of this reading call for a reconsideration of the privileging of multiplicity over unity in postmodern discussions of agency, since if multiplicity constructs unity, at least in some contexts of domination, then counterposing good postmodern multiplicity to bad modern unity constitutes a misunderstanding of the problem. It is more appropriate to look at the way notions of both multiplicity and unity operate politically. The fragmented subject is not in and of itself a guarantor of liberatory thinking or practice.

But this tells us little about what sort of fragmentation might be at work in the constitution of the sovereign, masculine subject. This subject's form of time consciousness, I will argue, is one site of a kind of temporal fragmentation, which legitimates rather than undermines domination. My interest in the question of time as related to sublime experience came out of a moment of suspicion regarding the cliché, one that I accepted until recently, that white time consciousness is linear.[14] After reading the work of Edward Said, Ward Churchill, and others, who discuss white people's propensity to identify others present in the now as moments of our own pasts,[15]

---

ausdrücklich ein. Nur indem man den "Widerstreit" von Einbildungskraft und Vernunft im Erhabenen berücksichtigt, trifft man den Kern dieses Gefühls. Pluralität und Kritik hängen eng zusammen. Das Erhabene ist auch von daher ein zutiefst kritisches Gefuehl.

14. For a more nuanced discussion of linearity and time, see Lorenzo Simpson, *Technology, Time, and the Conversations of Modernity*, especially pp. 50–56. "Through its promise of mastery, technological progress seems to make possible the realization of what I earlier referred to as the 'ideal of satisfaction.' Such an ideal, one of self-sufficiency, of autonomy, is traditionally tied to the attainment of a standpoint outside time, to the eternal present. yet technology presupposes an awareness of the openness of the future, of an experience and a conception of time as linear" (1995, 52). In my account here it will be the necessity of achieving a point outside time and space, that results in the fragmentation of the subject.

15. See Edward Said's 1978 *Orientalism*, especially pp. 55, 231, 235; and Ward Churchill's 1998 *Fantasies of the Master Race*.

I began to suspect that this was a strange linearity at best, one which requires a subject that is spatiotemporally fragmented.

The remarkable work of Johannes Fabian in *Time and the Other: How Anthropology Makes Its Object* broke open the question of time in anthropological discourse.

> Among the historical conditions under which our discipline emerged and which affected its growth and differentiation were the rise of capitalism and its colonialist-imperialist expansion into the very societies which became the target of our inquiries. For this to occur, the expansive, aggressive, and oppressive societies which we collectively and inaccurately call the West needed Space to occupy. More profoundly and problematically, they required Time to accommodate the schemes of a one-way history: progress, development, modernity (and their negative mirror images: stagnation, underdevelopment, tradition). In short, geopolitics has its ideological foundations in chronopolitics. (Fabian 1983, 143–44)

It is this history that forms the backdrop and milieu out of which, and into which, the discipline of anthropology and its particular time consciousness emerge. The object of anthropological inquiry is, according to Fabian, constructed through a temporal framework on which the discipline is founded, and which itself "belongs to the political economy of relations between individuals, classes, and nations" (Fabian 1983, x). Fabian concludes from this that "the construction of anthropology's object through temporal concepts and devices is a political act; there is a 'Politics of Time'" (x).

In a complex analysis of transitions in European conceptions of time— including most importantly its spatialization—Fabian constructs an account of the genealogy of anthropological or evolutionary time. This genealogy is intimately bound up with the history of travel, and particularly the secularization of travel in the eighteenth century, in conjunction with European colonial enterprises. "For the established bourgeoisie of the eighteenth century, travel was to become (at least potentially) every man's source of 'philosophical,' secular knowledge" (Fabian 1983, 6). Moving away from the notion of journeys as "pilgrimages, crusades, and missions," travel became a source of knowledge, and most particularly and peculiarly, a source of knowledge about one's own evolutionary history. "The philosophical traveler, sailing to the ends of the earth, is in fact traveling in time; he is exploring the past; every step he makes is the passage of an age" (Degerando 1969 [1800], 63).

This notion of travel as time travel is in essence a mistaking of space for time so that spatial distance becomes a kind of metaphor for temporal distance, and temporal distance is overcome through traversing space. I say "mistaking" space for time because the others that one encountered on one's journey did not actually exist in one's past but in their own present time. This present time, however different from the traveler's, coincided temporally with it. It was not, however, experienced as coinciding but rather as *in succession* to the traveler's own present.

This "mistake" characterizes the very epistemological approach of anthropology to its objects of inquiry. Fabian's genius is to point out that the connections between the emerging discipline of anthropology and European colonialism were epistemological. "One cannot insist too much that these links were epistemological, not just moral or ethical. Anthropology contributed above all to the intellectual justification of the colonial enterprise. It gave to politics and economics—both concerned with human Time—a firm belief in 'natural,' i.e. evolutionary Time" (Fabian 1983, 17). The very way that anthropology constructed its object was both embedded in and legitimizing for colonial practice. Anthropology "promoted a scheme in terms of which not only past cultures, but all living societies were irrevocably placed on a temporal slope, a stream of Time—some upstream, others downstream" (17).

The very terms employed in anthropological (but also political and economic) discourse about Others function to build an epistemology of time. "A discourse employing terms such as primitive, savage (but also tribal, traditional, Third World, or whatever euphemism is current) does not think, or observe, or critically study, the 'primitive'; it thinks, observes, studies *in terms of the primitive*. Primitive being essentially a temporal concept, is a category, not an object, of Western thought" (Fabian 1983, 17–18; emphasis added). Fabian's crucial insight is that "primitive" and its partner terms are historically and culturally specific, ideologically laden *ways of knowing*.

What is fundamental to this process of knowing is a "denial of coevalness" (Fabian 1983, 31). This is the foundational move that grounds the strange phenomenon, still with us today (as is evidenced in contemporary travel literature) of our propensity to identify others present in the now as moments of our own pasts. It is somewhat astonishing to realize that the European subject tends, to the present day, to experience him/herself as engaged in a kind of time travel when faced with certain others in the present.

We see that the "other" is both assimilated and dominated in this temporal casting back. Instead of a "not like me" designation, the other receives a "not like me now" designation, "but like me then." The copresence of the Other transmutes into a special kind of succession where moments of my own past are stored up in certain remote places and can be visited (thus recuperated) by me when I traverse space. The other is seen as inhabiting an anterior, less evolved, less developed stage of one's own evolutionary history. And here we come to a point that Fabian misses. This sort of assimilation of the Other to my time is also a kind of *internalization* of the other, who is cast not only backward in time but *inward*.

A splitting of the subject is necessary in order to accomplish these spatio-temporal acrobatics. The contradiction in the experience of knowing other peoples to exist contemporaneously with one's own and yet internalizing them as part of one's evolutionary past puts a certain strain on the Euro-masculine subject identity. I not only cast the other I confront inward and backward in time but also cast him/her there as *a former incarnation of myself*. I split myself, between this self now and that primitive self. The resultant multiplicity of the subject is a key part of how the temporality of relations to the other becomes ideologically potent.

This sort of time consciousness will be essential to the subjectivism of a thinker like Kant. Kant's resolution of the paradox of space is built upon the expansion of the subject's interior universe to include the object/woman/nature. His resolution of the paradox of time will be entangled with the tendency to cast Others present in the now downstream in time, but also inward. Again, the subject is expanded to assimilate, to *take in* Otherness.

My focus here is specifically on racialized Otherness. While we generally don't think of Kant as an early theorist of race, Emmanuel Eze points out that "the questions of race and of the biological, geographical, and cultural distribution of humans on earth occupied a central place both in Kant's science of geography and in anthropology" (Eze 1997, 3). We generally dismiss Kant's explicit references to Africans—including his infamous remark: "in short, this fellow was quite black from head to foot, a clear proof that what he said was stupid" (*OFBS* 1960, 113) as racist but unimportant to the body of his philosophical work, as other works in the history of philosophy in which the question of the racialized Other becomes explicit are now largely dismissed as products of a former age of naive prejudice. Yet the same concern is often repressed but operative under the surface of a more abstract argument. Here structures of "deep race" are at work.

Eze points out that race was not a tangential concern for Kant in any case since "throughout his career, Kant published voluminously in the subject area [of race]: at least five long self-standing essays . . . and two books" (3).[16] Kant, though well-known for his critical philosophical works, was actually a leader in the development of anthropology.

> Rarely is it noted that Kant devoted the largest period of his career to research in, and teaching of, anthropology and cultural geography. Before, during and after he wrote the better-known critical works, Kant researched, developed and regularly taught what he called the 'twin' sciences of anthropology and physical geography. Kant was the first to introduce geography into the curriculum of study at the University of Königsberg, in 1756. When he started teaching anthropology at the same university in the winter of 1772–3, it was the first such program of study in any German university. (Eze 1997, 2)

The number of courses Kant taught in anthropology and geography, moreover, far exceeded the number he taught in logic or metaphysics. Whether this reflects Kant's interest, or the interest of his students, it is clear that Kant was deeply involved in the establishment of this new field of study. The mere volume of Kant's work in this area, however, is not nearly so significant as the question of how certain structures of thought might cross over from Kant's explicit work on race into his epistemology, ethics, and aesthetics. Indeed, Kant's interest in race and the question of human cultural geography works itself out through certain structures of spatiotemporality that spill over into his aesthetics.

Kim Hall is one of the few feminist thinkers to read Kant's aesthetics in the context of European colonial expansion. In her article "*Sensus Communis* and Violence," Hall shows that the dominion the Kantian subject has over nature has implications for women and non-Western men who are considered closer to nature, and implicitly not included in the community of judging subjects (Hall 1997,

---

16. Kant's work on race/anthropology includes *Anthropology from a Pragmatic Point of View, On the Different Races of Man*, and the *Observations* themselves, a good portion of which is devoted to the question of race and national character.

263). Man's superiority to nature is the very foundation of the ideal of unlimited progress that is in turn foundational for Western colonial expansion (262).

Kant's glorification of the Western warrior (and war itself) as sublime adds to the legitimating function that Hall believes Kant's work plays in the justification of European colonialism.[17] The key passage here is well-known:

> War itself, provided it is conducted with order and a sacred respect for the rights of civilians, has something sublime about it, and gives nations that carry it on in such a manner a stamp of mind only the more sublime the more numerous the dangers to which they are exposed, and which they are able to meet with fortitude. On the other hand, a prolonged peace favours the predominance of a mere commercial spirit, and with it a debasing self-interest, cowardice, and effeminacy, and tends to degrade the character of a nation. (*CJ* 1928, 112–13)

By juxtaposing the "savage" to the "warrior" and making the "civilized" warrior the object of the "savage's" admiration, Hall argues, Kant reinforces colonial myths and justifies colonial and patriarchal violence (Hall 1997, 266–69). "For what is it that, even to the savage, is the object of the greatest admiration? It is a man who is undaunted, who knows no fear, and who, therefore, does not give way to danger, but sets manfully to work with full deliberation. Even where civilization has reached a high pitch there remains this special reverence for the soldier" (*CJ* 1928, 112). Hall argues that Kant exercises an ideological violence in that his work is not only informed by European colonial narratives, it rationalizes and legitimizes "patriarchal and colonial authority as well as the use of violence when that authority is threatened" (Hall 1997, 260).

In Hannah Arendt's *Lectures on Kant's Political Philosophy*, we find a more forgiving account of Kant's position on war. For Arendt, Kant's recognition of the aesthetic and even practical value of war (as a force that drives progress) is to be counterposed to his explicit condemnations of war in the sphere of action. War is, Arendt notes, not something that a rational agent could ever affirm as a course of action, yet the spectator of history cannot help noticing that war is intimately connected to progress, providing "one further spur for developing to the highest pitch all talents that minister to culture" (*CJ* 1928, 433). However different, both accounts link Kant's positive aesthetic valuation of war implicitly to *the structure of temporality* that underlies it by invoking the notion of progress. By making this temporal structure explicit, we will come a good deal closer to understanding what is at stake in sublime experience.

It is significant that the well-known passage that is the target of Hall's criticism appears in the context of Kant's discussion of the "dynamical sublime" (section 28). Here the "might of nature forces upon us the recognition of our physical

---

17. Hall seems to have made a mistake, or else opted for a very loose reading of Kant, when she says that the warrior is the "ideal of beauty." The warrior actually is an ideal of the sublime as opposed to beauty. The passage Hall cites takes place in the second moment of the Analytic of the Sublime. Because Hall blurs the distinction here between the beautiful and sublime, she skirts a primary way that gender is structured in Kant's text.

helplessness as beings of nature, but at the same time reveals a faculty of estimating ourselves as independent of nature, and discovers a pre-eminence above nature that is the foundation of a self-preservation of quite another kind from that which may be assailed and brought into danger by external nature" (*CJ* 1928, 111). Though Nature occasions the sublime because it "challenges our power," "our power" is "not of nature," thus nature is entitled to "no such rude dominion that we should bow down before it" (111). In fact some sense of safety in the face of nature's might is necessary in order to experience the sublime; "we must see ourselves safe in order to experience this soul-stirring delight" (112). The dynamical sublime is occasioned only "in so far as [nature] is looked on as an object of fear" (*CJ* 1928, 110), but paradoxically as an object that "has no dominion over us" (109). The "savage," not having overcome "our physical helplessness as beings of nature," (*CJ* 1928, 111) immersed in and at the mercy of the natural world, fettered by it, is awed by this fearlessness. It is the soldier's distance from and autonomy in the face of the natural world that makes the soldier the object of "awe." The might of nature "is here called sublime merely because it raised the imagination to a presentation of those cases in which the mind can make itself sensible of the appropriate sublimity of the sphere of its own being, even above nature" (112).

What is important here is that this entire scene is telling a story about spatio-temporal experience. Remembering that "civilization" and "savagery" are temporal notions, we see that distance from nature is the mark of the "civilized" because it has a place in time posterior to the time of the savage who is still immersed in nature. The "savage" is cast into an anterior time characterized by immersion in nature. But at the same time, the implication is that the "civilized" soldier's own past is reflected in the awestruck "savage." "Our physical helplessness as beings of nature," (1928, 111) is projected onto the "savage" and his "primitive" time, in order that the soldier may now inhabit a time where, in Kant's terms, "civilization has reached a high pitch," and he is no longer bound by necessity. In this evolutionary formulation "civilization" contains within it its own muted reference to an unciv-ilized past. Kant's civilization at "high pitch" evokes other times, through which the subject marches forward out of a savage enslavement to the natural world, a now superseded past. These stages are distributed in space across the globe, setting the scene for Kant's narrative of the encounter between the soldier and the "savage."

As Eze notes, in "the numerous writings on race by Hume, Kant, and Hegel, 'reason' and 'civilization' became almost synonymous with 'white' people and northern Europe, while unreason and savagery were conveniently located among the non-whites, the 'black,' the 'red,' the 'yellow,' outside Europe" (Eze 1997, 5). By the time Kant wrote his own *Anthropology*, what diverse Europeans of various nations have in common is their membership in the white race (*A* 1978). Even as early as the *Observations*, Kant refers to "the peoples of our part of the world" (*OFBS* 1960, 97) and "the other parts of the world" (109), constructing a European "us" over and against a non-European "them." But elsewhere Kant is even more explicit, in *On the Different Races of Man*, written in 1775, Kant describes four races of humans, all of whom come from an original "stem genus." The "stem genus" is the oldest, and thus the farthest along, on the evolutionary scale, or as Kant calls it in yet another context, the "color chain" (cited in Eze 1997, 61). Both the "stem genus" and the "first race" are white, the second race is American, the third race is black, the fourth race is Indian. These races are spatially distributed along a temporal line, a distribution that, to repeat the phrase from Johannes Fabian, "promoted a scheme in terms of which not only past cultures, but all living societies were irrevocably placed on a temporal slope, a stream of Time—some upstream, others downstream" (Fabian 1983, 17). European difference from others is *time difference*, conceived in terms of *spatial distance* (Fabian 1983, 16). Thus, even though Kant's explicit claims that "the tallest and most beautiful people on dry land are on the parallel and the degrees which run through Germany" (from *Physical Geography*, cited in Eze 1997, 59) and "humanity is at its greatest perfection in the race of the whites" can easily be dismissed as simple ignorance, this dismissal obscures rather than illuminates the saturation of his work by the *temporality* of this emergent white identity[18]—a saturation that crosses the line from his anthropology and social commentary to his epistemology and aesthetics.

Let's return for a moment to the beginning of the plot of the story that culminates in the temporal acrobatics in Kant's "Analytic of the Sublime," that is, to the first moments of the first *Critique*. As we noted with Irigaray above, Kant accepts the externality and existence of the world, it seems, only to underpin the inward powers of the subject. The genius and radicality of Kant's method is that he claims for the subject powers that seem on first (naive) consideration to belong to the natural world, without doing away with that world entirely. The first of these powers are, of course, space and time, which Kant subjectivizes as preconditions for the possibility of any experience whatsoever. Time is no longer immanent to the movements of the planets or the stars, the seasons, the rising and setting of the sun, the light and darkness or relative heat of a day. Space is no longer immanent to distance between places, to modes of travel between them, to motion. In short, space and time are no longer immanent to nature but are drawn into the expanding universe of the subject. This moment, when space and time are internalized and taken to be powers of the subject, is a crucial moment not only for Kant's epistemology but for his aesthetics as well. As Kant tells the story of the subject, the crucial turn of the plot, which hinges on the moment of internalization of space and time, sets the scene for further developments and is what necessitates the shattering of the subject in the "Analytic of the Sublime."

As we have seen, Kant's sublime is a feeling and an experience that allows the subject to think, though not to know, his own freedom. The price for this experience is a rupture in the relationship between the subject and his environment, which allows him to experience a heady independence from the natural world (*CJ*

---

18. "Emergent" may seem to be a misleading term, as it implies that something brand new is afoot. The colonial expansion that is the historical occasion for the construction of a racialized European identity began several centuries before Kant. By calling this identity "emergent" I don't mean to imply it was brand new but that it was undergoing constant development and revision, that it was still in its period of formation. I would contrast this to today since now this modernist racialization is undergoing a massive cultural "undoing" or "unmaking," which is not to say, of course, that more sophisticated or subtle forms of racialization are not taking its place.

1928, 262). But this rupture is at its deepest *a violation of space and time*. In the mathematical sublime, the imagination's efforts to comprehend as measurement the magnitude of the world (space) is at once an effort to comprehend "the successively apprehended parts at one glance" (259), that is, the world in time. In sublime experience, the imagination's effort to apprehend a seemingly infinite space, which is to comprehend a seemingly infinite time, "is pushed to the point at which our faculty of the imagination breaks down" (*CJ* 1928, 254). The imagination is ruptured when she fails to give spatiotemporal form to the formless in nature. "Since the time-series is a condition of the internal sense and of an intuition, [the effort to comprehend the mathematical sublime] is a subjective movement of the imagination by which it does violence to the internal sense—a violence which must be proportionately more striking the greater the quantum which the imagination comprehends in one intuition" (259). This violence *"removes the time condition"* (259, emphasis added), that is, loosens the hold of temporality on the subject. Reason, as the only faculty capable of comprehending infinity in one intuition, soars on this violence to a feeling of its "superiority over nature within, and thus also over nature without us" (264).

The subject himself is now shattered, as Kant seems to admit when he speaks of the "violence to the internal sense" and Lyotard so convincingly argues. One of the most concise formulations of Lyotard's reading in this regard is this one:

> The Sublime is a kind of gap, a breach in the self as given. It is the displeasure, almost the anxiety, that nothing will be given. . . . Then Kant says, that precisely on the occasion of this disorder, at the same time, an absolute magnitude or absolutely mighty idea of Reason is given. This doesn't permit the overcoming of the gap, but it (the idea) comes, so to speak, out of the clearing of this gap. In any case, it comes to a sort of "quasi"—he even uses the expression quasi-representation—of something, which is presupposed to be unrepresentable, namely an object of an idea of reason. . . . The real transcendental or critical content of that which Kant calls the Sublime, is rather the incapacity for synthesis. (*IE* 1989a, 321–22)[19]

The sublime experience catapults reason through a "gap" in the subject to an absolute autonomy that produces a feeling of the unnameable, the supersensible. Sublime feeling confirms a subject's destiny as autonomous, but the subject of sublime experience is not ever reunified, according to Lyotard.

19. My translation. The German text reads as follows:

Das Erhabene is eine Art Loch, eine Bresche im Gegebenen selbst. Das ist die Unlust, fast die Angst, dass nichts gegeben wird . . . Dann sagt Kant, dass gerade anlässlich dieser Un-ordnung zugleich eine absolut grosse oder absolut mächtige Vernunftidee gegeben wird. Diese erlaubt zwar nicht, das Loch zu überwinden, aber sie Kommt sozusagen aus der lichtung diese Lochs hervor. Jedenfalls kommt es zu einer Art "Quasi"—er benutzt sogar den Ausdruck "Quasi-Darstellung"—von etwas, was qua Voraussetzung nicht darstellbar, näm-lich Gegenstand einer Vernunftidee ist . . . Der eigentliche transzendentale oder kritische Inhalt dessen, was Kant das Erhabene nennt, ist viel eher das Unvermögen zur Synthese.

But in contrast to this reading, which sees no reunification of the subject and finds cause for celebration in its fragmentation, I read the Kantian sublime as a narrative of unity that is internally constituted by multiplicity. What I am arguing is that the moment of shattering that Lyotard emphasizes is not indicative of a failure of the subject to maintain its unity but is the very way the subject attains a new unity, once the unity that bound him to the natural world has been broken.

Because space and time are powers of the subject, if sublime experience loosens the hold these have on the subject, it is essentially freeing the subject from an abjected part of himself—rupturing the first unity of the subject. This is to say, the subject who is at the mercy of the natural world because he is of that world has a certain kind of "unity" but no freedom. His freedom is purchased at the price of this initial unity. To abject the natural world, he must also abject, violate in fact, an aspect of his very subjectivity, that aspect most connected to sense and thus to the material world.

But this shattering is the very event that allows him to rise to a new unity. He is freed to a region above space and time. But this very position "above" or "beyond" the spatiotemporal world demands a narrative, an explanation. It demands that the subject project his physical helplessness in the face of a powerful nature onto the non-European "savage," onto the feminine imagination, onto abjected others. These are, however, part of the very expanded inwardness of the Euro-masculine subject. The savage exists as a transcended moment of his own past. The feminine imagination as a transcended moment in the course of the ascendance of reason. The projection of these aspects of the self onto others and the internalization of these others is the very mechanism through which the subject both shatters and dominates, is plural and unified. The postmodern discovery that there is a latent plurality at the heart of the unified subject is an important one. What is missed is that this plurality, far from being the "meteor" that gives the lie to the unified subject, is its very mode of holding itself together.

But the Euro-masculine subject pays a high price for his projections. The expansion of his interior universe is purchased at the price of a degradation of and disregard for what is external, that is, what can't be reduced to him. He no longer lives in the time of the seasons or in the places of the natural world. The transcendental subject is everywhere and always, which is to say nowhere in particular, at no particular time—he is *displaced*. This subject who is without place desperately attempts to build and rebuild his identity through conquering, dominating, and exploiting other places. (One can read this as materially and structurally as one would like. Daily life in Europe, by Kant's time, was completely infused with the products and profits of colonial expansion.) For the Euro-masculine subject, *displacement is the price tag of freedom*. It is through this displacement that his destiny is felt, at the same time that this displacement is his destiny.

Because of the self-aggrandizing nature of the subject of sublime experience, he is incapacitated in his relations to others. He has trouble experiencing what happens as happening to someone else at all. This trouble is deeply connected with certain philosophical problems that have preoccupied philosophers of the Western tradition. Because this subject experiences power in the world as merely his own power mirrored back to him, he is always mistaking others for himself, and the places of others for his own. We might say he exists in a state of lethal confusion.

It is not the Euro-masculine subject who pays the highest price for this carefully cultivated and defended state of confusion, however. He demands place-lessness of others. As Casey notes, "the domination of native peoples was accomplished by their deplacialization; the systematic destruction of regional landscapes that served as the concrete settings for local culture" (Casey 1997, xii). This dispossession also involved the massive genocide and relocation of indigenous nations. To mention only one example, U.S. colonial policy seemed to involve a recognition of the importance of place for indigenous nations and a systematic and official effort to permanently sever the connections between particular peoples and particular places in order to destroy them (Stannard 1992). It is as if, in both Europe and the places it controlled, the link between people and environment, the reverence of peoples for their environments, was to be systematically undermined.

The temporal structure that consistently and relentlessly assumes a progressive, developmental, evolutionary direction to time, with the Euro-masculine located at the superior and temporally posterior end of this trajectory, justifies the severing of relationships to place. Because this other is part of an internal past that has already been superseded, their contemporary existence, and the places they inhabit, are important only as a kind of exotic tourist attraction for time travelers. Thus assimilation, genocide, and environmental destruction are entirely reconcilable since the other is understood in some important sense to be a moment in the development of the Euro-masculine subject that is already superseded, and others' places are places the European has already passed through and left behind on the way to becoming civilized.

During the last half of the last millennium, Europeans spread across the globe and waged war on the inhabitants of other continents and took their land. Who could represent the identity that was built in transoceanic conquests, broken loose from the particularities of any specific place, blasting whole cultures, languages, and peoples out of time? In the eighteenth century an explosion of interest in the sublime, in the attempt to name the unnamable, represent the unrepresentable, culminated in Kant's "Analytic of the Sublime." The "Analytic" placed a terrible power in the interior universe of a subject shattering across space and time, in horror and awe of himself.

In the late twentieth century, after nearly two hundred years of dust, in the midst of a new unrepresentable economic and technological conquest of space and time, the sublime reemerges. But today the "others" of Euro-masculinity seem eager to accept the gift of the fragmented subject as a panacea for the megalomania of the unified rational hero of the Enlightenment—not recognizing the play of multiplicity and unity that enable this displaced subject to sustain lethal fictions of autonomy and progress.

Postmodern multiplicity will accept some revisions, to be sure. As we will see in the next chapters, when the referentiality of language gives way to the self-referentiality of texts, the internal is "turned inside out," becoming the context rather than the content of consciousness. The inwardness of modern multiplicity is essentially reversed without enabling the postmodern subject to rebuild a relation to place. At the same time, the constituting activity of a now collectivized and externalized discursive subjectivity becomes the totalizing conceit that reaffirms the modernist fantasy of independence and sovereignty—now assigned to "subjectivity without a subject." The resultant unintelligibility of the external political world (and the others of that world), and of the natural world on which we depend, is the price we pay for a now postmodern fantasy of emancipation.

3

The Postmodern Sublime

If the sublime is the aesthetic notion proper to postmodernity, it is because it speaks to the spatiotemporal experiences that mark our time/place (in the developed "West") as postmodern. The death of history that is said to inaugurate the postmodern arrives when those who believe themselves to be the masters of time find themselves unable to "man" the flow of time, that is, unable to keep telling convincing stories about progress. The more distance is conquered to save time, to *gain* time as Lyotard would say,[1] the more we find ourselves at the mercy of time. Today we live, as David Harvey and others have pointed out, in the *instant*, that is, in the time of instantaneous gratification of desire, of instantaneous obsolescence, instantaneous global communication, the instantaneous image (Harvey 1990).[2] These conquests of time and distance (I can communicate with my friend in Brazil in the matter of a moment) don't free us from time (yet I can't find the time to make the call). We experience ourselves, in daily life, as slaves to time in fact, rushing from morning to night in order to be on time, to not waste time. As Casey notes, "we are lost because of our conviction that time, not only the world's time but our time, the only time we have, is always running out or down. All time, it seems, is 'closing time.' No sooner have we settled in somewhere than we hear 'Hurry up, please! It's time!'" (Casey 1993, 7). Postmodern sublime experience will reflect the pleasure/displeasure of this paradox of mastery and enslavement, the paradox of contemporary temporality.

For Kant, as we saw in the last chapter and as Lyotard reminds us, sublime experience "removed the time-condition," that is, threw the subject into a kind of

---

1. In postmodernity, Lyotard notes, "success comes from gaining time.... Reflection is not thrust aside today because it is dangerous or upsetting, but simply because it is a waste of time. It it 'good for nothing,' it is not good for gaining time" (D 1988, xv).
2. See particularly Harvey's "Time-space Compression and the Postmodern Condition," in *The Condition of Postmodernity* (1990).

out-of-time and beyond-time, where the mechanism of nature and the time of sense experience no longer limit. In postmodern accounts, by contrast, the sublime is the very experience of the time condition. It traps the subject in the instant. But there is an escape here as well, for this very entrapment will be the way to a discursive freedom. Because we exist discursively only in the moment, the bindings that tie the now to a before and after are loosened, and a profound temporal contingency (freedom) envelopes the subject. Both accounts see the subject *freed from the phenomenal time of succession*. Lyotard's fascination with the Kantian sublime is due in part to the fact that the experience of the sublime is "not situated in succession" (*LAS* 1991, 135), and thus it prefigures the rupture in succession that is a defining structure of contemporary temporal experience.

The other structure of contemporary experience that must be important to our inquiry here is that of our relation to place. While the modern sublime was theorized with constant reference to nature, the postmodern sublime is theorized almost exclusively in relation to art, which as Lyotard reminds us, no longer imitates nature (*LR* 1989b, 206). If the modern sublime involved "an aesthetics of denaturing" (*LAS* 1991, 53), that is, worked its disruption in relation to our home in nature, the postmodern sublime will work its disruption in the context of con-temporary experiences of highly constructed relations to place, where long periods elapse in which we may not notice the natural world at all. Climbing from sealed buildings into sealed automobiles, from underground parking lots into yet more sealed buildings, our evenings focused on television or computer screens—we are emplaced in a world of flat surfaces, saturated by language and images, rather than a world where weather, landscape, or planetary motion are centrally important. Perhaps the modern abjection of the natural world has blossomed into the com-plete repression of this world in postmodernity, where we assuage the pain associ-ated with the loss of a home in nature with the acquisition of a home in the world of signs. So, in a sense, the price Kant paid for resolving the paradox of necessity and freedom, a natural world which we dominate and are alienated from, is the same price we pay today. If Jameson is right, "postmodernism is what you have when the modernization process is complete and nature is gone for good" (1991, ix).

No figure has been so important in the resurgence of interest in the sublime than has Jean-Francois Lyotard. His recuperation of this aesthetic experience from Kant has made it a central notion for postmodern theory, in fact. My own interest in the notion comes about because of a suspicion: that the sublime is at work in feminist postmodernism as well, though not explicitly. Making the workings of the sublime explicit is simply part of "thinking what we are doing," in Arendt's words.

A closer look at Lyotard's late work will help to bring to light both what is disturbing and what might be important in feminist appropriations of the sublime. I begin by contextualizing Lyotard's treatment of the sublime in terms of his broader project of developing a "philosophical politics" of "bearing witness to the *differend*." I then look more closely at Lyotard's reading of the Kantian sublime and at his discussion of language using the famous example of "Albert." My questions are, throughout, What happens to place in Lyotard's philosophical politics? What political possibilities are opened or closed in the process? A final discussion of one of Lyotard's essays on feminism, or as he terms it "women's struggles," will prepare the way for looking at how the postmodern sublime is at work in feminist thinking in the next chapters.

Lyotard's Philosophical Politics

In his major philosophical work, *The Differend,* Lyotard's purpose is a political one. The central concern of his later work (his early work is not at issue here) is with the role of philosophy after the linguistic turn. It is to "set up a philosophical politics" (*D* 1988, xiii), in fact, a politics of reflection on language and power. Influenced by Wittgenstein and the Kant of the third *Critique,* he will propose that it is the role of a philosophical politics to "bear witness to the *differend*" (xiii), that is, to the absolute and irresolvable heterogeneity of distinct "phrase regimes." This involves an ability to see and articulate the differences/disputes that characterize encounters between incommensurable ways of speaking about things. It will require an attentiveness to the rules of distinct language games, which are in each case immanent to the game in question. The philosopher's role is to bear witness to the way that "a wrong results from the fact that the rules of the genre of discourse by which one judges are not those of the judged genre or genres of discourse" (xi), though the only sign of this wrong may be the inability of one of the plaintiffs of the case to speak. Lyotard hopes to show "that the linking of one phrase onto another is problematic and that this problem is the problem of politics" (xiii).

It is his concern for "the problem of politics" that sets Lyotard's work apart from that of so many of his contemporaries. The concrete historical circumstance that illustrates Lyotard's text is that of historical "revisionism," particularly Faurisson's denials of the existence of the gas chambers at Auschwitz. His approach is one of reflection, where "reflection requires that you watch out for occurrences, that you don't already know what's happening. It leaves open the question: Is it happening" (*D* 1988, xv). He will not attempt, then, to prove that Faurisson is wrong, or in any way to counterpose a discourse of "proof" to Faurisson's denials. In fact, it is the very role of such discourses that becomes the central focus of the inquiry, in part because Faurisson presents himself as a seeker after proofs. Lyotard paraphrases Faurisson: "In order for a place to be identified as a gas chamber, the only eyewitness I will accept would be the victim of this gas chamber: now, according to my opponent, there is no victim that is not dead; otherwise, this gas chamber would not be what he or she claims it to be. There is, therefore, no gas chamber" (*D* 1988, 3–4). The revisionists appeals to "the cognitive rules for the establishment of historical reality and validation of its sense" (57), and immanent to this phrase regime, Lyotard argues, they commit no injustice.

The discursive violence occurs when the rules of one phrase regime are imposed upon the other. The harm comes in this case from treating the objects of history (here, the gas chambers), as if they were strictly observable in the way that the objects of cognitive science might be. The rules of the game of a juridical cognitivist discourse are imposed as if they were the "real" rules that result in "real" knowledge of "reality." But reality is "at play" in "all the other families of phrases" as well, though differently (*D* 1988, 55). For Lyotard, of course, reality is itself phrase-bound: "reality is not what is 'given' to this or that 'subject,' it is a state of the referent (that about which one speaks) which results from the effectuation of establishment procedures defined by a unanimously agreed-upon protocol" (4). The "protocols" of a cognitivist phrase regime, with its pretensions to universal validity, silence other phrase regimes. The silence Faurisson encounters in his search for an "eyewitness" to the gas chambers, is itself a sign of harm, one that is attended to only if we "bear witness to the *differend*." For the revisionists, the very fact that they are "not worried by the scope of the very silence they use as an argument in their plea" is itself a kind of violence because only "by this does one recognize a wrong done to the sign that is this silence and to the phrases it invokes" (57).

Lyotard's analysis of the double bind created by the imposition of cognitivist rules across genres of discourse is one that coheres in significant respects with feminist analyses of masculinist legal discourse as it applies to cases involving crimes against women, like sexual harassment. Here the "harm" resulting from the harassment is that it disempowers a woman, or takes away her agency. Yet the mere fact that she brings a case in court shows that she acts as an agent and that no such harm has taken place.[3]

Lyotard's contribution to a radical politics is his stepping back from the rush to judgment, his recognition that the particular discursive regime that is cognitivist or juridical creates silences and injustice, never on its own terms of course, but in terms of other discourses. His philosophical politics call for the development of a new competence (or 'prudence') in the face of such silences, an ability to listen for and to such silences, to recognize them as signs of the suffering that is alleged. We "must break with the monopoly over history granted to the cognitive regimen of phrases, and . . . must venture forth by lending [an] ear to what is not presentable under the rules of knowledge" (D 1988, 57).

This plea is a fitting one, particularly if addressed to those in positions of power who might insist on the authority of the "cognitive regimen of phrases." It is fitting because it "fits" with the humbling of the Euro-masculine subject that is so central to the dawning of postmodernity, and it is in that respect a courageous position for a philosopher of Lyotard's stature in the West to take. It is also fitting because the *differend*, for Lyotard, is what destabilizes the totalizing procedures of grand narratives, or "metalanguage." Without a place to stand in the "really real," which underlies specific phrase regimes, the authority of the cognitive phrase regime is humbled—since the speakers in this regime speak a particular and local language without privileged access to an ontology of truth, just like everyone else.

While Lyotard's insistence on curbing the megalomania of cognitive/juridical models of knowledge is to be commended, there is an ambivalence at the heart of Lyotard's philosophical politics that compromises its efficacy as a politics of justice in relation to the historical injustices that preoccupy social movements. "Bearing witness to the differend," cannot fulfill its promise of becoming a philosophical

3. This is one of the major insights of Catharine MacKinnon, in fact, putting Lyotard in good company indeed.

politics if the witnesses continue to understand themselves to be without place in a world that exceeds language. The dislocation of the subject of sublime experience that Lyotard celebrates, I will argue, is the very thing that prevents the philosopher from "bearing witness to the differend" in any effective way. Lyotard's call to a philosophical politics is in danger of becoming a call to another species of intellectual idealism even though Lyotard is opposed to this! A closer look at Lyotard's reading of the sublime will help to show why.

Lyotard's Sublime

The classical reading of Kantian Aesthetics emphasizes teleology, that is, the introduction of the regulative Idea of an objective finality in nature, which is the key to the reunification of the field of philosophy (which Kant has split into pure and practical reason). Lyotard's reading is a postmodern one because it emphasizes the failure of this project yet elevates this failure to an extremely significant place in our own efforts to address contemporary concerns. For Lyotard, Kant's "Analytic of Aesthetic Judgment" is "a propaedeutic to philosophy, a propaedeutic that is itself, perhaps, all of philosophy," because it teaches us, "the secret of the 'manner' (rather than the method) in which critical thought proceeds in general" (*LAS* 1991, 6). This secret "manner" of proceeding is aesthetic, that is, reflective. In other words, in order for the subject of cognition to do its work, which largely consists of "domiciling" its objects under categories, it must feel itself thinking (52). The categories of the subject of understanding are underwritten by the heuristic process of "feeling thinking experiences" (30), that is, "the feeling pleasant and/or unpleasant that thinking has about itself" (30), which "seems to be the nerve of critical thought as such" (26). Indeed, "by itself the category is blind" (38), so the very power of the knowing subject to know its object is unleashed only by sensation, which is to say only in the relation between the aesthetic and the cognitive, in which the aesthetic partner is primary (40).

Among the two aesthetic experiences that Kant discusses, Lyotard believes that the sublime has the most relevant lessons to teach a postmodern reader. While the beautiful promises "everyone the happiness of an accomplished subjective unity" while it "allows one to hope for the advent of a subject as unity of the faculties, and for a legitimation of the agreement of real objects with the authentic destination of this subject, in the Idea of nature" (*LAS* 1991, 159), the sublime is "a meteor dropped into the work" of this happy project. The beautiful is an expression of the harmony of the imagination and the understanding, but the sublime is what brings us to a sharp awareness of the incommensurability of imagination (the power of presentation) and reason (the power of cognition). "This conflict is not an ordinary dispute," Lyotard reminds us, "which a third instance could grasp and put an end to, but a 'differend,' a *Widerstreit*" (124). The two powers are heterogeneous, absolutely heterogeneous in fact, since reason is concerned with "the absolute of the infinite," while imagination concerns itself with "the absolute of the finite" (126). What the experience of the sublime does is to make us feel the *differend* between these heterogeneous regimes (234). When the imagination tries to step up to the task that reason sets for her (knowing full well that a presentation of such might or magnitude all "at one glance" is not possible), that is, when she tries to speak in the language of reason, her failure produces the sensation of the sublime, which is the sensation of the *differend* (152).

As noted in the last chapter, the failure of the imagination occurs in the transition from an attempt to apprehend successive parts or moments of a might or magnitude (which the imagination is quite capable of doing and is what the understanding might demand) to an attempt to comprehend all of the parts "at one glance." It is this second attempt that entails "an abuse, a violence," "the destruction of the temporality proper to all presentation" (*LAS* 1991, 143), that is, the temporality of succession. This violence will also be the violence that shatters the hope of a unified subject.

Time, as we know, is the form of inner sense, it is "not only indispensable to the presentation of an object in intuition, it is a 'condition of the internal sense'" (*LAS* 1991, 143). Thus this violence not only brings the imagination to her knees, or if Lyotard is correct, to her death, but "strikes a blow at the very foundation of the 'subject.' Taste promised him a beautiful life," Lyotard reminds us, "the sublime threatens to make him disappear" (144). This blow to the unitary subject is, of course, Lyotard's evidence for his contention that "it is very difficult to classify Kantism among the philosophies of the subject" (146).

Lyotard's reading of the Kantian sublime is postmodern in its emphasis on the underbelly of pleasure/displeasure doing its secret work in the process of cognition itself, in its celebration of the demise of the phenomenal time of succession, in its feeling for the absolute incommensurability of heterogeneous regimes of phrases, and in its discovery that the subject of sublime experience is a shattered subject. It is also postmodern in its account of place.

In its postmodern rendition, sublime experience is produced by and produces a movement of displacement, what Lyotard calls an "ontological dislocation" (*LR* 1989b, 206). This is the humbling experience that gives the lie to the universalist pretensions of the cognitive phrase regime, that shows that reality is at play in other phrase regimes as well, and that there is no privileged access to an ontology that exceeds the reality at play within regimes of phrases that could be the foundation for arbitrating between them. The postmodern sublime is at first the feeling of terror experienced on the edge of the abyss between regimes of phrases.

How is this also an experience of exhaltation? The sensation by which one is gripped at the moment when the "real" dissolves into a bare absence between regimes of phrases is also the experience of *emancipation from necessity* understood as the necessary referentiality of language. In other words, it undoes the relation between words and things. The clash between heterogeneous language games, the absolute incommensurability of the games, the lack of any common ground from which to arbitrate between them, leaves one awash in sheer difference. When we realize that reality is a function of signs, is at play within but not between regimes of phrases, we are emancipated from the tyranny of the real. The "unnameable" or "unrepresentable" in postmodernism is experienced as a flash of recognition of the radical contingency, of the absolute indeterminacy of signs.

Lyotard's critique of Kant is this: when faced with the incommensurability of "heterogeneous regimes of phrases" Kant resorts to the "Idea of nature." Kant "sets into orbit outside the sphere of the perceptible all those 'objects' that are not objects of knowledge" (*LR* 1989b, 350–51). These elusive objects, which we cannot know, nonetheless guarantee that regimes of phrases deploying the same names are commensurable, are related at the base, that is, in nature. Lyotard finds that "if we do away with this overly consoling Idea, we are left with the naked convulsions of the differends" (341).

Lyotard uses the example of two sentences, one descriptive and one a command: "That door is closed," and "Close that door." Each sentence presents a different universe, one in which the meaning, the sender, and the addressee are all different in the different regimes. Lyotard's assertion of this difference is based on a difference in expectation and situation. The "entity" who is the addressee of a command is expected to act differently than the "entity" who is the addressee of a description; the "entity" who utters a command is situated differently than the "entity" who utters a description. If the sender and the addressee change, then so does the referent. "Doesn't a descriptive sentence call up its referent differently than a prescriptive sentence? Isn't being the object of a piece of information entirely different from being the object of some future transformation" (*LR* 1989b, 342)? Since, for Lyotard, the referent is "an instance in the universe presented by a phrase (and what else could it be?)" (342), it, like the other instances, changes when language regimes change. Different language regimes constitute, or set into play, the reality of the same referent (here "door") differently.

Philosophy's mistake has been to see across these different instances a unity of substance. Lyotard's other example is even more poignant—the example of an entity named "Albert." He takes the sentences "Albert is going to leave Marie," and "Albert, think before you act," and "What courage Albert has," and the sentence Albert himself utters, "I think it would be best if I left Marie" as shifts in instance across heterogeneous phrases, which "seem to complete the dissolution of the identity of that entity who answers to the name of Albert" (*LR* 1989b, 314). Yet philosophers have taken "Albert" to be a self-identical substance, a real referent that is "taken up" in different regimes of speech while it remains essentially the same across them. But for Lyotard, as soon as I write, " 'Albert' is a self-identical substance, a real referent that is 'taken up' in different regimes of speech," I have introduced yet another regime, yet another instance, yet another Albert.

> In respect to philosophical inquiry, the situation of that referent often causes the investigator to admit with no further debate the reality of the entity in question, and to conclude that the various enunciations cited are only variations on the meaning allowed by the substance or substratum called Albert, which is from that moment held to be real. This is an error. The investigator's phrase is the "nth" (here, the fifth) in a series along the lines of "What then is the reality of Albert?" This sentence, which belongs to the interrogative regime, has in itself no privilege enabling it to endow the entity named Albert with a real identity. (*LR* 1989b, 342–43)

Philosophy, unconscious of its own nature as "phrases about phrases," mistakes an instance of speech, here "Albert," "put into play" for its meaning, with an entity, Albert, "put into play" for its reality. It mistakes a different sort of phrase regime for a cognitive one and erroneously believes the cognitive phrase regime to provide access to something like the "real truth of Albert." Kant's objects of nature are, for Lyotard, such "overly-consoling" appeals to a "real truth." Philosophy's new self-consciousness about its nature as "phrases about phrases" allows it to recognize its "referents" as meaningful instances within speech regimes rather than real substance.

This realization entails, however, the "ontological dislocation," which Lyotard describes in relation to sublime experience. These descriptions can be read as accounts of our postmodern relation to place, where the subject who is at home in a world of signs incommensurable with other sign-worlds is also radically alienated from the natural world. This subject must indeed experience the "referent" as an "instance in the universe presented by a phrase." Lyotard's parenthetical "what else could it be?" (LR 1989b, 342) betrays the commonsense quality that this insight takes on in contemporary discourse.

Yet Lyotard's notion of an "ontological dislocation" itself points to a place/ implacement that exceeds language. When we "put out of play" an excessive ontology (meaning not reducible to language) in the experience of the *differend*, is it a mere fiction that we are putting out of play? If so, this is not an ontological dislocation but a discursive one since what we put out of play was born of language in any case. But it seems that an excessive ontology is already "in play" in language—and not as a mere phantasm produced in language, but as a sensation of place that underlies the very experience of dislocation. If we experience ourselves as dis-located, then we have some sense of "ontological location" that is prior to, and a precondition for, the experience.[4] Perhaps Lyotard's "ontological dislocation" is felt so poignantly because of the deep sensation of, or at least longing for, the location against which such dis-location works.

This dislocation *in place* is achieved *through time*. Lyotard claims that "to judge is to open an abyss between parts by analyzing their differend" (LR 1989b, 326)—an abyss that is a no-place for the subject. But what is it that we are opening the abyss in? As should be clear by now, "the abyss" is opened in time. The benefit of sublime feeling, which for Lyotard is the same as the benefit of criticism in general, is in "the convulsion in which 'before' and 'after' *lose their co-presence* in…discourse (LR 1989b, 325; emphasis added),[5] a convulsion in which the

---

4. I am writing in agreement with and essentially making the same point as Merleau-Ponty. In his famous preface to *The Phenomenology of Perception*:

> For if I am able to talk about "dreams" and "reality", to bother my head about the distinction between imaginary [or discursive] and real, and cast doubt upon the "real", it is because this distinction is already made by me before any analysis; it is because I have an experience of the real as of the imaginary, and the problem then becomes one not of asking how critical thought can provide for itself secondary equivalents of this distinction, but of making explicit our primordial knowledge of the "real." (Merleau-Ponty 1962, xvi)

5. "Co-presence" is Lyotard's term to name what he takes to be an illusion, that the "Albert" of one sentence (now) is somehow co-present with the "Albert" of another sentence (yesterday) and another (tomorrow). For Lyotard, our linking of these instances across time is a fantasy of a co-presence that would only be possible were "Albert" Albert, i.e., real substance.

"Albert" of my sentence here is set adrift in the now of this instance of speech, where the Albert of that instance before and the Albert of that instance after "lose their co-presence." For Kant, time was a power on the subject side of the subject-object relation, yet time and space were intuitions that were bound up with sense experience in relation to nature. For Lyotard, it seems, nature is completely absent from time. The temporal "movement" of the sublime is a kind of sense experience that takes place wholly in relation to language. In fact, postmodern time is precisely the terrifying sensation of the absence of nature, that is, of a no-place where nature used to be, which opens up between this Albert and all those others.

The temporality of Lyotard's sublime is perhaps best articulated in his well-known essay "The Sublime and the Avant-Garde."[6] The faddishness of art today is in contrast to the role of art in the nineteenth and twentieth centuries, where "with the advent of the aesthetics of the sublime, the stakes of art . . . was to bear witness to the fact that there is indeterminacy" (*LR* 1989b, 206). This was the indeterminacy of the "here and now," Lyotard argues. Citing the work of Barnett (Baruch) Newman, who painted pictures with titles like "here" and "now" and wrote an essay entitled "The Sublime is Now," Lyotard's question is how the sublime can be understood to be "here and now." Sublime art is art that takes up the task of "bearing pictorial or otherwise expressive witness to the inexpressible" (199); such art confronts "the possibility of nothing happening" (198) and becomes itself the event (*Ereignis*) that holds this possibility in suspense. This is why the sublime, for Lyotard, is an "agitation," an "intensity," over the abyss since "here and now there is this painting, rather than nothing, and that's what is sublime" (199). But the painting bears witness to the possibility of nothing happening, to the ontological tenuousness of the here and now. The "intensification" produced in the sublime experience of the indeterminacy of the now, defeats the will, which would like to "affirm its hegemony over time" (211). For Lyotard, "the avant gardist task remains that of undoing the presumption of the mind with respect to time. The sublime feeling is the name of this privation" (211).

The presumption of the mind with respect to time is that this now is connected in some determinate way with a before and an after—that is, that each instant is bound in phenomenal, which we might also call natural, time. The time that accompanies a single entity through changes of birth, life, and eventually death, that is, the time of mortality, is here unbound (as indeed, it was in the Kantian experience of the sublime as well). Now there is nothing to tie Albert-before to Albert-now to Albert-at-some-future-moment. Albert is free in the instant, which is to say in his absolute particularity. Each Albert is through and through particular, loosed from the constraint of some substantial or essential Albert. In

---

6. This essay is primarily a lament about the role of the artist in postmodernity. Artists have lost their way and become fascinated by incessant innovation; art is driven by the market, by fad, engaged in the production of the "cheap thrill" rather than the *Ereignis* (event). As such the sublimity of art has been displaced onto the sublimity of the capitalist economy, which is regulated by an unpresentable Idea, infinite wealth, and power.

fact, the "entity" named Albert changes identities faster than he can say his own name.

The theme of "ontological dislocation," however, is celebrated, rather than interrogated in Lyotard's account. At least it is not deeply interrogated as a question *of place*. This question is important because it is *the here* that is capable of binding the now to a before and after. The "here" can only do this work of binding if it is more than a point on an abstract spatial grid (i.e., if it is a lived place). "Here is Albert!" I turn around, and turn back again, and though he may have moved across the room from my desk to my bookcase, I still can say "There is Albert!" with complete confidence. The here and there are bound in place so that the now of the first phrase and the now of the second can be bound in time. Certainly the relation between space and time can be strained by movement or travel (our memories are often connected deeply to specific places so that they fade more quickly if we move). When hurricane Katrina hit the Gulf Coast, she destroyed place to such an extent that she unbinds the before and after for the survivors. They report looking about and being unable to place themselves, not knowing where they are (even though they are wading through the streets of their own neighborhood in New Orleans, now under water). This sensation must surely also be experienced as a rupture in time. The lives lived before Katrina are irrevocably changed after Katrina. And when time is ruptured, so is narrative. The incomprehension on the faces of the residents of New Orleans, even those in safety, is the embodied sign of the sublime—they walk about on the other side of the limit of the presentable, caught in the moment (for the moment), which cannot be presented in speech. They certainly may speak in the manner of "this happened" and then "that happened"—but it is clear to everyone, and certainly to the speakers themselves, that their words do not, cannot, represent the might or the magnitude of what is happening.

Albert's time is the time of the instant, not the time of succession. The unbinding of the before and after bespeaks an unbinding in relation to place as well. Because he is radically dis-placed, disoriented in both space and time, there is no possibility of metalanguage about Albert, there is no theory of Albert. Indeed, there is no natural world, no place to underwrite such a theory.

Place and the Differend

Lyotard's philosophical politics comes to a standstill because he does not attend sufficiently to the question of place that is completely entangled with the story he tells about time. If "what is at stake in a literature, in a philosophy, in a politics perhaps, is to bear witness to *differends* by finding idioms for them" (D 1988, 13), where is it that we stand when we find these idioms? In a neutral in-between? There is no such place for Lyotard.

The four instances of speech that constitute a phrase universe are the addressee, addressor, referent, and sense. The witness won't then, be any of these, won't be, that is to say, located either in the universes of the "phrases in dispute" or in the space between them, which is a mere abyss. The crucial political question is, Where will the witness stand? The witness is placed some mysterious where, not inside or in-between but dispersed among the regimes of phrases.

Linking the phrase regimes is inevitable, Lyotard tells us, though a number of linkages are always possible, and none is prescribed by the regimes themselves. "Inside a genre of discourse, the linkings obey rules that determine the stakes and the ends. But between one genre and another, no such rules are known, nor a generalized end" (D 1988, 30). Inside a genre of discourse, we might say, necessity reigns, while between genres there is freedom (in its postmodern form as discursive contingency). But again, who lives this freedom? By what means is it deployed? How can it be lived except in the creation of yet another phrase regime that is every bit as untranslatable as the regimes of the original dispute? *Where is the witness?* The freedom of the instant, of an unboundedness in time, has also unbound her from place.

Let's imagine that the witness is Albert. If Albert (can he do this, for Lyotard?) enters into the phrase regime of the revisionists, he will see that it has its logic, its regimen, by which the argument of the revisionists commits no injustice. If Albert enters into the phrase regime of the survivors, he will see that it has its sense, that its silences are the sign of a wrong, that an injustice has been committed. And if Albert finds an idiom, initiates, that is to say, another phrase regime, with no more authority than the first two, which recognizes the *differend* of the first two, this is how he "bears witness." But what has Albert done (where has Albert gone)? He has merely dispersed himself among heterogeneous regimes of phrases. The Albert of the first phrase regime, the Albert of the second, and the Albert of the third, will be as at odds with one another as the regimes themselves (the reality of Albert is put into play differently in each regime).

Lyotard's philosophy fails to become a philosophical politics because Albert can't answer the crucial question "Is it happening?" except within the idiom of a particular regime. He has no ground on which to stand in order to insist that "Yes, it happened," nor can he claim, "and it matters to all of us."

Solidarity with victims of great crimes or tragedies requires bearing witness to the *differend*, but not only that. Lyotard identifies the problem of politics as primarily a problem of the "linking of one phrase onto another" (D 1988, xiii), but this is only a preliminary problem. The problem of politics is the problem of relations between persons who, while bound in particular regimes of phrases, are never absolutely bound there. A transformation would require more than a holding-neutral and recognizing the terms of the dispute, it would require a coming-over-to-the-side-of the victims, who are not, after all, regimes of phrases, but persons with whom I (must) share a (natural and political) world.

If, in the experience of the sublime, Albert finds himself humbled, finds that the cognitive phrase regime in which he has put all his faith is but one regime among others; if he discovers the possibility of sense without mastery in bearing witness to the *differend*, this development is certainly to be celebrated. But if Albert becomes so fascinated with the *differend* that he loses the capacity for solidarity, he will make no contribution to a liberatory politics. If Albert is caught up in the temporality of the phrase, where one instant gives way to the next and the now loses its relation to the before or after, he will not contribute to efforts to make historical sense of injustices. As tempting as it might be for a feminist to see the development that turns Albert into a humble man as a positive one, if Albert is simply engaged in a narcissistic fascination with his own experience of humbling, he will not be an ally to anyone but himself.

Solidarity would require something more. If translation is impossible when face-to-face with an Other, learning a new language is only terribly difficult. Why not understand the feeling of the sublime, the terror at the edge of the abyss, the silence of the Other, as a call to undertake the difficult task of learning to hear and speak anew. This is not a call for a new metalanguage, exactly. Nor is it a call for good translators (although a good translator should never be underestimated). Even less is it a call for the proliferation of "little narratives." It is a call to enter the place of the other.

This is not to be understood metaphorically. An exemplary instance of what is meant might be the courageous travel of a woman like Kathy Kelly, founder of Voices in the Wilderness, who (among many other things) organized brigades from the United States to travel to Baghdad and bear witness to the aerial bombardment of the city by the U.S. military.[7] The group's belief that "where you stand determines what you see and how you live" amounts to an understanding that "finding an idiom" to present the unpresentable depth of human suffering and injustice, in some circumstances, requires a terrible and radical relation to place. The brigades of international witnesses place themselves in the very places where injustices are occurring. The name of the organization itself, "Voices in the Wilderness," is an implicit recognition that the place of this new idiom is both dangerous and lonely yet might give birth (beyond metanarrative and mininarrative) to meaningful political speech. These voices will have an answer to the question, Did it happen?—an answer that could make a political difference, and not just to them.

Of course, while some circumstances seem to require the sort of radical travel to the places of Others that Kathy Kelly has undertaken, nothing could be clearer today than that, at least in terms of the global environment, all of us already live in the same place. This place already enables an idiom that is capable of "bearing witness" across extraordinarily different material and ideological locations. If the oil and coal industries, assisted by U.S. politicians, have been able until very recently to sustain the fiction of a meaningful countervoice to the overwhelming world consensus about global warming (consisting of "It is happening!"), it was certainly to be expected that this countervoice would eventually have to concede (as it finally seems to be doing). In this case, place exerts a pressure on regimes of phrases that becomes decisive at some moment—that determines, eventually, what we see (though certainly not yet how we live).

"One of the Things at Stake in Women's Struggles"

This brings us to the question of what political difference the experience of the sublime makes in feminist thinking. What, after all, if Albert were a woman?

---

7. See the group's Web site at www.vitw.org and Kathy Kelly's book *Other Lands Have Dreams: From Baghdad to Pekin Prison.*

Certainly the sublime has not become an explicit notion in feminism, even in feminist postmodernism. But if when we talk about the sublime we are talking about a central feature of the spatiotemporal experience of our times, then surely feminism will have its own version of the sublime?

Fortunately for us, Lyotard has not been entirely silent on the question of women and feminism. We may be able to read his remarks on "women's struggles" in light of his theory of the sublime and thus gain some orientation for our study of feminist postmodernist texts in the next chapters. When Lyotard wrote "One of the Things at Stake in Women's Struggles," he must have either explicitly decided on self-parody or forsaken his own critical senses entirely. I can't decide which, in spite of reading the little essay a number of times. To conclude his reflections on "Women's Struggles," he writes:

> Deceitful like Eubalides and like realities, women are discovering something that could cause the greatest revolution in the West, something that masculine domination has never ceased to stifle: there is no signifier;[8] or else, the class above all classes is just one among many; or again, we Westerners must rework our space-time and all our logic on the basis of non-Centralism, non-finality, non-truth. A United Nations vote denounced Zionism as racism, to the great scandal of the West which suddenly found itself in the minority. One day a UN vote will denounce as male sexism the primacy accorded theoretical discourse to the great scandal . . . of us all. (*LR* 1989b, 120)

My trouble with Lyotard's essay begins with his presumption. He presumes to do precisely what he presumes to identify as what feminism has or should have or is in the process of making impossible: he takes for himself the "right to decide meaning." And even more: the meaning he decides on for "women's struggles" is precisely the upshot of his own contribution to contemporary thought, which is the heralding of the demise of theory in the face of "the *differend*" —so he puts himself in the company of feminists by identifying "what is at stake" in women's struggles as precisely what is at stake in his own. Of course if "the right to decide meaning" is removed through the demise of theory in general, then women will not be in a position to decide meaning either—even to decide that theory should be denounced as "male sexism."

To be fair, Lyotard has apparently set out in part to defend the honor of a particular feminist, Luce Irigaray, against the accusation that she has failed to maintain the distinction between the world of signs and the world of the flesh. And he has done this at a time when Irigaray's own stature as a major figure in contemporary French philosophy was not well-established enough to make such a defense popular. Her accusers miss the point, he argues, since "this movement

---

8. This is an extremely interesting part of Lyotard's claim, but one that I won't take up explicitly here. If Albert turns out to be a mere sign, but not a sign *of anything*, it seems that feminism will champion the things for which there are no signs. This is a reinscription of the division between speech and matter, with men and women on their usual sides of the divide, but a reinscription even as the very relation between the two is dissolved. Two sides of the same coin, if the coin dissolves, may well collapse into the same thing anyway—a sign without a referent is as much a bare particular as an entity without a sign.

solicits and destroys the (masculine) belief in meta-statements independent of ordinary statements" (*LR* 1989b, 120). In other words, "there is no signifier." In fact, "The Destruction of Metalanguages Is at Stake in the Women's Struggle" (*LR* 1989b, 118) is the subheading for the last section of Lyotard's essay. Metalanguage is the language of masculinity, Lyotard reminds us, language that takes for itself the right to legislate meaning across incommensurable regimes of phrases, never realizing it is utterly trapped within its own. But here Lyotard claims that all theoretical treatment of the relation between men and women will be written in this language and consequently will reinscribe the relation rather than revolutionizing it. Feminists, apparently, aren't in the business of doing theory at all but are rather nullifying the very possibility of theory by recognizing the impossibility of metalanguage.

There are a host of frightening little claims that accompany this larger theme: that men really would like to be little girls who are "like savages" (again, to be fair, Lyotard is not talking about real little girls but the ones adult men imagine and define themselves against—but now the distance between the signifier—Lyotard's little girls—and the ordinary—real ones—is reinstated, and who are the savages?) and that "truly civilized women are dead women, or men" (He is following Irigaray, but again, these aren't real women, I take it, but women remade in the masculine sign world). Indeed the language of philosophy admits of only two possibilities: women either are "relegated to the borders" of philosophy or die to be reborn as men if they dare to enter.

What feminists have done, if Lyotard is correct, is to recognize a complicity between the political and the philosophical. (But didn't Marx do this as well?) "The complicity between political phallocracy and philosophical metalanguage is made here: the activity men reserve for themselves arbitrarily as fact is posited legally as the right to decide meaning" (*LR* 1989b, 119). Is it self-parody or simply the inevitable carrying out of the law that Lyotard then tells us what feminism means? And that feminism means precisely the demise of theory? Feminists don't enter the symbolic order, they bring it down. But in not entering it, they remain, for Lyotard, "deceitful like realities," that is, like Kant's objects that pretended to guarantee the transition from one "regime of phrases" to the other but in the end had no relation to the phrases at all. In other words, the traditional association of women with everything "banished outside the confines of the corpus socians," that is, "savagery, sensitivity, matter and the kitchen, impulsion, hysteria, silence, maenadic dances, lying, diabolical beauty, ornamentation, lasciviousness, witchcraft and weakness" (114) is reinscribed here. That Lyotard might value these things is perhaps to be appreciated—but nevertheless, we are left wondering what feminists are doing when we are thinking and writing. Lyotard's answer would be, perhaps, that we are doing the same thing he is.

It is certainly true that feminist postmodernists have taken up the banner of the demise of metalanguage. They have taken up this banner in the United States out of a dispute within feminism, a dispute about what it means to speak of women or for women or about women and whether the metalanguage required in this speaking is always noxious or merely necessary. Feminist postmodernism has taught us that the "women" feminists speak of are as caught in the instantaneity of postmodern time as Albert, as confined to the particularity of the instant, of the context of the solitary speech act. There can be no theory of women, certainly not a metatheory, because there can be no metalanguage about women. And here we find the answer to the question we posed above, "What if Albert were a woman?" It seems that Albert is.

The Idea of feminism, that is, women's liberation, is as unpresentable as the Idea of freedom was for Kant. Feminist postmodernism has taken this insight and transformed the task of feminism from one of making concrete the idea of women's liberation to one of pointing out its indeterminacy. A historical/cultural/political project has been turned into a discursive practice, that is, the project of showing the mistake of metalanguage. This is a crucial turn, the linguistic turn in the context of feminism, the crucial turn of feminist postmodernism. But this turn, I will argue, comes at the cost of a kind of forgetfulness about what is at stake in women's struggles. In fact, I would insist that what is at stake in "women's struggles" is not masculinist metalanguage at all, but women.

4

The Stakes of Feminism and the Feminist Postmodern

Now we must rephrase Lyotard's question slightly: instead of asking what is at stake in women's struggles, we ask what is at stake in the feminist struggle over the alliance between feminism and postmodernism. Could it be that what is at stake is *what is at stake*? At its deepest, the debate may be precisely about what feminism is for. The two-decades-old struggle over whether the alliance between feminism and postmodernism benefits or harms the feminist project is really much more about what the feminist project *is*.

The criticism that feminist postmodernism is apolitical or antipolitical, that it undermines rather than promotes goals proper to feminism, has been restated in various ways in various contexts. A good summary is to be found in Jane Flax's 1992 rejoinder to these criticisms, "The End of Innocence":

> "You cannot be a feminist and a postmodernist," I was told. Postmodernists are a- or even antipolitical. They are relativists; if we take them seriously, any political stance will be impossible to maintain or justify. Feminists must generate and sustain a notion of truth so that we can adjudicate conflicts among competing ideas and legitimate the claims of (some) feminist theorists and activists. Since postmodernists believe there is no truth, conflict will only be resolved through the raw exercise of power (domination). Postmodernists' deconstructions of subjectivity deny or destroy the possibility of active agency in the world. Without a unitary subject with a secure, empirical sense of history and gender, no feminist consciousness and hence no feminist politics is possible. Since postmodernists believe meanings are multiple and indeterminant, if you write clearly and comprehensibly you cannot be a postmodernist. In fact, postmodernists write obscurely on purpose so that no one outside their cult can understand them. One must choose between total acceptance or rejection of their position. Acceptance entails abandoning feminism or annihilating its autonomy and force, subordinating it to a destructive and inhospitable, male-dominated philosophy. (Flax 1992, 446)

Flax's formulation is perhaps a bit of a caricature, but it nevertheless provides a quick review of many of the central themes of the conflict.

Elsewhere the conflict has been articulated as a matter of foundations. Particularly in the 1995 volume *Feminist Contentions* (structured as a series of essays and critical responses between Seyla Benhabib, Judith Butler, Drucilla Cornell, and Nancy Fraser), we see the debate move from one about feminism and postmodernism to a more specific conflict between critical theory and poststructuralism to an argument over foundations. Benhabib's question, "Can feminist theory be postmodernist and still retain an interest in emancipation?" frames the debate. For Benhabib, "A certain version of postmodernism," what she calls the "strong version" of three theses in postmodernity—the Death of Man, Death of History, and Death of Metaphysics—"is not only incompatible with but would undermine the very possibility of feminism as the theoretical articulation of the emancipatory aspirations of women" (Benhabib et al. 1995, 29). In other words, the strong version of these three theses—that there is no subject, there is no history, and there is no truth—amounts to a subversion not only of patriarchal conceits but also of the very possibility of feminism as well.

Butler's rejoinder begins with a contestation of the use of the term "postmodern" but goes much further, implicitly reworking the very definition of feminism itself so that Benhabib's definition of feminist theory as "the theoretical articulation of the emancipatory aspirations of women" no longer holds as a common ground between the two. This conflict is never brought to the surface of these *Feminist Contentions*, where the explicit debate about foundations turns for the most part on the possibility or impossibility of a "unitary subject"—and the relation of the subject to "power." My project in this chapter is to recuperate and bring under critical scrutiny the other sense of foundation that is implicitly but not explicitly contested in this and other of Butler's early texts—that is, the stakes, the purpose, of feminism itself.

It is important to add a clarifying note here. I find Butler's early work to be extremely challenging in the best sense, even as I find it to be mystifying in the worst sense. This is the kind of philosophical thinking that shakes people, that destabilizes deep-seated assumptions (I experience this nearly each term with my students) and rejuvenates a commitment to making sense of the world in new ways. Yet these early texts turn on certain foundations that I find more than a little troubling, even as they contain moments of confusion or ambivalence that prefigure and push toward a rather dramatic "turn" in Butler's very recent work. I would tentatively characterize this turn as a "phenomenological turn." Her early work (up through the 1997 and 2000 texts, *The Psychic Life of Power* and *Antigone's Claim*) can be distinguished from her very recent work (inaugurated by *Precarious Life*, 2004) by a shift in foundations. The periodization of the work of a living thinker is always tenuous business, of course, doubly so when the "turn" is so recent and when one anticipates the annoyance of the thinker herself—so I offer this characterization with some trepidation. What one actually finds is not an absolute departure but a kind of crescendo of strain (1997b, 2000) followed by a breakthrough, which seems to be brought about by certain historical events (9/11 among them) in concert with the textual tension that was already building. While in chapter 8 I turn to Butler's recent work quite enthusiastically, in this chapter and in chapter 6 I engage Butler's early work in order to clarify some central stakes (or mis-takes) of feminist postmodernism.

My effort is to do this, at least to some extent, on Butler's own terms, so I will begin by acknowledging and responding to her insistence that the term "postmodernism" is misleading and masks a "ruse of authority," that distorts rather than clarifies the issues at hand. Second, I argue that establishing the feminist postmodern over and against a foreclosed "essentialism" amounts to a disavowal of the realm of necessity. A dual conception of "nature" as "human nature" and the natural world is foreclosed at the moment that inaugurates the textual space in which feminist postmodernism sets to work. This disavowed realm returns on the inside of Butler's theory as a discursive "nature," which makes constant trouble in regards to the subject's agency, the subject's freedom. Third, I will show how Butler's approach to the relation between extradiscursive being and speech authorizes the dis-placement of feminism from its foundation, but not a foundation in the unitary subject so much as a foundation in a certain set of historical projects. This central moment of unraveling in Butler's work is an implicit "sublime" experience, where both temporality and the relation of speech to place mirror those found in Lyotard's notion of the sublime. Finally, it becomes clear that the return of the repressed realm of necessity (or otherwise said, the repressed relation to the earth) in Butler's early texts, its return as discursive *determinacy*, pushes toward exactly what Butler turns to in her later work: the theme of embodied vulnerability in relation to other persons. This is to say, it pushes toward something that always exceeds the discursive.

What's in a Name? Saying "Postmodern"

Butler rejects the use of the term "postmodern" in the sweeping way I use it here. "Who are these postmodernists?" she asks. "Is this a name one takes on for oneself, or is it more often a name that one is called if and when one offers a critique of the subject, a discursive analysis, or questions the integrity or coherence of totalizing social descriptions" (Benhabib et al. 1995, 35)? The term is used to communicate a fear of something dangerous and unruly. It gathers up a myriad of divergent positions—including postmodernism and poststructuralism, which includes deconstruction, French feminism, Lacanian psychoanalysis, work drawing on Foucault, cultural studies, and so on—and presents them as if they are essentially the same (36). This is an "effort to colonize and domesticate these theories under the sign of the same, to group them synthetically and masterfully under a single rubric, a simple refusal to grant the specificity of these positions that provides an excuse not to read, and not to read closely" (4). The collapsing of such diverse theories into a unitary "postmodernism" is authorized by what Butler calls a "Hegelian trope," the view that "historically a set of theories which are structurally similar emerge as the articulation of an historically specific condition of human reflection." This trope serves to falsely unify diverse theories under the assumption that they "symptomatize a common structural preoccupation" (5). Yet Butler's use of the term "Hegelian" as a kind of curse word is similar to the most dismissive use of the term "postmodern," offering as it does no argument for why we shouldn't believe that the immersion of writers of theory in specific, and widespread, material conditions should not constitute, at least in large part, certain concerns as more central than others. An effort to articulate this coherence cannot be presumed in advance to be falsifying rather than illuminating.

What, after all, of writers who do claim the name "postmodern" and do see postmodernism as a widespread and identifiable cultural movement? Butler contests Benhabib's use of Lyotard, whose book *The Postmodern Condition: A Report on Knowledge* does precisely this, as an example of what postmodernism is, "he cannot be made into the example of what all the rest of the purported postmodernists are doing," she writes (Benhabib et al. 1995). She would presumably object, as well, to my own "lumping together" of her work and Lyotard's. I am not, however, using Lyotard's work to debunk Butler's, without reading it, but rather to elucidate a certain kind of aesthetic experience that is at the center of Butler's work, but inexplicit, and that will be traced here in Butler's own texts.

Butler does admit of a possible coherence between poststructuralism, post-modernism, and other "powerful criticisms" that get lumped under the term "postmodern." "If postmodernism as a term has some force or meaning within social theory, or feminist social theory in particular, perhaps it can be found in the critical exercise that seeks to show how theory, how philosophy, is always impli-cated in power" (Benhabib et al. 1995, 38). For Butler, if there is such a thing as postmodernism, it is not something to which one can ascribe a set of positions "as if it were the kind of thing that could be the bearer of positions" (36). She says the same of poststructuralism, which is a term she is at least slightly more comfortable with. "Poststructuralism is not, strictly speaking a position, but rather a critical interrogation of the exclusionary operations by which 'positions' are established. In this sense, a feminist poststructuralism does not designate a position from which one operates, a point of view or standpoint which might be usefully compared with other 'positions' within the theoretical field" (Butler and Scott 1992, xvi). The coherence of the various theories that get called "postmodern," for Butler, is this critical interrogating role, a role that differentiates them from "positions."

What are the consequences of defining poststructuralism or postmodernism as modes of interrogation and asserting a difference between modes of interrogation and positions? As a feminist, I am immediately uncomfortable with this claim of a no-place beyond position, a position-less-ness from which to criticize or interrogate other positions. Poststructuralism becomes a kind of neutral tool, it "can be used," it has "no necessary political consequences . . . but only a political deployment" (Benhabib et al. 1995, 41). The advantage for poststructuralism of not being a position is clear since positions lay down foundations that must be brought into question. Poststructuralism is that part of a "social theory committed to democratic contestation within a postcolonial horizon" (Benhabib et al. 1995) that is no po-sition and thus has no foundation. It can itself remain uninterrogated, even as it interrogates the foundations of that very "social theory" in which and by which it is "used." It is readily apparent that for Butler, at least in this context, the "social theory" whose foundations are to be interrogated is feminism, and the neutral tool, itself beyond interrogation, is poststructuralism or postmodernism.

Postmodernism, then, has a job to do vis-à-vis feminism. The job is to show how feminist social theory is "always implicated in power," while postmodernism itself is simply a "movement of interrogating that ruse of authority that seeks to close itself off from contest" (Benhabib et al. 1995, 41). Of course by defining poststructuralism (or postmodernism) as the very movement of this interrogation *of* feminism, it cannot be contested *by* feminism. Feminism is a social theory, here reduced to a set of positions in contrast to postmodernism. Feminism loses its power as itself a *mode of interrogation* while poststructuralism is freed from critique and freed from political consequences. It is what corrects or checks feminism, what puts feminism off the wrong path.

This seems to me nothing less than precisely the kind of "ruse of authority" Butler is at pains to deconstruct. By whose authority is postmodernism or post-structuralism (and Butler herself is using the terms interchangeably at least on this point) removed from the field of contestable positions and granted this no-place? If, as Butler teaches, the fearful aspect of these divergent theories is in their critical capacity, and if "it is this movement of interrogating that ruse of authority that seeks to close itself off from contest that is, in my view, at the heart of any radical political project" (Benhabib et al. 1995, 41), why should this project stop at what we have perhaps inadequately called "postmodernism," whether or not it is primarily a mode of interrogation? After all, we subject modes of interrogation to interrogation all the time (the feminist interrogation of scientific method comes to mind).

If we refuse the reduction of feminism to a set of positions and insist that feminism is also a mode of interrogation, then feminism will also interrogate postmodernism. Here I am accepting Benhabib's formulation: feminism interrogates out of a concern for the "emancipatory aspirations of women," at least some women somewhere. Postmodernism seems to me to interrogate out of another concern entirely, which can be described most briefly as the dismantling of modernist metanarratives. Feminism, then, has a job to do vis-à-vis postmodernism as much as postmodernism does vis-à-vis feminism. If various postmodern theories have laid down certain common foundations in spite of their differences, and I believe they have, it is important that feminists "find a way to bring into question the foundations [these theories are] compelled to lay down." In what follows, I look for the foundations of the early Butler's postmodernism, a postmodernism deployed in order to bring into question the foundations of that "social theory" called feminism.

Butler claims that her task is not an "antifoundationalist" one. "Rather, the task is to interrogate what the theoretical move that establishes foundations *authorizes*, and what precisely it excludes or forecloses" (Benhabib et al. 1995, 39). This will be my task in this engagement with Butler's own position, and I do believe she has one. What does Butler's poststructuralism authorize in feminism? What are the foundations it lays down? What is excluded or foreclosed in this laying down?

The Foundations of the Feminist Postmodern

What kinds of "foreclosure" define feminist postmodernism? The term "foreclosure" is an important one for Butler, and I'm deploying it in the way that she does. Butler argues in *Excitable Speech* that "language constitutes the subject in part through foreclosure, a kind of unofficial censorship or primary restriction in speech that constitutes the possibility of agency in speech" (*ES* 1997a, 41). In other words, our very agency is constituted in and through the prohibitions that define us. What and who we are enabled to be is constitutively connected to what and who we are forbidden to be. As Butler teaches us, borrowing the notion from Freud, what is foreclosed becomes "something that happens only under the official sign of its prohibition and disavowal" (*PLP* 1997b, 139). What are the foreclosures that enable a feminist postmodernist to be one? What do we postmodern feminists define ourselves against?

When Butler concedes that postmodernism is a name that might represent a kind of coherence and that this coherence has to do with a mode of interrogation of foundations and what foundations authorize, she is implicitly setting post-modernism against "essentialism."[1] Butler's own early work turns on these mo-ments of contestation. In *Gender Trouble* she contests the essentialism of sex and gender; in "Contingent Foundations" she contests the essentialism of notions of the subject; in *Bodies That Matter* she contests the essentialism of our notion of "matter"; in *Excitable Speech* she again contests the essentialism of the subject, now a subject injured by speech; in the *Psychic Life of Power* she contests, among many other things, the essentialism of the boundary between inner and outer and of heterosexual love. These works are all complex and can't be reduced to these moments of contestation—yet they would hardly be possible without them. In-deed, one of Butler's important contributions to feminist postmodernism has been to take the feminist critique of essentialism to levels of sophistication that far outstrip other efforts.

I argued in my introduction that the term "essentialist!" has come to function more as a dismissive accusatory than as a meaningful critical term. This is a widespread cultural phenomenon that is not true for Butler, who generally has not deployed the term in this simplistic way. If we look for the foundational exclusions of Butler's poststructuralism, however, we find essentialism. Essentialism provides the very limit against which postmodern theory works. An "essentialist" is every-thing a "postmodernist" is not. A forbidden essentialism is the "constitutive out-side," of feminist postmodernism, what is excluded, and in that exclusion gives an identity to what it is excluded from. The word "essentialism," whether we know what we mean by it or not, operates as the sign of a primary prohibition that "bestows existence" on feminist postmodernism.

Essentialism is itself rendered unintelligible at the same time that it constitutes the intelligibility of what it is excluded from. It ceases to have meaning for femi-nism in a number of ways: first, the term becomes so flexible and all-encompassing that almost anything can come to be categorized as essentialist; second, any essence talk begins to seem nonsensical for feminism, or even antifeminist; and third, we become unable to articulate, or even investigate, what might be essential to our lives as persons. The problem with all this is simply that in our flight from

---

1. By 1998, Butler is herself urging caution abut the dismissive use of terms like "essentialism," as noted in the introduction.

essentialism, we are *dumbfounded before the question of essence*, but not freed from it. (On the contrary, essentialism creeps back in under the guise of its undoing, as we will see below.) In the course of this flight, we profoundly misunderstand ourselves and the project of women's liberation.

More than providing a limit against which the postmodern is defined, the foreclosure of essence inaugurates the very site or space in which postmodernism works. This is the space that is opened up "over the abyss," in Lyotard's discussion of Albert, where the disruption of any connection between words and extra-discursive referents, between "Albert" and any existing Albert, leaves one agitating above a now gaping absence. This is the space of the sublime, the space of terror/exhilaration where the referent is recast as an instance of speech rather than an extradiscursive thing that stands in some relation to speech. In feminist post-modernism, the name most necessary to the feminist project, the name "women," is freed from an extradiscursive reality to "agitate over the abyss."

The price we pay for entering this space is very high. As Butler points out at another moment in her work, foreclosure is also a "preemptive loss" (*PLP* 1997b, 23) that throws the subject into a kind of unending melancholy. For Butler, the preemptive loss that inaugurates the subject is understood at least in part as a loss of homosexual love. This is "a loss which cannot be thought, cannot be owned or grieved" (24). But there is another loss that is gestured toward yet unspoken under the sign of "essentialism." How can we trace this loss?

"Essentialism" is deployed most commonly in feminism as a gesture of con-tempt for a belief in an essential "nature" of women. A central contribution of feminism to philosophy, at least in what we call the West, has been its disruption of the stories of "human nature," and "women's nature," that justified women's subordination. Feminists sensitive to the ways resignifications of "woman" in feminism have reinscribed notions of "nature" along race and class lines have contributed a similar disruption to feminist narratives of "women" that legitimate race and class oppressions or exclusions. These are the "natures" that are at stake on the surface of feminist postmodernism, and the struggles over race, class, and sexuality in feminism are often evoked as supporting postmodernist positions.[2]

But only feminist postmodernism defines itself as the antithesis of any belief in "natures" whatsoever. Previous efforts saw specific attributions of "nature" to be misogynist, racist, and wrong, and often relied on counterassertions of a "nature." For example, to legitimate struggles for equality or self-determination, feminists

2. There is some disingenuousness to "claiming" these struggles as legitimating of the postmod-ernist project since leading thinkers among feminists of color also disagree about the role or efficacy of postmodernism vis-à-vis feminism. At least one would need to acknowledge these disagreements and make some argument for why postmodernism and antiracist or anticolonialist struggles are necessarily linked in this way. The evoking of antiracist struggles within feminism as support for postmodernism seems to me to serve the simple purpose of warning the critical reader against a critical stance vis-à-vis postmodernism since this presumably places one within the camps of the racist white women's movement. This tendency is particularly strong in Butler's and Scott's introduction to their 1992 col-lection, *Feminists Theorize the Political*.

argued that women are just as rational by nature as are men. Latino/a activists and thinkers have argued Latinos/as are as capable of self-government by nature as any other race. Many social movements have argued that people by nature acquire their most important traits through socialization rather than biology. Alternatively, and more problematically, some accounts affirmed differences in nature but attempted to revalue the "natural attributes" of the subordinate group. Feminist postmodernism distinguishes itself from these efforts by defining itself over and against the "essentialism" that would have recourse to any notion of "nature" at all. "Nature" in this sense is foreclosed in feminist postmodernism, and this founding foreclosure is, at least in part, what limits and bestows identity on the field.

I have come to suspect that this founding foreclosure in postmodern theory actually depends on and obscures another. For what would it mean to say that persons have no nature at all? Beyond the claim that biology is not or should not be social/political destiny in terms of gender or race differences, this position seems to see persons as without relation to the natural world.[3] This second foreclosure amounts to a reiteration and reinstantiation of a prior and long-standing foreclosure that has accompanied Western philosophy since its inception. Far from marking a radical departure from the modernist tradition, I'm arguing that postmodernism actually carries over a founding prohibition from modernism. This is the foreclosure of the material world, the earth, as the ultimate condition of possibility for life itself. For the postmodernist, to be sure, this emancipation is purportedly not in service to an unveiling of human "nature" or destiny as it was for Kant but is a freedom from that "nature" as well. Yet this second freedom depends on the first, on a fantasy of a world made of consciousness, limited to consciousness, dependent on consciousness—now of course the *externalized and collectivized consciousness* we call discourse. Here discourse, both product of and productive of human subjectivity, is phantasmatically freed from what Arendt called "the quintessence of the human condition," that is, the planet itself. "Earth" becomes here merely another term in the intertextual universe we inhabit, fully dependent on this sign-world of human making. This dramatic reversal, where the earth is dependent on us but we are independent of the earth, is perhaps the quintessential metatheory of Euro-masculinist philosophy.

The same metatheory reemerges in postmodernism translated into an exchange of the relation between words and a world for the self-referential world of the text. This is an inwardness turned inside out. It requires the foreclosure of our relation to the natural world, but like all foreclosures, this one involves a dramatic loss. What does it mean to disavow a relation that we live moment to moment, to disavow what Arendt called "a free gift from nowhere," to disavow our dependence on breath and light and warmth? What does it mean to lose this first love?

---

3. A symptom of this shift is our new understanding of biology as simply what we make of it. Phenomena as diverse as cosmetic surgery, the manipulation of and patenting of genes, the genetic alteration of species, and cloning all seem to bear witness to a transformation in our relation to our own biology and the biological processes of the world. Here "biology" is drawn up into the world of human making, and the space outside of human making that we call "nature" is impoverished even more.

I read the emphatic anti-essentialism of postmodernism, in part, as a disavowed grief for the loss of a primary love for our planet,[4] because a love for our planet would entail an acknowledgment of our utter and inescapable—that is, our essential—dependency in relationship to it.

The feminist postmodernist flight from essentialism is also, of course, a flight from the realm of necessity. In earlier moments of the Western philosophical tradition, the realm of necessity was devalued, was what had to be overcome or projected onto others (wives, slaves, etc.) in order to do philosophy or experience freedom. Feminists, for the most part, have accepted this devaluation but argued that women's humanity justified their emancipation from this realm as well. Feminist postmodernism completes this project. When life becomes art, world becomes text, and nature becomes culture, then sex becomes gender and necessity melts away into discursive freedom. But if I gain this home in language only when nature in both senses is foreclosed, then the price of liberation is a home in both the natural and the social worlds. I lose the footing, the place to stand from which and through which something that exceeds the inwardness of the postmodern discursive universe, something that calls to me from beyond the confines of the discursive, resists its totalizing tendencies. Certainly this resistance is present to me as an excess on the inside of the discursive universe; this call makes itself heard on the inside of the chain of signification that binds me, which is simply to say that language itself seems ever to resist our efforts to seal it off entirely.

We might think of postmodernism as that set of ideas that not only abjects the realm of material (as opposed to discursive) necessity but renders it unintelligible. If the realm of necessity is unintelligible, "the political" must be as well.[5] As one example, that struggle so central to feminist politics, the struggle for material equality, is inextricably tied to our materiality, to the relationship of dependence between persons and our planet—if we were freed from the need for material sustenance, material equality would not be a central aspect of struggles for social justice at all. In saying this, I'm claiming that the realm of necessity is the ground or space on which inequalities are built and struggles for equality are waged. When equality is severed from this ground or space, it ceases to make much political sense—so how we engage the philosophical question of necessity and freedom will be key to how we engage the question of equality. It is this essential relationship between humans and our planet that makes equality matter.

There are two strands or themes I find important here that run through our engagement with the question of necessity and freedom in the feminist postmodern. One strand is internal to Butler's theory itself, and one strand has to do with the broader social-political climate in the United States. Let me take up the second one first. In the United States, freedom has been understood precisely as

---

4. Of course earth is not to be reduced to a mere "planet," but I emphasize the planetary aspect of "earth" to emphasize as well our brute, material dependence in relation to it.

5. This is the same point Martha Nussbaum argues when she says that a kind of essentialism is necessary as the basis for a "global ethic and fully international account of distributive justice" (1992, 205).

freedom from limitations, not freedom from necessity per se but from a kind of necessity that might be imposed by another person, or a government. Particularly strong in the U.S. American tradition is the notion of freedom of expression, a kind of discursive freedom that seems to escape entanglement with necessity in the brute sense of breathing, drinking, and eating. This is a kind of freedom that also escapes the material issues of equality since presumably anyone can be as free to speak as anyone else, no matter what the material inequalities between them. Now we know that this isn't true, but that is the story we are told so that discursive or expressive freedom can be legally declared without doing anything about material inequalities. When George W. Bush responded to the attacks of 9/11 by sloganizing "freedom has been attacked and freedom will be defended," he meant to divorce the issue from the material circumstances of brutal inequality that are suffered across the globe, in large part because of international economic and political policies pursued by the United States.

Traditionally in the United States, freedom is divorced from necessity, and questions of equality are severed from questions of freedom. Instead, questions of equality are taken up much more under the rubric of another philosophical question, that of the one and the many. Addressing the question of equality in this way has two consequences for feminist politics. First, it plays itself out politically in terms of struggles over exclusion and inclusion, in terms of the false or real universalizing of rights. Who gets to be human? Who gets included or excluded from places, opportunities, or legal protections? These are real struggles, yet framing the discussion in this way leaves us defining and redefining categories like "human" or "woman," and alternately deconstructing these same notions ad nauseam. It leaves us searching for a kind of minimal definition for inclusion in the category, as Martha Nussbaum does when she attempts to define the human by means of a minimal list of functions that are essential to human life and serve to distinguish humans from other creatures (including, she admits, possibly the severely disabled) (1992).[6] What remains misleading in these discussions is the effort to categorize, rather than to give a *descriptive account of our relation to the realm of necessity*, one

---

6. There are some senses in which my own project shares a great deal with Nussbaum's. She argues that "the legitimate criticisms of essentialism still leave room for essentialism of a kind: for a historically sensitive account of the most basic human needs and functions... without such an account, we do not have an adequate basis for an account of social justice and the ends of social distribution" (1992, 205). Though I agree with this, I disagree with Nussbaum's attempt to reclaim essentialism through a normative definition of the category of human rather than to provide a descriptive account of the essential relation of dependence between persons and places, as I do here. As noted in note 31 to the introduction, she admits that defining humans in terms of basic capacities involves "enormous potential for abuse" and historically has been rife with such examples.

> Therefore we should, I think, proceed as if every offspring of two human parents has the basic capabilities, unless and until long experience *with the individual* has convinced us that damage to that individual's condition is so great that it could never in any way, through however great an expenditure of resources, arrive at the higher capability level. (Certain patients with irreversible senile dementia or a permanent vegetative condition would fall into

which we share as persons not only with one another across all kinds of lines but with other species as well. This is to say that we exchange, again, real questions about life and how to live it in relation to one another for questions about how to speak about one another. We reduce the question of exclusion and inclusion to a question of language.

Consequently, framing the question of equality in terms of "the one and the many" eliminates the need to deal with material, economic, and social inequalities that define the relationship of various social groups and individuals to this brute realm of necessity. We forego attention to this realm in favor of formalistic and legal equality, that is, in favor of a discursive equality where discursive means what the law says or what a sign says or what admission requirements say. Put differently, this kind of equality restricts speech where speech would declare "Men only!" or "Whites only!" but does not address the unequal access social groups have to the necessities that define our relationship to the planet, to clean air, clean water, good food, light, warmth, shelter, and so on. Feminist postmodernism in the United States grows up and develops in a political context, then, where equality is already understood to be of the realm of the discursive rather than of the realm of the material.

The other strand that runs through an engagement with the question of necessity and freedom is internal to postmodern theory and has to do with the foreclosure I mentioned above, the foreclosure of the realm of necessity where a fantasized freedom from necessity is accepted as the precondition for doing philosophy at all. In postmodern theory, necessity is, like everything else, discursive. It is discursive determinacy, the "chain of signification" that binds the subject in discourse. In Butler's theory of subjectivation, borrowed and reworked from Althusser and Foucault, the first moment is a moment of determinacy that constructs the subject, bestows existence on the subject.

The second moment is a moment of discursive contingency that births the subject's agency, which I will discuss in more detail below. For now, a brief overview of the problem must suffice. In Butler's theory of subjectivation determinacy, which I take to be necessity in its postmodern form, eventually melts away in favor of discursive contingency. This melting away happens through the very temporal and ontological elusiveness that mark Lyotard's sublime. First, there is a contingency of context, of what kind of discourse, when and where and under what

---

this category, as would certain very severely damaged infants). It would then fall to other moral arguments to decide what treatment we owe to such individuals, who are unable ever to reach the higher capabilities to function humanly. (1992, 228)

If we set ourselves to the task of a descriptive account of dependency, and what enables or protects our relation of dependency on the planet, the point is not to decide who's in and who's out of the category of human but to articulate what humans actually share with, and how humans depend on, other living beings—this opens the field rather than closing it.

conditions of power construct the subject—agency will always be a result of local and specific matrixes of discourse. (When I say "women" in a university in New York, it will not mean the same as if I say "women" in a university in Nigeria, there is no ontology of women to bind these two instances of speech together.) The second sort of contingency is the temporal contingency of Lyotard's Albert. (If I say "Albert" now, this will not be the same Albert as if I say "Albert" at some other moment.) The conditions of discursive power that found the subject also found the subject's agency, through these contingencies. These contingencies of time and context, these iterative contingencies, are *the sites* for agency. As Butler writes, "if conditions of power are to persist, they must be reiterated; the subject is precisely the site of such reiteration, a repetition that is never merely mechanical" (*PLP* 1997b, 16). It is in reiteration, in the temporal and contextual gaps between one citation in the chain of signification and another, that we find the kind of contingency that leaves a space for agency.

But what has been foreclosed, as Butler herself teaches us, always returns. That realm of necessity, which has been foreclosed to create a discursive universe will return as a constant source of trouble within it. The point on which Butler has most often been criticized, where she has been extremely hard pressed to formulate an adequate response, is in regard to her efforts to explain how the subject has agency at all. The subject's very agency is due, for Butler, to a vulnerability, it is an agency that seems wholly unrelated to the subject's own will or conscious intention. This agency is *given* in discourse, quite without the subject's consent, and exercised, seemingly unwittingly, and without any guarantee of efficacy. The subject is dependent, even for its autonomy, on discourse. What does it mean to exercise agency in the context of this moment-to-moment dependence? Can there be an adequate theory of agency based on a reduced notion of freedom as mere discursive contingency?

To add to the difficulties, Butler doesn't see the primary discursive vulnerability of the emergent subject merely as a kind of dependence, she conflates discursive dependence with subordination.

> Bound to seek recognition of its own existence in categories, terms, and names that are not of its own making the subject seeks the sign of its own existence outside itself in a discourse that is at once dominant and indifferent. Social categories signify subordination and existence at once. In other words, within subjection *the price of existence is subordination.* Precisely at the moment in which choice is impossible, the subject pursues subordination as the promise of existence. Assuming terms of power that one never made but to which one is vulnerable, on which one depends in order to be, appears to be a mundane subjection at the basis of subject formation. (*PLP* 1997b, 20–21; emphasis added)

This is why Butler's discussion of hate speech is so mystifying. The "injury" of hate speech is only intelligible, I believe, if we understand this speech to exceed the boundaries of mere speech, that is, simple name-calling, and attach itself to the historical and material subordination of targeted groups. But for Butler, the "injury" of hate speech is in the end no different than the primary injury that produces the subject in language in any case. Butler detaches injury from its material and historical conditions and reattaches it to a generalized process of discursive subject formation. Here the victim of hate speech seems to owe, at least at that moment, their very existence as a subject to the perpetrator of the crime, who bestows this existence, albeit unwittingly. Thus this primary dependence on language, which is for Butler a *subordination* in language, is the unfortunate but necessary condition for becoming a subject. The harm of the injury is converted surreptitiously into a kind of ultimate benefit. If dependence always means subordination, subordination is merely a sign of this dependence—out of which agency emerges. But this is a strange kind of agency at best. This subject is not free in any recognizable sense of the word and cannot "act" in the way we commonly understand "action." This is not a subject in possession of free will, at least not the sort of free will that, when exercised, might result in reasonably predictable consequences. Even if such a dependent subject might, as Butler puts it, assume "a purpose unintended by power" (*PLP* 1997b, 15), it remains in a state of discursive vulnerability that is never overcome (*ES* 1997a, 26). In fact, it is unclear if this subject is the sort of creature that might "assume a purpose" at all since her agency is bestowed under conditions of vulnerability, and her actions are not likely to be efficacious, at least in the sense of realizing a conscious purpose.

And indeed, the fundamental dependency of the subject on discourse, the subordination of the subject in discourse, binds this subject every bit as inextricably to an essence, as modernist accounts of the subject did. This subject *has an essential foundation in language*. Necessity, foreclosed to inaugurate the space of the postmodern, returns to plague the discursive subject within the postmodern. What is prohibited is reinstantiated inside the system that defines itself on the basis of that prohibition. It returns on the inside of that textual universe in the form of an essential and universal subordination of subjects in language—a necessary subordination. This is to say that even this discursive subject, this instance in speech, *has a nature*; its nature binds it to discourse and in discourse. This is a "nature," nearly unrecognizable, a shadow of the sort of nature that might bind one to nature. Yet this very shadow nature will be what points the way back to nature, as we will see at the conclusion of this chapter.

For now, suffice it to say that the essentialism that was foreclosed in the inauguration of the textual space in which Butler's theory works reemerges as an internal tension *within the theory itself*. In what does the subject's agency consist, after all, given this condition of "primary vulnerability and susceptibility" (*ES* 1997a, 26) in language, given the return of the repressed, of necessity? What sort of freedom does this subject exercise? What is it, after all, that the postmodern subject is freed from, if she is freed at all? What is it that she is freed for?

Freeing the Terms: The Sublime Is What Feminism Is For

What the term "liberation" in "Women's Liberation" means has always been part of the contested ground of feminism. This question is necessarily linked to another, What is it that women need to be liberated from? If the source of women's oppression is economic, then liberation might mean equal pay for equal work or nontraditional employment or socialism or communist revolution. If the source of women's oppression is their role in mothering, liberation might mean finding technological alternatives to the womb, enlisting men equally in caring for children, access to abortion and contraception, or eschewing mothering altogether. If the source of women's oppression is compulsory heterosexuality, then liberation might mean more choice in matters of sex, political lesbianism, lesbian separatism, an organized and asexual boycott of the institution of heterosexuality, or working to make heterosexuality better by taking on a more daring and active role in bed. If the source of women's oppression is colonial expansion and racism, then women's liberation might be thought to follow naturally from national liberation or the reclaiming of precolonial cultures. If the source of women's oppression is the domination of nature to which women are thought to belong, then liberation might mean a revaluing of those things we associate with nature, an assertion of women's rationality over and against an irrational nature, or a more political and historical environmentalism. If the source of women's oppression is patriarchal religion, women's liberation might mean a recuperation of goddess traditions, church reform, or atheism. If the source of women's oppression is a repression of the female self, then liberation will mean self-expression through therapeutic communities, in art, or through protest. And if the source of women's oppression is men, then men will need to be changed, overthrown, or disposed of in some way to achieve women's liberation. "Women's Liberation" has taken all of these paths, many of which are not mutually exclusive, some of which are, and none of which is as simplistic as I've rhetorically outlined them here. It has been contested at every turn both from within feminism and from without.

Little surprise, then, that an implicit contentiousness about the meaning of women's liberation underlies the debate about feminism and postmodernism. This contentiousness is not new, though here it takes on a new form. For perhaps the first time, we find a position that claims a place *within* feminism from which to doubt whether some form of liberation from some oppression, for some women, somewhere is at issue in feminism at all. Feminist postmodernism authorizes this position as a feminist one for the first time, and thus must authorize a new purpose for feminism. For the early Butler, at least, women's liberation in whatever contested form, ceases to be at issue in feminism, ceases to be the point of feminism. What takes its place?

Again, the contention in *Feminist Contentions*, focuses in large part on the subject of feminism rather than its purpose. The arguments tend to cluster around the status of the subject, while an assumed commonality about feminism's project unravels in these discussions even as it goes unremarked. I want to trace several moments of this unraveling in Butler's response to Benhabib's criticisms of the postmodern in her essay "Contingent Foundations."

Butler responds to the accusation that she has undermined feminism's subject, undermined our ability to "speak of women" in a crucial passage of her initial answer to Benhabib. She speaks of two necessities that must be reconciled: (1) a necessity to speak of and for women, and (2) the need to keep the notion "women" open, unspecified. "I would argue that the rift among women over the content of the term ought to be safeguarded and prized, indeed, that the constant rifting ought to be affirmed as the *ungrounded ground* of feminist theory" (Benhabib et al.

1995, 50; emphasis added). Here feminist theory attains both a new (ungrounded) ground and a new project, that is, safeguarding and prizing the rifting of "women," the term. The shift I am bringing to the fore has here its first moment. The "rifting" of women over the term "women," a contentiousness that feminists suffer through in the belief that the stakes are more than the term itself, that the stakes are women, at least some women somewhere, becomes the point rather than part of the process of feminism.

The passage continues: "To deconstruct the subject of feminism is not, then, to censure its usage, but on the contrary, to *release the term* into a future of multiple significations, to emancipate it from the maternalist or racialist ontologies to which it has been restricted, and to give it play as a site where unanticipated meanings might come to bear" (Benhabib et al. 1995, 50; emphasis added). A term, "women," takes the place of women as the object of emancipation. The term is what is freed, what is "given play." What is it emancipated from?

In the above passage, Butler is suggesting a limited emancipation; the term is emancipated from the "maternalist or racialist ontologies" it has tended to carry around with it. But as we read on, we find that the term is undergoing a broader emancipation, from its relation to a fixed extradiscursive referent. This emancipation, moreover, guarantees a kind of reduced agency, a sort of discursive "liberation." "Paradoxically, it may be that only through releasing the category of women from a fixed referent that something like 'agency' becomes possible. For if the term permits of a resignification, if its referent is not fixed, then possibilities for new configurations of the term become possible" (Benhabib et al. 1995, 50). Here, there is a liberation of the "category of women" from existing women as a definable or fixed category of entities. This liberation enables an expansion of possibilities, of the possibilities of "new configurations of the term."

Again, we might be tempted to read this passage in a limited sense; it is only a fixed referent that the "term" is emancipated from, that is, it may still have an extradiscursive referent, but one that changes or is in flux in some way. So far, Butler has only said that real existing women are not easy to pin down, may change, or the category may come to include those not previously included, or to exclude some who were previously included. At this level, Butler's argument is for a recognition of gender flexibility. But Butler takes us beyond this limited "emancipation of the term" as well: the problem with feminists' speaking of women has been that:

> in effect the signified has been conflated with the referent, whereby a set of meanings have been taken to inhere in the real nature of women themselves. To *recast the referent as the signified*, and to authorize or safeguard the category of women as a site of possible resignifications is to expand the possibilities of what it means *to be* a woman and in this sense to condition and enable an enhanced sense of agency (Benhabib et al. 1995, 50; emphasis added).[7]

---

7. In one passage later in the debate that makes up *Feminist Contentions*, Butler concedes that the purpose she imagines for feminism "to expose and ameliorate those cruelties by which subjects are produced and differentiated" (Benhabib et al. 1995, 141) is not the only goal appropriate to feminism.

This passage contains a complex and equivocal account of the relation between being and speech that is difficult, if not impossible, to unravel, but a close look will point to the difficulties of the move Butler is attempting to make here.

First she suggests that we "recast the referent as the signified," that is, that "women" the term be taken to mean what the speaker means by "women" the term rather than as designating any existing women. Here Butler is severing extra-discursive being and speech-being by recasting the referent as an instance of speech, exactly as Lyotard did in regard to Albert. (What else could it be?) Second, she attributes to this emancipated term, now freed from its extradiscursive moorings and contained within discourse, the power to multiply the possibilities *of being* for women. But where are these possibilities? In speech? Outside of speech? She gives no account of how a term might have the power to open possibilities in extradiscursive being once speech and extradiscursive being are severed. How does one suddenly move from a signified into anything other than speech-being when this is precisely the link that has been broken when you have transformed the referent into the signified? Without some relation to what exceeds discourse, how does a mere term leap into extradiscursive being? If an emancipated term can have such an impact on being beyond discourse, certainly it must have retained some important relation to this being in the course of its emancipation?

Of course, one important aspect of what it means for "women," the term, to be freed from it referents is that it is cast into a kind of temporality that only terms, not referents, have. Extradiscursive referents exist in a now that is bound by natural time, bound in a past and a future. Terms (following Lyotard) exist in a bare instant, in the now freed from the trappings of a before and an after. In fact, Butler's "enhanced sense of agency" in discourse requires just the sort of temporality that underlies Lyotard's sublime experience, because it is the possible dis-loyalty of the term now to past instances of the term that opens up the possibility of resignification. Only terms can be liberated from succession and trapped within the instant of a single utterance. Only terms are instances (of speech) in an instant (of time).

Here I have stated things too simply and must step back to acknowledge that there is ambivalence in Butler's work on the question of temporality. On the one hand, Butler is at pains to show that the "ruse" by which subject's appear to author, as if from nowhere, their own actions or intentions, is a temporal one. This ruse is based precisely on the apparent lack of a relation between this moment and a past and future. Much of the debate about the subject, Butler points out, hinges on whether the subject is seen as posterior to power (as an effect of power) or anterior to power (the subject exists first, then employs power). For Butler, "the subject is

---

"I concede that this is not the only goal, and that there are questions of social and economic justice which are not primarily concerned with questions of subject-formation" (141). Yet, for the most part, the normative tone of her project is very strong. Perhaps the biggest problem with Butler's concession of other political purposes is that it remains unclear, if one were to accept what she says of language and subjects in her early work, how feminism is to have any purposiveness whatsoever, any orientation from which to struggle for justice.

itself a site of this ambivalence in which the subject emerges both as the effect of a prior power and as the condition of possibility for a radically conditioned form of agency" (*PLP* 1997b, 14–15). The subject is, on this reading, a site of temporality, in which the time of the subject doubles back on itself but in this doubling back recuperates a before (power prior to the subject) and an after (power as an effect of the subject) in the now. There is no subject-in-the-instant here.

On the other hand, in Butler's account of how the subject exercises its agency, it is precisely through a certain risk, a rift, an unpredictable break in the relation of the before and after in terms. Agency, for Butler is evidenced in the way that terms are resignified, that is, in the iterability of terms. Because there is no guarantee that each new speaking of "woman," for example, will reinscribe past significations, because a new speaking of woman inhabits a new space and time, a new context; agency is possible. Agency consists precisely in the misappropriation of terms, where terms assume "a purpose unintended by power," that is, refashion themselves in the now in a way that is not determinatively bound to a before and not predictive of an after. Here we see that the "chain of signification" itself operates based on a certain "ruse of authority," the ruse of authority that sees a determinate connection between before, now, and after. Indeterminacy means, for Butler, giving the lie to this ruse. Indeterminacy is the unlinking of before and after, the surrender to now. Temporal indeterminacy constitutes the freedom (agency) of the subject in the "chain of signification."

Of course, for many of us, the temporal unlinking Butler advocates is both convincing and confusing. Certainly the resignification of terms, including "woman," has always been a crucial activity for feminism. When Beauvoir wrote that "One is not born, but rather becomes, a woman" (Beauvoir 1952, 301), who could doubt that the power of that one historic sentence was in its resignification of "woman"? Yet there are two aspects of Beauvoir's resignification that seem to be lost in Butler's version. First, the power in Beauvoir's resignification is itself locked in a tension between the before and the after of the term, and second, that tension is not only in the before and after of the term but also the before and after of the lived lives of women in relation to the term. The tension is powerful because the "term" woman breaks with its temporal determinacy in Beauvoir's sentence, disrupts the determinant link between the before, the what-we-have-assumed-women-to-be, and the after, the what-women-might-turn-out-to-be. It does so, however, in the context of a certain purposiveness that grounds the shift in an uncovering of a (more than discursive) ontological possibility for women and immediately reknits the connection between the before and after in a new pattern. The term *does not shed its historicity, nor its connection to the living women it exists in relation to,* but reconstitutes the possibilities of both, and reconstitutes them precisely as an expression of what Benhabib termed, "the emancipatory aspirations of women."

Butler's temporal breech, on the other hand, is a sustained breech, a breech that wants to linger in the moment of rifting and disruption, a breech that refuses the consolation of a reconstitution of the temporal stream. It also refuses the "overly consoling" idea of "the emancipatory aspirations of women," which connects the phrase to some living women, somewhere. Butler's new "ungrounded ground" has, to be sure, its own purposiveness. "That such foundations exist *only to be put into question* is, as it were, the permanent risk of the process of democratization" (Benhabib et al. 1995, 51, emphasis added). Butler's rifting rifts only to reproduce the possibility of more rifting.

But it is hard to imagine that this purposiveness, this orientation toward eschewing purpose, will provide a direction for feminism that helps articulate "the emancipatory aspirations of women." Indeed Butler admits that it may not. "That the category is unconstrained, even that it comes to serve antifeminist purposes, will be part of the risk of this procedure" (Benhabib et al. 1995, 51). Certainly Butler's claim is that the same risk is run by feminism that doesn't eschew foundations. But Butler's ungrounded feminism leaves us with no means whatsoever of distinguishing a feminist from an antifeminist purpose; indeed, how could there be an antifeminist purpose if the mere multiplying of the possibilities of resignification is the new orientation of feminism? Every resignification will affirm this new purpose, willy-nilly, without regard to its specificity.

Freeing a term from its referent, or recasting the referent as the signified, produces a kind of aesthetic terror and delight. The experience of this recasting is the experience of the postmodern sublime, which involves both a dissolution of any place except a discursive one and a surrender to the temporality of the instant. In discourse, the internality of modernism is turned inside out, becoming the context rather than the content of consciousness. When the referent is recast as the signified, it is cast into discourse, and the ties of the before and after are dissolved in the temporality of the instant. The freed terms "rift" over the abyss, linger there, and the very experience of this lingering is what feminism is for.

For Lyotard, as for Butler, the "benefit" of this recasting is that in the liberation of the term from its referent, and its escape from the ties of the before and after, the possibility of a flowering multiplicity of meanings is produced. As Christine Pries has noted the "critical moment" of the sublime is in its multiplicity. "The feeling of the sublime is plural, and that is in itself plural. This means, it isn't only plural because it has taken on the most varied forms at various times, that are all present in 'our' concept of the sublime, but rather it is also plural in itself, split, and irreducible.... Plurality and critique cohere closely. The sublime is therefore a deeply critical feeling" (Pries 1989, 25, my translation). Multiple significations, especially unruly ones, become the benefit, the point, the stakes of feminism, which now exists merely to produce and reproduce this sublime experience of the liberation of the term.

What is authorized, then, by the laying down of these new foundations? First, the relativism that Butler denies is evidenced as the very stakes of her theoretical work, as the very thing that is authorized in the laying down of the foundations of this new position. Butler gives us no explanation for why plurality in itself should be a goal appropriate to feminism, but her work authorizes this goal as if it were beyond the need for legitimation. Second, this signals a fundamental shift in the feminist project. Without the emancipatory aspirations of women, without the freedom of women rather than terms at stake, embracing multiplicity might just as well mean embracing multiple forms of subordination as it does multiple forms of liberation. Indeed, the two amount to the same thing since, once the terms are liberated, the multiple contents they are given bear witness to their indeterminacy, bear witness to "freedom"—whatever those contents might be. The foundations of postmodernism authorize this shift in the feminist project. Third, the laying down of the foundations of feminist postmodernism authorizes these changes as changes *within* feminism. In other eras we would have seen any move to disconnect feminism from "the emancipatory aspirations of women" as antifeminist; now this disconnection happens from a site that has been carved out as internal to feminism. We are to set the terms free, set them free without regard to whether or not there are any women, anywhere, who are or still want to be freed as well.

"Getting Back into Place"

When Butler writes that the point of freeing the terms from their referents is "to expand the possibilities of what it means *to be* a woman" (Benhabib et al. 1995, 50), this is perhaps a sign of the pressure exerted within her work by the loss of a home in a world that exceeds speech.[8] Of course Butler's freed terms can never expand possibilities for living, breathing women, if the severing of the relation between "women," the term, and women, is the very condition of the possibility for their emancipation. Once you've left the women of the feminist struggle behind, how do you, willy-nilly, get them back?

The answer, one suspects, is that there has been no real leaving behind. There is an excess, a resistance, that can't be siphoned off from speech, at the very heart of speech, that refuses to break with speech. Foreclosed, it becomes a melancholic presence haunting discourse from the inside—gesturing continuously toward an outside. Perhaps the postmodernist mistake has been to allow a central insight about the referentiality of language, the insight that language does not reliably mirror the things to which it refers but also constitutes them in some way, to exceed itself. If we accept that there is no referentiality in this mimetic sense, must we accept that there is no place outside of speech whatsoever? Must this excess and resistance be reduced to mere absence, to an abyss over which language and the discursive subjects upon which it bestows existence agitate?

Not only must we not accept this radical cutting off of being and speech; we don't, in fact, accept it at all. We live a connection between place and speech in our most mundane daily practices. Our speech, whether written or verbal, is inextricably tied to breath, to warmth, to light, and to nourishment. If speech does not mirror extradiscursive being, it may well be because the Other is there on the inside/outside of speech, which is the very condition for the possibility of speech. Even if we were to accept that our nature is discursive, this postmodern nature would itself point to a beyond discourse, to a place in which to be. The very discursive nature that emerges on the inside of Butler's feminist postmodernism pushes toward a more-than-discourse, resists the reduction to mere discourse, exceeds itself and opens out toward something radically irreducible to us. Butler's

---

8. The title of this section is the title of Ed Casey's 1993 book in which he attempts to break open a phenomenology of place.

discursive nature heralds, in fact, the return of a repressed primary dependence. This nature is, perhaps, nothing more than that primary dependence on the planet, on what is outside consciousness and prior to consciousness, projected onto a discursive screen.

In this chapter, I have tried to show how the centrality of the sublime in feminist postmodernism displaces the feminist project. Particularly, it displaces an orientation toward "the emancipatory aspirations of women" with an orientation toward the emancipation of terms. In feminist postmodernism only words are freed, but women never are. These moves depend on a "ruse of authority" that sets postmodernism up as a mode of interrogation vis-à-vis feminism while removing it from the field of positions to be interrogated. They depend on a foreclosure of "essentialism," which serves as the mark of a repressed relation to the natural world. This repression returns on the inside of feminist postmodernism as a kind of discursive essence and a kind of trouble over the relation between speech and an "outside" to speech. Such trouble exerts pressure on the text. And this pressure necessitates a return to what has been foreclosed.

The paradoxes of time and space are hard at work in feminism, as elsewhere. Where is the feminist subject? She is dispersed in discourse, without a place to stand in either the natural or the political world. The words she most needs— "women," "emancipation," "liberation"—are trapped within the instant, having lost a home in time. She herself is unbound from a before and after, and unable to rebuild a place in time. She lives in the constituting consciousness of the modern subject, now turned inside out, become context. This is the postmodern shelter, offered to refugees of the hurricane that has ravaged the subject's ties to nature, her ties to a place not trapped in language. Inside, secure from the winds, she experiences a heady kind of freedom. But the hurricane shakes the house, debris keeps falling to the floor. She rushes around, nailing things back into place but can't quite keep up with the destruction. What's worse, someone has locked the doors from the outside.

5

Interlude: Postmodern Goods

Sublime Experience in Feminist
Celebrations of Pornography

Now reference and reality disappear altogether, and even
meaning...is problematized. We are left with that pure and
random play of signifiers we call postmodernism.

—Fredric Jameson

The world of pornography is mythological and hyperbolic,
peopled by characters. It doesn't and never will exist.

—Laura Kipnis

We have seen that however much hard core (pornography)
may claim to be a material and visible thing, it is still
fundamentally a discourse, a way of speaking about sex.

—Linda Williams

Though tensions over racism, class, and sexuality are often cited in connection
with the feminist postmodern turn in the United States, the conflict over pornography was at least as central in setting the stage for feminist interest in discourse theory. The claim that pornography is fantasy or fiction, that pornography
is speech, and that to associate it with violence or oppression amounts to a naive
equation of fantasy and reality, lends itself to the development of discursive theories of pornography. It puts pornography on the side of discourse. As the argument goes, because pornography is materialized in images and words, it is
"representation" rather than "reality." The developments in postmodern theory
that throw the referentiality of speech into question seem particularly pertinent to
dismantling political positions that protest pornography's harm based on an implicitly referential theory of the relation between representations and realities.[1] If

---

1. I do not attempt, here, to criticize the view that sees antipornography theories as necessarily in
league with naive theories of reference—though such criticism is certainly warranted. In fact, prominent

we were to search high and low for a concrete case to illustrate the political impact of the linguistic turn on U.S. American feminism, we would find no better example than the "pornography debates."

The "anti-anti-pornography" position in feminism was at first based on free-speech arguments and did not necessarily claim that pornography was harmless (only that censorship was more harmful). It certainly did not insist that pornography was beneficial to women. This quickly changed, however, as postmodern perspectives provided some feminist thinkers who were adamantly opposed to anti-pornography theory and practice with a way of framing and articulating their criticisms. While there is currently little to no visible anti-pornography activism from feminists in the United States, what we might call "pro-pornography feminism" has developed out of the "anti-anti-pornography" position. Now a handful of feminist university professors are engaged in the study of pornography, not as a genre of literature in which the master narratives of male supremacy or the domination of women are to be deconstructed but as a rich source for narratives of *the liberation of desire* from a repressive antisex orthodoxy; that is to say, as a rich and positive resource for feminism.

These feminists believe they have found in pornographic texts a site of social protest that speaks to their concerns. Particularly, they see pornography as a genre of literature (film, etc.) in which sexual/moral *normativity* is defeated. Pornography's contribution is in "dismantling the very idea of the norm," in the words of Linda Williams, who is one of the founders of what she calls "pornography studies" (Williams 1989, 117–18). "Normativity" is a term that is often deployed as if its negativity is self-explanatory. Its force turns on a host of implicit associations that add to its efficacy as a code word for all that is wrong with the feminist anti-pornography movement. "Normativity," in these accounts, is both the name for dominant social models of sexuality and for feminist models that rely on some notion of what sexuality *should* be. These critics accuse anti-pornography feminists of holding onto a romanticized notion of a natural female sexuality that is gentle, equality based, and less genitally focused than male sexuality. "Normativity" carries with it, then, not just the connotation of an ethical imperative, or of a normalizing practice, but the full force of "bad essentialism." Pro-pornography accounts insist unequivocally on the social construction of sexuality, as do most anti-pornography accounts, but whereas anti-pornography feminists see pornography as implicated in the construction of sexuality as a site of women's oppression, pro-pornography feminists believe that the very notion of oppression, in this context, contains a hidden appeal to an essential female sexuality.

Little wonder, then, that pro-pornography feminists have taken up the banner of the simulacrum over and against what they believe to be the unwarranted consolation of an essential, natural, or real female sexuality that is damaged by the

---

antipornography theorists have a complex and sophisticated approach to the question of the relation between words and reality that tends to be deeply constructionist. The rhetoric of the antiporn movement sometimes obscures this complexity, but it is clearly to be found in the written work of Catharine MacKinnon, Gail Dines, and other antipornography activists.

culture of pornography. There is, they argue, no real sexuality prior to its construction. Pornography teaches this lesson, in fact. "Normativity" is dismantled in pornography, which means that our outmoded faith in a pre-social real is too, since that is what sexual norms appeal to as a way of gaining ethical force.

But it is not only the fantasy of a pre-social or natural real that is dismantled in the linguistic turn as it concerns the pornography debates. It is the social/political/material real as well. Or to state the problem more precisely, it is any real that exceeds the discursive, whether in the realm of nature or in the realm of politics. It is the world outside of pornography that disappears as feminists turn to immanent textual analysis on the genre's own terms. It is as if such writers are trapped within one of Lyotard's language games, recognizing and affirming the immanent regimen of the game but with no place to stand outside of pornography from which to critically evaluate it.

The theorists of "pornography studies" are not, as they imagine themselves to be, free of normativity, they are caught up in the normativity of pornography itself, interpreted through a postmodern lens. They are caught up, that is to say, in the sublime experience of the dissolution of what exceeds or resists the text, and this dissolution itself becomes a regimen, that is, a new source of normativity. This is, indeed, the political harm that the linguistic turn has brought to feminism. Recognizing that harm requires standing some place that is not internal to the pornographic text. It demands an affirmation of *somewhere else*.

TV World

One spring my seven-year-old daughter's second-grade class was returning from a field trip on foot through a busy section of urban San Francisco. The twenty children with their teachers and chaperones rounded a corner and encountered two San Francisco police officers, guns held to the heads of two men who were face down on the sidewalk. The police had removed the men's pants (I suppose to search for guns or drugs). The class proceeded past this event to the crosswalk and returned to school. The teachers, anxious about the effect witnessing the event might have on the children, entered responsibly into a "debriefing" conversation with them. Perhaps predictably, the primary response from the children was exhilaration; when asked what they thought of what they'd seen the most common response was, "Cool! Just like on TV!" Not only that, the few students who responded "as if" the event were real, were teased for being upset. I was left wondering later what it meant that the children saw the event as akin to another TV experience. Why were those who "read" the event as real, rather than fiction, ridiculed?

As a feminist long-involved in the feminist pornography debate, on the now unpopular anti-pornography side, my daughter's experience with her classmates evoked for me the jarring encounters I have had with pro-pornography feminism. My sense had long been that the conflict was fundamentally about the status of "the real," about a change in, or a contradiction in, our relation to "the real." I have come to believe that rather than arguing about whether or not pornography is real (meaning in this context whether it is an industry with a process of production and consumption implicated in gendered social and political hierarchies that are harmful to women) or a text (a "mere" fantasy whose meaning is always indeterminate but emerges nonetheless in a "readable" fashion in the play of signs and must be deciphered through immanent critique), the task is to trace how it becomes unreal.[2]

The fictional "texts" of television were a way for the children to "read" an event on the streets of San Francisco as only more fiction. It became a TV text in which, and this was the exhilarating part, they were *involved*. It seemed to me that the children's experience had somehow robbed them of that place outside TV, a place from which they might have been able to distinguish (immediately, affectively) between this event and a TV spectacle.[3] The texts of TV had produced, in true postmodern form, a sort of seamless self-referentiality.

The children also described what they saw as "Just like TV!" I suspect, because its *intensity* was familiar to them. They had experienced the same physical sensations time and time again in front of the television screen. This intensity is produced in the tension between horror and exhilaration that one experiences when the border between the real and fiction is momentarily dissolved, as it must necessarily be when bodily sensations (especially dramatic ones) accompany the television experience. Such feelings of intensity mark the experience as sublime, as an agitation between terror and exhilaration that has come to function as "the good" for much of postmodern theory.

This is the experience that is celebrated in feminist defenses of pornography that are informed by postmodern theory as well. The sublime intensities pornography has to offer, especially to women, are "the good" and the "ought" that function as the anti-ethics of pro-pornography feminism. These "postmodern goods" render a feminist politics in relation to pornography unintelligible.

Here, I trace how sublime intensity displaces the U.S. American feminist political project, by seeming to evacuate the very space of the political, in two pro-pornography feminist books. Yet these texts have their normativity, and their politics. Linda Williams and Laura Kipnis have both become well-known for their passionate defenses of pornography. Both authors clear the ground of the extradiscursively real by relocating the discussion of pornography in a fantastically self-referential place (the "text" for Williams, or an untranslatable "private language" for Kipnis). They relocate the discussion of pornography within the pornographic text. For both authors, I argue, a kind of sublime intensity marks the experience of this relocation, which occurs when the simulacrum transgresses and colonizes the real. Any normativity founded on some footing outside the pornographic text is destabilized in the process. This

2. To reiterate what is perhaps by now obvious, there is a dual sense of "the real" that is undermined in postmodern accounts: the real as social and political structures that are at least in part extradiscursive (i.e., material) and the real as an extradiscursive ontology. This chapter is primarily concerned with the first sense of the real.

3. A tendency toward such a "televisionization" of reality is certainly linked to the amount of time most children spend watching TV, which in the accounts I've read ranges from 5 to 7 hours *each day*. This is 35 to 49 hours each week—equivalent to a full-time job.

destabilization is celebrated as the power and political importance of pornography and becomes the new norm, pornography's own "ought."

In fact, the "intensities" of pornography produce, against the grain of anti-pornography criticisms, their own account of pornography's "real truth." Otherwise stated, these intensities now stand in for "truth" itself, as that toward which feminist thinking strives. My point here is not simply to reassert the relation between pornography's words and images and extradiscursive reality but to point out that doing away with that relation by eliminating one of its terms is hardly the solution to its mystery. As Jameson notes, "To raise the issue . . . of the fate of the 'referent' in contemporary culture and thought is not the same thing as to assert some older theory of reference or to repudiate all the new theoretical problems in advance. On the contrary, such problems are retained and endorsed, with the proviso that they are not only interesting problems in their own right but also, at the same time, symptoms of a historical transformation" (Jameson 1991, 94). So instead of celebrating the sublime intensity pornography produces as some long misunderstood "real truth" of pornography, I see it as a clue to a truth about ourselves and the conditions of contemporary life.

Pornography as Discourse

Linda Williams, by her own account, becomes successful by writing "the first book to deal with the history and textual form of moving-image pornography" (Williams 1989, ix). She credits herself with being a founder of a new field of study "that might be called pornography studies" (ix). In this field, a proper study of pornography will find the meaning of the genre through discourse analysis rather than in an abstract political principle (free speech).[4] It will find the meaning of the genre inside the text.

Entering the Text

Williams formulates her purpose in *Hard Core: Power, Pleasure, and the "Frenzy of the Visible*," as finding out "what pornography is." "The feminist rhetoric of abhorrence," writes Williams, "has impeded discussion of almost everything but the question of whether pornography deserves to exist at all. Since it does exist, however, we should be asking what it does for viewers; and since it is a genre with basic similarities to other genres, we need to come to terms with it" (Williams 1989, 4–5). For Williams, the question of "what pornography is," is a textual question and is best answered on pornography's own terms.

---

4. This differentiates new defenses of pornography from old ones as mentioned above. Earlier defenses were almost invariably premised on the abstract principle of free speech and were more hesitant to argue that pornography is in itself good for women. This insight I owe to Maureen Sullivan who formulated it very well in her essay at the 1998 Duke University Women's Studies Program Lecture Series, "Who's Zoomin' Who? Feminism, Pedagogic Porn, and Auto-Essentialism."

To enter into the text, Williams will engage in a preemptive bracketing that sets the meaning of pornography apart from both its context and its content. For Williams, approaching pornography as a genre means bracketing its context, that is, moving it out of the messy material world where questions about the conditions of pornography's production, the social impact of its consumption, and the extraordinary profits it generates impinge. In fact Williams writes, "however much hard core may claim to be a material and visible thing, it is still fundamentally a *discourse, a way of speaking* about sex" (Williams 1989, 229, emphasis added). Focusing on pornography as text will also mean bracketing its literal content. Now it is not the content of pornography's speech but its form that is the bearer of its meaning. This double bracketing is what inaugurates the textual space in which Williams's theory works.

"Text" is a foundational notion here. To begin to understand what it means, we can look closely at a brief passage in Williams's critique of the feminist anti-pornography film *Not a Love Story*. The film, which among other things critically examines the role of the penis in pornography (often portrayed as a weapon, as threatening, etc.), fails for Williams because the penis is conflated with the phallus. "The problem with *Not a Love Story* is that it proceeds as if suppressing the 'dick' could solve all the sexual problems of patriarchal power. By showing us the penis in its attitude of threat over the passive female victim, the film uses explicitness to mock and demystify the symbolic power of the phallus" (Williams 1989, 266). The film, in other words, draws a connection between the *content* of pornography and its *context*. Put simply, it attempts through a critical "reading" of penises in pornography to understand a relationship between the penis functioning as a sign (phallus) and the context of gendered social power (or in clearer terms, male supremacy).

The film presumes that it is not a mere accident that very real penises on real men[5] stand in for "the phallus" in a pornographic scene and that this non-accident has to do in some complex way with men's social power over women. This critical mocking examination is meant to demystify the penis and turn it back into a usually limp bit of flesh, at the same time leaving in stark relief how the penis functions as a sign (phallus) of something socially real (gendered power). Williams's response is to be insulted on the penis's behalf, reminding us that the penises in pornography are "quite spectacular." She seems to think that it is the explicitness and visibility of pornographic representations of the penis as an organ that are objectionable to feminists rather than the social power attached to penises as signs.[6]

---

5. These men are the actors, paid for the parts their penises play in the various scenes, or the amateur makers of pornography themselves, who employ their girlfriends or other women they are close to in scenes that prominently feature their own organs as well.

6. Williams seems also to worry that penises are actually quite necessary for sex. "While the physiology of sex is not likely to change, its gendered meanings can" (Williams 1989, 267), she argues, though the "physiology" of sex certainly does change with different sexual practices, many of which don't involve penises, spectacular or not, at all. This is a strange argument coming from Williams, who elsewhere rejects all notions of "natural" sexuality.

This feminist critique of explicit pornography fails... precisely in its attack on the literal organ of the penis. Satisfied simply to deride the organ of presumed male power itself rather than the system of oppositions by which the symbolic meaning of the penis is constructed, the critique does not even approach *the discursive root of the problem* of pornography and sexual representations for feminism.... In attacking the penis we seem to attack the phallic authority that it symbolizes as well. But the tempting conflation of meaning between the two accedes to the impossibility of change. (Williams 1989, 266, emphasis added)

Yet the feminist "attack" on the penis in *Not a Love Story*, which is really a critical reading of the social power that this organ seems to carry around with it in pornography and life, is precisely an attack on the phallic authority it symbolizes. There is no assumption that the actual organ created the problem, no assumption of a "natural" connection between the organ and the context of social power, no call to massive political protests involving penectomy in this critical feminist film. The penis is not attacked apart from how it functions as a symbol of social power but precisely *because* it functions as such.[7] Implicit throughout is the sense that the bond between social power and men's penises is not a necessary one.

Yet Williams reads this as a conflation of the organ with the sign. What Williams accepts here are two important theoretical positions associated with postmodern theories of language: (1) that there is an ontological distinction between signs and their referents and (2) that this distinction essentially seals signs into a sign-world, that is, inaugurates a purely discursive space in which signs work. For Williams, a text is precisely this kind of sealed discursivity. Yet there is no reason to accept that an ontological distinction between signs and their referents (i.e., that the being of a sign is a distinct form of being from the being of a referent) seals signs off from referents entirely, and there is no argument in Williams's account as to why we should accept this conclusion.

Judith Butler addresses just this presupposition in her critical work on Lacan (*BTM* 1993, 77–91). She takes issue precisely with the idea that the penis and phallus are so radically distinct and notes that this claim is based on the ontological distinction between the thing and its symbol we've just mentioned—that is, the being of a thing and the being of its symbol are assumed to be radically different kinds of being. "The phallus symbolizes the penis; and insofar as it symbolizes the penis, retains the penis as that which it symbolizes; it is not the penis.... The more symbolization occurs the less ontological connection there is between symbol and symbolized.... Symbolization depletes that which is symbolized of its ontological connection with the symbol itself" (83–84). Butler's critical move is to ask, "What is the status of this particular assertion of ontological difference if it turns out that this symbol, the phallus, always takes the penis as that which it symbolizes" (84)? The connection that binds the phallus to the penis is one of "determinate negation," such that "the phallus would be nothing without the penis" (84). For Butler,

---

7. The more subtle feminist point that the "phallus," or male social power, constructs the organ, i.e., determines something important about how the actual organ is lived and experienced by both men and women, seems to be lost on Williams entirely.

the attempt to radically differentiate the phallus and the penis fails. "It is not enough to claim that the signifier is not the same as the signified (phallus/penis), if both terms are nevertheless bound to each other by an essential relation in which that difference is contained" (90). There may well be an ontological difference between a penis and a phallus, but "difference" cannot be presumed to mean an insurmountable gulf that puts the two effectively out of any sort of relation to one another (and this whether the phallus is a mere signifier or indeed the "supreme signifier" as Lacan so enthusiastically claimed).

To take Butler's reading a step further, the "essential relation" that binds the penis and the phallus, and which contains their "difference," is a relationship to actual gendered social power. In this context, gendered social power is symbolized by both the phallus and the penis and configured in specific ways so that the complexity of the relationship between the organ, the organ as a symbol, and the symbol of the phallus can't be disentangled. If a pornographic image includes a man "brandishing" his penis, is the penis an organ or a symbol? Doesn't this brandishing function precisely at that moment to evoke the relationship between the organ and the symbol, that is, to reinscribe the penis as the phallus, as a mark of male social power over women?

This is, I suspect, what is so disturbing to Williams—that this "phallic authority" is presumed in *Not a Love Story* to be "real" in the sense that it is implicated in a more than discursive context of gendered power relations rather than *discursive* in the sense of something sealed within a "system of oppositions" among signs. What I mean by this is that real penises employed as signs are assumed to refer to social and political authority, that is, the content of pornographic images is thought to be in relation to the social context in what for Williams is always dismissed as a "naive" sense. "For these naive realists, to see a woman phallically penetrated, bound, gagged, tortured, or (as presumably in *Snuff*) murdered for male sexual pleasure is tantamount to watching a real woman present in the viewer's own space-time continuum being victimized by these outrages" (Williams 1989, 201). One might be legitimately horrified by such things, of course, whether or not the very real woman in the picture is "in the viewer's own space-time continuum." Williams's various attempts to explain why these women aren't real (there is a contract, she's faking the pain, or perhaps she's into it) are brief and halfhearted. She states for example, "the violence of masochism is contractual. In all three types of sadomasochistic pornography described above— amateur, sadie-max, and aesthetic—violence invariably arises out of an agreement between dominator and dominated" (212). How Williams can possibly purport to know whether or not persons in these scenes, shot in living rooms, studios, and many other settings all across the world, have all made voluntary agreements to be bound, gagged, tortured, and so on, is never explained. Here she herself naively assumes that the *pictures*, which purport to represent sado-masochism, unproblematically reflect the *activity* of sadomasochism, which is by most definitions necessarily contractual. "We would do well to remember, therefore, that the phallus is fundamentally not real and not possessed by anyone" (Williams 1989, 166), she writes. The phallus is a sign, is form; the penis is merely an organ. If the sign of the phallus seems to refer to some real social content, this is a mere distraction for naive readers, it is primarily a sign referring to other signs. The root of the problem is "discursive," not social. On Williams's reading, feminists have mistaken a problem of textuality for a problem of the social world. This is the world that must be bracketed if we are to understand pornography on its own terms.

Williams's effort will be to map out developments within the genre, to tell the story of the liberation of female desire through pornography, drawing on the sign systems of psychoanalysis. But how is she to do this when quite apart from the social realities of masculinist domination, the images and words, the contents of the pornographic texts are themselves quite misogynist? To affirm the value of pornography for feminism, she will have to take the additional step of denying that what pornography seems to mean is what it actually means. After bracketing the context of pornography, she brackets the misogynist *content* of pornographic images. The apparent social power depicted there, where men consistently dominate women, does not mean what it seems to mean; it always means something else. "The apparent hard-core literal meaning of these images always means something other or more than what they seem to say," she announces. Here Williams's work can be characterized as Jameson characterized Saussurean structuralism: "meaning . . . is generated by the movement from signifier to signifier. What we generally call the signified—the meaning or conceptual content of an utterance—is now rather to be seen as a meaning-effect, as that objective mirage of signification generated and projected by the relationship of signifiers among themselves" (Jameson 1991, 26). What pornography *seems* to say about women and men is, for Williams, an objective mirage that feminists have been susceptible to. The deeper discursive meaning is liberatory. This principle is announced as a kind of starting point. Rather than concluding after sustained reflection and argument that what she admits to be the misogynist "literal content" is not relevant to "meaning," Williams simply brackets pornography's literal content from the beginning.

In both moves, the move that brackets context and the move that brackets content, the problem of the relationship of representations of gendered power to actual gendered power is simply sidestepped. This kind of preemptive bracketing closes the text off from extradiscursive reality in the political sense. This is what Jameson has called reification in its most advanced, now postmodern, form. Jameson argues that the logic of reification has invaded language, discourse, and culture and become "a force whose logic is one of ruthless separation and disjunction," splitting content off from form. Form is elevated and content is debased. For Jameson, this sort of reification is both figure and effect of the other sort of reification, which we saw in Williams's bracketing of social realities: "the 'effacement of traces of production' from the commodity thereby produced" (Jameson 1991, 314), that is, the effacement of the context of the material world and the inequalities that are evident there. Of course this is very close to the feminist criticism of the philosophical tradition in aesthetics in which the notion of a rarified realm for art removed from gendered relations of power is also rejected.

I am suggesting along with Jameson and those feminist critics that the elevation of form (here, phallus as sign in a system of signs) and debasement of content (gendered social power) in texts, and the ignorance we live in about how the material realities of our daily lives are produced, are signs of our times. Though

I am not imputing some kind of conscious motivation to Williams, I am arguing that the impact of her analysis is precisely to affirm the deep disjuncture we experience between the social structures that build our worlds and our daily experience of living in them. Indeed, for Williams, the women and men used in pornography, the conditions of their employment, the international multibillion-dollar industry and the profits it generates are not part of pornography's truth. And neither is pornography's content, which so explicitly affirms gendered social power.

The New Meaning of Pornography

Yet in the absence of content, having debased content and liberated form from it, is there a new meaning that replaces this "naive" meaning? Williams has an answer for this: "As discourses of sexuality name, identify, and ultimately produce a bewildering array of pleasures and perversions, the very multiplicity of these pleasures and perversions inevitably works against the older idea of a single norm—an economy of one—against which all else is measured" (Williams 1989, 115). If feminists look for the "seeds of a different sexual economy," within the reigning sexual economy, instead of protesting it, "we will be on a path that leads to the representation of sexual pleasures becoming grounded in an economy of abundance rather than scarcity, of many rather than one" (117). Indeed, because the literal content of pornography has been repressed along with its troublesome ethical questions, here we see the emergence of a new content in Williams's work. Form itself, by way of multiplicitous signs referring to each other, a kind of cacophonous and directionless speech, has returned as a new content.

This new content, *pure multiplicity*, is what has political power for Williams. Just as for the early Butler, the feminist project becomes a quest "to release the term[s] into a future of multiple significations" without regard for the content of those significations. The value of pornography is in its multiplying of discursive/ sexual possibilities without regard to the content of those possibilities. For both authors *a plurality without orientation* is the product of good postmodernist thinking.

The plurality of sexual discourse in pornography leads, it seems, to a mixing and matching, a blurring of the lines, of various sexual identities. Williams enthuses:

> Contemporary video pornographies have something for every conceivable sexual predilection. Yet it would be a mistake to assume that these pornographies arise simply to cater to already-constituted strictly compartmentalized, sexual orientations. More significantly, with the proliferation of categories, there is also an accompanying fluidity of appeal, a cross-fertilizing of eroticized polymorphous perversions. To me the most striking feature of these recent video pornographies is the extent to which unitary categories of identity begin to cross and blur. (Williams 1989, 304)

This crossing and blurring is just the kind of destabilizing "intensity" through which the normativity that characterizes a particular sexual predilection can be destabilized. Multiply identifying with all kinds of people having all kinds of sex is *in itself* good for us, *in itself* liberatory, because it destabilizes the sexual norms we live by and in and through which we build a sexual identity. Here "liberatory" is simply a function of quantity, without regard to the "misogynistic regimes of sexual relationships" (30) Williams herself admits predominate in contemporary hard core. If this multiplicity has a coherent message, it is "the importance of transgression and excess" (10), which we learn with the "cross-fertilizing of eroticized polymorphous perversions" (304).

The political stakes of this freedom do not remain unannounced by Williams. If we "discipline ourselves" to like what's in all kinds of pornography, to identify with the rapist and the victim, the sadist and the masochist, the pain and the pleasure, we will be able to "join the sexual marketplace as consumers" ourselves. This "democratization" of the marketplace brings with it a new kind of citizenship—"the new diversity of sexualities and the spread of perversions, of 'diff'rent strokes for diff'rent folks,' bring with them greater sexual citizenship for women, the potential for breaking down hierarchical oppositions, and a general movement toward a degendered libido" (Williams 1989, 274). The values of a globalized economy are here celebrated: the reduction of citizenship to consumption, the preparation of the consumer to desire the product. According to Williams, what is politically important about the "polymorphous perversions" of pornography for feminism is that they teach women, too, to want and buy pornography.

Need we ask what kind of world these new sexual citizens, degendered libidos straining toward transgression and excess, inhabit? This will be a consumerist paradise of sublime intensities, where the traditional pornographic normativity—"Consume!" "Transgress!"—holds sway. Here we exist in the economy of, in the *textuality* of, pornography itself, which gradually invades and disciplines a new real, a bodily real.

Sublime Intensity

The political power and cultural importance of pornography consist for Williams in this: when "representation of sexual pleasures" becomes "grounded in an economy of abundance," the "dismantling of the very idea of the norm" (Williams 1989, 117–18) ensues. On my reading of Williams, this occurs through a kind of sublime experience of intensity felt when the flesh-and-blood body itself is taken up into the pornographic text.

Williams explicitly links the experience of viewing pornographic videos "remote control device in hand" with Baudrillard's notion of the "'ecstasy of communication' in which simulacra replace the real" (with the caveat that, unlike for Baudrillard, here the body is not superfluous) (Williams 1989, 304). In interactive hard core available on the Internet, Williams finds a similar blurring between "virtual" and "real" bodies. Here "a sustained simultaneous dividedness of attention and blurring of the distinction between the virtual bodies on screen—one of which is now presumed to be 'my' own—and my own 'carnal density' here where I sit before the screen" (Williams 1989, 312), produces an experience of the dissolution of the difference between life and text. This is not, Williams argues, to be seen as a radical departure from the way other genres of pornography work, but rather virtual pornography teaches us something about how most pornography works. The important function of pornography is, then, to dissolve the distance and the limit between the body and the text, to involve the body in the text, and ultimately to textualize the body.

Indeed, there is an interesting progression in Williams's work. At first it seemed as though she sets out to read the meaning of pornography off the text of the body. The fact that pornography "moves us" is a key starting point, "But proper or not, at this stage in the contemporary proliferation of discourses of sexuality it seems helpful for all of us ... to agree at least that we are moved, whether to anger or to arousal, by these images of hard-core pornography" (Williams 1989, xvii). But later in Williams's book, it is pornography that inscribes itself on the body. Williams ends up seeing the meaning of the body's responses as something pornography constructs: "pornographies are becoming part of the process by which spectators *discipline themselves* to enjoy different varieties of visual and visceral pleasure—pleasures that are both produced in the imagination and felt in the body" (315, emphasis added). When pornography moves us, we learn, it is building its own meaning, and here Williams begins to tread on ground that looks strangely like the radical feminist critique.

In fact, if there is a coherent radical feminist theory of the relation between pornographic representation and social reality, it has to do with how pornographic discourse can socialize real sexual response to misogyny and how this is built out of and reinforces the misogynist content of social life. For decades anti-pornography feminists have been arguing that pornography, like all cultural products, socializes us, and because it works on sexual response, it socializes sexuality in the body— primarily male sexuality (even now men are still the major consumers and producers of pornography, Williams concedes).[8] Because it socializes (or in post-modern terms "disciplines") sexual response to misogynist content, pornography is implicated in the whole complex of gendered social power that is the target of feminist theory and activism. That Williams uses the new term "disciplines" and discards the older and possibly less precise term "socializes," hardly changes the fact that she has willy-nilly reintroduced the theoretical tenets of the anti-pornography position she has disputed from the outset.

Indeed, though she has formerly bracketed the misogynist content of pornography, Williams can't help conceding her disappointment over this content at times. The grand narrative of liberation she has constructed as the story of pornography's development as a genre has not been borne out by the content of recent developments on the Internet.

> As a feminist historian of porn I find it just a little depressing to see the extent to which, for all its exalted "interaction," this pornography consists primarily of men doing things to women and women, for all their verbal aggressiveness, having things done to them. The man "plays" upon the virtual bodies of the women. ... There is a strange poignancy about a pornographic woman who knows she is "just a piece of ass in a software package." (Williams 1989, 311)

---

8. Williams celebrates the fact that women are consuming more and more pornography, however.

It depresses me too. The difference between Williams's reading and a radical feminist reading consists only in this: recognizing that pornography socializes sexuality and the body to pornographic contents, radical feminists connect this socialization to gendered social power. That this connection has been too simplistically causal at times should not belie the need to work out just what kind of connection there is, in all its complexity. But having done away with normativity and raised the banner of "diff'rent strokes for diff'rent folks," having witnessed the evacuation of the space of the extradiscursively real, Williams would be hard-pressed to argue now that there is anything harmful about "a piece of ass in a software package," other than that it depresses her. Locked into a textual universe, where real social power must not come into play, Williams must deny any connection between the sign-world of pornography and the material world where harm takes place.

To do this, Williams makes an argument that is far beneath her in a single paragraph she devotes to debunking the claim that there is a connection between pornography and sexual violence.[9] She claims pornography "does not generate rape . . . for the simple reason that feminists have done such a good job of showing that rape is not pleasurable for the person who is raped. Rather pornography's speculation about pleasure would seem, first and foremost, to generate only more, and different, pornography" (Williams 1989, 276). Because women don't like to be raped, pornography does not generate rape. This would be something like arguing that cars can't cause air pollution because air pollution isn't pleasurable and driving is! Williams cites no testimony, no sociological evidence, no scientific study, not a single statistic to support what can only be called a silly claim that not liking something impacts what causes it.

Freed from the need for such cumbersome things as evidence, set adrift in the sign-world of the text, she must still somehow negotiate the strange connection between the body (for her "the real" is the body) and the sign-world. The body, moved, constructed, and disciplined by pornography, must ultimately be displaced—put out of place—must itself enter the world of the sign where it is safely sealed off from the world in which men often do harm women. Instead, as if Williams actually imagines that signs, not people, are producing pornography and having the sex from which pornography is made, she informs us that "pornography, by formulating sexual pleasure as a problem, with solutions involving the need for further sex and further speculation about that sex, begets pornography" (Williams 1989, 276), not sexual violence.

Williams manages to overcome her depression about the misogynist content of even brand-new pornography and to distance herself again from any connection with a radical feminist critique of this misogynist content by elevating formal elements of the new "interactive" Internet porn to something like its "true

9. She mentions the issue at other points in the book, but this is the only place I found in her book where she actually attempts a refutation of the feminist claim that pornography plays some complicated part in generating rape in some cases.

meaning." Recognizing that the "intensity" this pornography offers is in "an un-canny dispersal" of the self, "a new kind of mobility, a blurring of the boundaries between here and there that in no way escapes the body" (Williams 1989, 312), Williams locates the "good" of even this depressingly misogynist pornography in sublime experience. Here the displacement of the body and consequent displea-sure/pleasure occur again on the border of the real and the text, in a movement that displaces the sexual subject/body into the text. The problem Williams set out to address, the problem of the relationship between body and text, is relocated now *within* the text. The sign has not escaped the body but rather *engulfed* it. (It was the modern subject that had this tendency to engulf things; here discourse, which is what has become of that subject, keeps doing the same thing.) Once taken up into a sign-world, the body loses any footing in the social world, where harm takes place. There is no longer any place to stand outside pornography from which to question the regimens of pornography's phrase regimes. Williams is thus able to disable a feminist critique of pornography as related to harm.

Though Williams decries normativity, this does not stop her from arguing, in the end, that pornography should exist because "pornographies are becoming part of the process by which spectators discipline themselves to enjoy different varieties of visual and visceral pleasure" (Williams 1989, 315). The "ought" here has to do with sex that is to be superabundant, multiplicitous in its methods, and free of any norms. "Diff'rent strokes for diff'rent folks" is to be the motto of the new sexual citizenship (274). It is the break from normativity that produces the intensity proper to pornographic experience and makes looking at all that depressingly misogynist pornography worth it. Yet the normativity of pornography itself returns as the new "ought" for feminism. We ought to seek experiences that destabilize the real, intensities that break us out of the confines of any normativity. That this is itself a grand and sweeping norm seems lost on Williams.

The Politics of the Text

Texts that are intended to be more popular than scholarly, such as Laura Kipnis's passionate defense of pornography, *Bound and Gagged: Pornography and the Politics of Fantasy in America*, trade on the same destabilization of the social reality that more academic texts do. For Kipnis, it seems, the sublime disjoining of words and world overtakes the text itself and critically impacts the very intelligibility of her project.

Kipnis's book is, on her own account, a quest to discover "what violent fantasy means." Reading her work, the more interesting question for me became, What does "meaning" mean? Kipnis constructs an implicit theory of meaning that goes through some extraordinary evolutions across the two hundred pages of her book, which I trace here briefly. What is important about these evolutions is that they reflect a fragmentation in our notion of meaning that seems to be a generalized part of life under postmodern conditions.

Let's look at her first meaning. Initially, Kipnis sets out to solve the puzzle of the relation of fantasy to reality. But instead of inquiring into that relation, Kipnis, like Williams, relocates the problem and dissolves the relation of fantasy to reality instead. She argues that asking what violent fantasy means is equivalent to "asking what person x or y experiences when viewing or constructing a violent fantasy" (9). The meaning of pornography is only to be found in individual lives, she tells us; they will reflect private emotional landscapes. "Given how complex, idiosyncratic, and counterintuitive these meanings prove to be, it strongly suggests that no generalization about what violence means or why viewers are attracted to it is supportable" (13). As for Williams, the conditions under which pornography is produced, the profits it makes, and how it is consumed play no part in this notion of meaning. Meaning is in a mental container and not generalizable. That gets us up to page 13.

Kipnis's second theory of meaning is clearly influenced by postmodern notions of language games, or phrase regimes. Meaning here is constructed in private languages spoken by subcultural groups, such as gay male sadomasochists, and is untranslatable. It is a function of the "customs, values, and language" of the group, of their "rules and etiquette," that is, meaning is something that emerges in relationships between people, but only between people who share a local language (61). The implication is that any attempt to "translate" these meanings to a more dominant language is bound to fail and will end in repression. This is on page 61.[10]

Meaning has already begun to exceed the limits of the mental container. This excess will crescendo throughout *Bound and Gagged* so that sometime later she writes, "pornography is not just an individual predilection: pornography is central to our culture" (161). It is "the royal road to the cultural psyche" (162), provides "a detailed blueprint of the cultures' anxieties, investments, contradictions" (164), and is working-class revolution in progress (162–63). No more private languages here, now the meaning of pornography belongs to all of us. This is all between page 161 and 164.

On page 206 we find out that, ultimately, pornography is civil disobedience.

These multiple and contradictory meanings all coexist for Kipnis in a sort of fragmented way. They reappear at will in the text. When she needs to diffuse questions of harm, pornography is contained in a monadic mental space. When she wants to argue that we all really need and want pornography, it is civil disobedience. Let me say that I think Kipnis's fragmented notion of meaning, where it assumes different shapes at will and without explanation in her text, isn't just bad scholarship and shoddy argumentation, though it is that. It is also a sign of our times. I am suggesting that what marks postmodernity is just the sort of fragmentation and confusion we see here. This is what tends to happen to meaning in life and theory under postmodern conditions, for academics and second graders alike.

But whatever its form and function, and this is Kipnis's central claim, pornography ultimately isn't real. "The world of pornography is mythological and hyperbolic, peopled by characters. It doesn't and never will exist, but it does—and this is part of its politics—insist on a sanctioned space for fantasy" (163). The

---

10. Interestingly, Kipnis's defense of Daniel Thomas DePew, a gay male sadomasochist caught in an FBI sting operation to catch producers and consumers of child pornography on the Internet, is precisely an exercise in translating such a "private" language, even as she argues that such languages are not translatable. This incoherence remains unproblematized.

"sanctioned space" of pornography undergirds the incoherence of Kipnis's multiple theories of meaning, functioning as a kind of bottom line.

The sublime experience that dissolves the category of the real takes on, for Kipnis too, the character of an imperative. The only law pornography obeys is that law that says "Transgress!" Kipnis tells us enthusiastically. She and other defenders of pornography see its value in how it shocks and explodes, they think, normativity. But the imperative "Transgress!" has become a new norm, a new ought. The "sanctioned space" of pornography owes its sanctity to its strict obedience to this imperative.

Pornography, like other texts, becomes a kind of strange site of purification, where everything that enters leaves the messy material universe behind. As Jameson noted, "So it is that political power becomes a 'text' that you can read; daily life becomes a text . . . consumer goods are unveiled as a textual system . . . war becomes a readable text" (Jameson 1991, 186). Everything that seems material is transported to the magical sign world—not necessarily intentionally.

Kipnis's tendency, too, is to transport everything that pornography touches into its "sanctioned space." Here, we find a stark example of the political stakes of such an approach, of the political consequences of losing any footing outside the text. She doesn't argue explicitly in her book that child sexual abuse is also a text, but the way she "reads," or better "writes," incidents of child sexual abuse, they do take on the irreality of pornographic fantasy. Here, the fact that, for Kipnis, pornography is a discourse and a language game, in spite of its heroic performance in the political sphere, seems to return on the very word choice and syntax she uses to discuss incidents of child sexual abuse.

Dean Lambey was one of two men arrested for conspiracy to kidnap, rape, film, and murder a child in the first FBI investigation of child pornography on the Internet. Kipnis argues that both Lambey and his "accomplice" Daniel DePew were entrapped, and there is a good deal of evidence to support her argument. But it seems that the exhilaration of the postmodern sublime, the exhilaration produced when the simulacrum colonizes the social world, works its magic on the very sentences Kipnis writes to tell Lambey's story. The reader is lulled into a sense that Lambey not only was a victim of police entrapment but also inhabits that sanctioned fantasy space of pornography. Everything Lambey does somehow inhabits that world too.

Kipnis informs us that the shy, ineffectual Lambey has a "guilty interest in children." He is "according to his own reports, a somewhat nervous and ineffectual pedophile. He seemed to have mostly confined himself to furtive fondling of sleeping boys he manages to come in contact with, terrified of being caught" (15). Three pages later we learn, "his mostly unsatisfactory sexual experiences with boys seem to have been confined, to date, to fondling and a few episodes of oral sex" (18). Kipnis writes about the children Lambey would like to abuse sexually in what appears to be Lambey's own language, they are "young prospects." She tells us Lambey doesn't really know "how to make the right moves" on his "young prospects." She refers to the topic of Lambey's and the FBI agents' conversations as "the kiddie sex arena" (15). Her language and glib tone are exactly the same when she talks about incidents of child sexual abuse or the "fantasy world" of pornography.

Her language is in fact the same as the language of the pornography so that she creates the sense that not only Lambey's fantasies but also the kids he abuses inhabit the sexy sign-world where everything is dangerous and no one gets hurt.

When she talks about child pornography, the existence of which would clearly undermine the idea that fantasy and reality inhabit entirely separate worlds, we learn that it, like all pornography, doesn't really exist; "contrary to mythic reports about vast underground child porn rings," she tells us, child pornography is "largely unavailable, even if you're zealously searching it out" (14). We learn a few pages later that both Dean Lambey and the FBI agent have some, since they exchange pornographic pictures of children. If someone as shy, bumbling, and ineffectual as Lambey can get a hold of child pornography, we might think anyone could—but a sort of "glossy skin" slides over this incoherence.

Kipnis herself seems to experience a sublime destabilization here. She seems to have lost access to any place outside the pornographic text from which to observe and evaluate its harm. Without such a place, she takes up the fantasy language of pornography to rewrite the reality of child sexual abuse as a discursive, in this case also a pornographic, event.

The "postmodern condition" may well be the condition under which children are trapped within a TV world, unable to find a place to stand outside TV from which to experience an event in their own neighborhood as life rather than text. It may well be the condition under which academics can stake out their territory within the sign-world of pornography and sacrifice any place outside the pornographic text from which to see children who've been sexually abused as anything other than "young prospects" for "ineffectual pedophiles" that "don't know the right moves."

In feminist celebrations of pornography, there is no effort to dismantle the Euro-masculinist projects of mastery, nor to dismantle the master narratives that support the subordination of women to men. The melting away of the social world that occasions entrance into the discursive universe of pornography becomes both its justification and purpose, fulfilling as it does the imperative to be anti-essentialist at all cost. Consumers of pornography can "perform" their inessentialism by adopting the multiple subject positions portrayed. The writers of this feminist postmodernism don't deconstruct pornography's "phrase regimen," they strive instead *to think in terms of it*, to follow its internal logic, to experience its intensities.

But just as Lyotard's "philosophical politics" failed to become a politics at all by eliminating the possibility of political solidarity with victims of historical wrongs, pro-pornography feminism fails to be feminist when it offers women no place to stand outside the pornographic text from which to bear witness to the harm pornography does to women. Caught up in pornography's language game, loyal only to the norms of that game, these feminists sacrifice the externality required for a feminist reading of pornography. This is not to say that an immanent reading of pornography cannot be part of a feminist approach, only that it cannot be the whole of it.

Feminists must insist on the radical *excess* of feminism vis-à-vis the Euro-masculinist projects and narratives of mastery—whether these are pornographic or not. This exteriority is never "pure" or absolute. It is as often a corruptive influence on the inside of the master projects and the master narratives as much as it is a countervoice that haunts them from outside. Perhaps it is too often complicit with them and too often compromised in its relation to them. But it is also, if it is to be feminist, always an excess, a resistance, a kind of trouble that unsettles these projects. It is a disruptive force that always gestures toward something else, toward somewhere else.

But if we are to affirm this resistance, where are we to start? For many feminists the point of departure has been "the body," or "the materiality of the body." As we have seen, Williams's virtual body is a body without place in any meaningful sense of the word. It is without political place because any site in the sign-world it lays claim to can be easily exchanged for another (normativity is its taboo). But the bodies we live still refuse to be confined within any text about the body. We do not succeed in experiencing our bodies as mere products of discourse even if we believe them to be, because our bodies *experience* as well as being the objects of experience.

6

Talking Back to
Feminist Postmodernism

What's Wrong with Discursive Bodies?

> If the body is a metaphor for our locatedness in space
> and time and thus for the finitude of human perception and
> knowledge, then the postmodern body is no body at all.

— Susan Bordo

If the current fascination with the sublime has to do with an uncritical celebration of our contemporary experience of being caught up in a world saturated with language, then what part does the body play in this experience? Given that the body is our "organ" of experience, don't the sublime dis-placements and dis-locations that we have been preoccupied with throughout have to work their magic through the body? If, as so many have acknowledged, the body is what gives us place, then isn't it only in the flesh that we can live the experience of *dis*-placement?[1]

But if one thing is clear in feminist postmodernism as the new millennium begins, it is that bodies themselves are texts. And textual as they are, they are no longer the place where oppression and liberation are lived in the flesh and blood. They are sites of play, sites of performance, sites of catachresis. As "sites"[2] they provide a pseudo-place for an intellectual activity, that is, textual analysis, but they can neither be said to be in place, nor can they be said to give us place in the usual sense of the word. A postmodern body is subject to intensities, inscriptions, and

---

1. I am taking the term "talking back" from a section of Judith Butler's *Bodies That Matter* where she tries to distinguish mere repetition from a kind of repetition or "performance" of gender that is "a kind of talking back" or resistance (1993, 132). She is attempting here to talk about resistance as something that takes place in the "slippage between discursive command and its appropriated effect" (122). I mean my use of the term to imply both an appropriation and a making over of feminist postmodernism.

2. This notion of "site" as opposed to "place" is a technical distinction in the work of Edward S. Casey. It is important throughout both *The Fate of Place* and *Getting Back into Place*.

dissolutions, but it is not to be found somewhere, some concrete where. It is not a body that orients us to a concrete place—only, if at all, to a virtual space, a textual space. Certainly the question, Where is the postmodern body? seems jarring. But isn't this in itself a bit shocking? A body, this body or that one, is after all so much in and of place, so dependent on place.[3]

I am interested in a feminist account of the body that returns it to its flesh and blood, while taking into account the theoretical developments that turned the body into a text. It is idealism in its postmodern form that we will have to confront in order to bring the body out of its textual playground and back to earth. If modern idealism expanded the inner world of the sovereign Euro-masculine subject, post-modern idealism turns this world inside out but continues to expand it so that everything, including life itself, is engulfed by the postmodern text.

Confronting postmodern idealism does not mean reasserting our faith in the object-body of the empiricists, a faith that still undergirds many feminist political efforts in relation to the body. It is the object-character of the body, which is affirmed both in intellectualist accounts (an object-body is constituted by consciousness or discourse) and in empiricist accounts (the body is a material object caught up in relations of mechanical causation), as Merleau-Ponty pointed out nearly six decades ago. Borrowing from Merleau-Ponty, I will suggest that corporeal consciousness, the reversible body-world relation, which is the foundation for subjectivity as well as objectivity, is the place to begin to understand what's wrong with discursive theories of the body.

What's wrong with discursive theories of the body will have to do with the inefficacy of such theories in the face of unprecedented levels of global environmental destruction. These theories are of little assistance in our efforts to articulate our relationship to the planet we inhabit in a politically meaningful way. The textual body, or in some accounts the virtual body, has little relation to the body of the earth; it seems in fact to be the realization of that quintessential Euro-masculine fantasy of emancipation from necessity, where "necessity" serves as a negative marker for the relationship of dependence between bodies and places. A textual body need not breathe or drink, eat or suffer—it is pure (virtual) desire. A new feminist account of the body will call for a re-marking of the relation of the body (and thus of the subject) to the realm of necessity.

History Notes on Feminism and the Body

Long before the body became a text, feminists found it was already fraught with problems. Variously theorized as the place where oppression left its mark, or where liberation might begin, women's bodies, whether objectified, violated, pleasured,

---

3. While I don't mean to deny the phenomenological account of body that makes place dependent on body (see for example Casey 1993, 199, and Merleau-Ponty 1962), I do want to stress the other side of this relation, which is, certainly for both of these authors, reversible. The dependency of the body on place is to be emphasized precisely to break through the subjectivism that is so overwhelmingly central in philosophical accounts that have inherited so much from idealism.

overworked, underpaid, wholly natural, socially constructed, or given by the goddess were of central concern to second-wave feminists.

The centrality of the body in feminist protest needs little explanation. The particularities of women's bodily existence have notoriously functioned as the central justifications for women's subordination to men, at least in cultures of the Euro-masculinist West. Women's alleged closeness to, or enslavement to, the processes of the body, has been contrasted to men's fantasized freedom from this realm, their freedom for intellectual, political, or spiritual life.

The feminist response to this close association between women and the body has often been, certainly in the context of second-wave feminism in the United States, to try to set women's economic, social, and political subjectivity over and against our bodily lives. It is freedom from the bodily realm that frees women *for* subjectivity. At the same time, the clear recognition that having a body controlled by someone else, legally or otherwise, prevented women from attaining subject status, has meant that the body has remained at the center of feminist protest. The form of this protest has often been in keeping with the attempt to maintain a distance between women as subjects and women as embodied beings. Subjectivity means, just as in patriarchal accounts, gaining control over a body-object. It has tended to rely on notions of the body as property, even as the treatment of women's bodies as the legal property of men has been decried. Much of feminist political and legal activism has centered on insisting, "My body is my property!"[4] Of course, if my body is my property, I am not my body, I am a subject-owner of an object-body.

Early second-wave women's liberation politics called for social policies that would give women control over their own bodies, particularly when it came to reproductive freedoms and sexuality, but also in connection with "women's" work. Closely on the heels of this call came another: the demand to end violence against women. First the rape crisis movement then the movement against domestic violence addressed the social situation of women who were victims of male violence. The issue of women's control over our bodies was connected with broader issues of sexual socialization, male dominance, economic disenfranchisement, housework, and sexuality as a center of women's oppression. A burgeoning lesbian feminist movement theorized lesbianism as resistance to male domination and androgyny as embodied resistance or "conscientious objection"[5] to feminine socialization.

In the 1980s, the question of women controlling their bodies got even more complex. Much of this complexity hinged on whether or not many of the things

4. I do not mean to imply, here, that there weren't many feminist theorists who had much more complicated notions of bodily existence. The work of Adrienne Rich, Audre Lorde, Mary Daly, and a host of other thinkers were early examples of work that did not rely on any notion of body-as-property. Here I am claiming that feminist activism, especially where it centered on legal reform, tended to rely on a faith in the body-as-property approach.

5. Sheila Jeffreys, in her account of early lesbian feminism, refers to lesbian feminists as "conscientious objectors" to gender. She also argues that "[l]esbian feminists have always been radical social constructionists in their approach to lesbianism" (1996, 361, 367).

women were doing with their bodies were seen as expressions of women's control over their bodies or lack of it.[6] Was it an expression of women's control over their bodies to sell them in pornography or prostitution? Could a woman choose—was it in fact an expression of her control over her body and thus liberating for her to choose—"violation" in the form of masochistic sex? Could traditional femininity be liberating if a woman chose it? Could the decision to change her sex surgically and hormonally be an expression of her right to control her own body? These questions entered what came to be called "the sex debates" in feminism with a vengence. To oversimplify a bit, how one answered them determined which side one was on. "No" to all of the above made one a radical feminist—the other side called you "antisex" or "cultural feminist" or "victim feminist," and later "essentialist." "Yes" to all of the above made one a pro-sex feminist—the other side called you "sex libertarian" or "antifeminist."

These questions, and the 1990s, brought a new complexity to feminist philosophies of the body. The "wayward desires" of women who were feminists, the vast array of lived bodily experiences that some women celebrated and others criticized, made it impossible to reduce the problem of the body to the problem of who controlled it from the outside, that is, legally. The body could no longer be considered to be property, mere matter, owned and controlled by the conscious and willful intentions of the mind.

The "pro-sex" feminists "won" the rhetorical battle, at least in academic feminist contexts in the United States. Their focus on "polymorphous perversion" in a rabidly individualist and voluntarist cultural milieu secured what can only be called a hegemony in U.S. academia for "pro-sex" feminism. Their notions of the body cohered more comfortably with postmodern theories than other feminist notions. Postmodern accounts tended to stress a definition of the body as primarily the seat of libidinal (here understood as antirational) impulses, the liberation of which was important in the liberation of women. In more recent feminist postmodernist accounts, our bodies have become sites of social inscription that we nevertheless may refashion as modes of self-expression or protest.

One mark of the change in how bodies are viewed in the context of feminist thought is the collapse of the central conceptual paradigm that distinguished sex and gender, a collapse that occurred initially both inside and outside of the new feminist postmodernism. The old feminist distinction between sex (as natural and biological) and gender (as social and cultural) was a distinction that fit nicely with the "My body is my property!" approach to feminist protest. The natural body was the property, and the gendered body was what the previous (patriarchal) owners had done to it. But social constructionist accounts recognized gender's influence in

---

6. I am leaving out the important role played by the enthroning of desire over reason in postmodern theories more generally. "Control" may be a misleading term since a right to express wayward desire does not necessary correlate on first glance with a notion of "control"—but even so, having the right to desire in feminist postmodernist accounts, whether or not by way of unbridled expression, certainly meshes with early feminist claims that women should have the power to decide their bodily destiny, in sex and pregnancy.

how sex itself was defined, articulated culturally, and lived.[7] There was no getting away from gender, no natural sex beyond gender, to which to return.

The value of these insights for feminism should not be underestimated. Initially, change was fought for on the field of gender. But sex always returned as that natural, God-given, immutable fact of women's existence. Women have babies. If they don't have babies, at least they can. This is what sex is, and sex is pre-social. Therefore every social policy that could be justified by reference to "real" sexual differences was. It was essential for feminists to question the sanctity of what was defined as pre-social sex. As Catharine MacKinnon put it: "To limit efforts to end gender inequality at the point where biology or sexuality is encountered, termed differences, without realizing that these exist in law or society only in terms of their specifically sexist social meanings, amounts to conceding that gender inequality may be challenged so long as the central epistemological pillars of gender as a system of power are permitted to remain standing" (MacKinnon 1989, 233). Gender became the primary of the two terms for feminists, but not as a superstructural formation of natural sex. Neither gender nor sex were seen as natural. Sex was a function of gender.

This critique was extended so much in postmodern accounts that the gendered body today is not only cultural rather than biological, constructed rather than natural but also textual rather than material, or in accounts such as those of Kipnis and Williams in the previous chapter, virtual rather than real. Gender is contingent, malleable, and performative. It is not particularly intransigent. Such cultural "performances" as drag demonstrate that there is no "original" or "authentic" gender or sex to play around with since sex is gender, and all gender is gender play.[8] The gendered body has become, in feminist postmodern accounts, the quintessential simulacrum, the copy for which there is no original. Today, much of academic feminism understands the body to be a discursive site. The body has turned into a text.

I will argue that these new approaches circumscribe the fullness of corporeal life as much as the "My body is my property!" approach did. While one view relies on a notion of body as passive matter to be acted on by cultural forces, the other views the body as a product of consciousness, albeit consciousness in its collective and dis-

---

7. For both Catharine MacKinnon, a radical feminist influenced most directly by Marxism and the central figure in radical feminist theory in the academy, and Judith Butler, the central figure in the establishment of feminist postmodernism, the collapse of this distinction is key to their theoretical work. Both argue that the intelligibility of sex is constructed through the social conventions of gender (MacKinnon 1989, *BTM* 1993).

8. A classic formulation of this idea can be found in Butler's 1991 essay "Imitation and Gender Insubordination." She gives credit to Esther Newton for the insight that drag "enacts the very structure of impersonation by which *any gender* is assumed" (1991, 21). This has profound implications for our understanding of gender; "[d]rag constitutes the mundane way in which genders are appropriated, theatricalized, worn, and done; it implies that all gendering is a kind of impersonation and approximation. If this is true, it seems, there is no original or primary gender that drag imitates, but gender is a kind of imitation for which there is no original; in fact, it is a kind of imitation that produces the very notion of the original as an effect and consequence of the imitation itself" (21).

cursive postmodern form. Neither approach begins to describe how it is that our bodies are lived, how it is that we live embodied in a place-world that sustains us.

Judith Butler and the Textualization of the Body

Though one cannot attribute all of the positions in the above paragraph to the early work of Judith Butler, no feminist has been more influential in the development of feminist postmodernism in the United States than she has. As we will see in the next chapter, Butler's thought not only establishes certain foundations for feminist postmodernism but also ends up exceeding and disrupting them—finally pushing toward a radically materialist account of embodied subjectivity. Here I focus on a particular moment in Butler's work that has been important in the transformation of feminist epistemology. We might characterize this transformation as moving from an epistemology focused on the project of unmasking patriarchal appearances to get to the truth underneath them to an epistemology of the simulacrum, where thinking unmasks the appearances only to find itself at the edge of an abyss of absence.

I want to take a closer look here at how this epistemology functions in Butler's early book on the body, *Bodies That Matter: On the Discursive Limits of "Sex."* I am interested in a critical reading of Butler's notions of interpellation, of "constitutive outside," and of her deconstruction of the notion of matter, not simply in order to say what I think she got wrong, but because a critical reading of her work can reorient us in relation to the question of the body.

In *Bodies That Matter*, Butler sets out to deal with some of the trouble that her former book, *Gender Trouble*, left unaddressed. She is responding to criticism that her earlier work left out "the material body."

> The question was repeatedly formulated to me in this way, "What about the materiality of the body, Judy?" I took it that the addition of "Judy" was an effort to dislodge me from the more formal "Judith" and to recall me to a bodily life that could not be theorized away. There was a certain exasperation in the delivery of that final diminutive, a certain patronizing quality which (re)constructed me as an unruly child, one who needed to be brought to task, restored to that bodily being which is, after all, considered to be most real, most pressing, most undeniable. . . . And if I persisted in this notion that bodies were in some way constructed, perhaps I really thought that words alone had the power to craft bodies from their own linguistic substance? (*BTM* 1993, ix–x)

Here Butler contrasts her own position to two distinct positions: one objectivist (the body is "most real, most pressing, most undeniable"), the other subjectivist ("words alone . . . craft bodies from their own linguistic substance"), and elides the difference between the two in the process. By doing this, Butler implicitly paints her interlocutors (who are worried about the extreme subjectivism of her position) as believers in "brute matter," setting herself up to reply to their criticisms with a classic constructionist view. The problem with this approach is that it allows Butler to leave aside the problem of the *subjectivism* that has plagued Western philosophy since Descartes and of which feminists have been justifiably skeptical. This inattention will plague Butler throughout her reply. Instead of taking up the question of the extradiscursivity of matter, the question of how matter might exceed or resist discursive constructions, she focuses instead on questions of agency and materialization.

Butler sets out to look more closely at what it means for agency when we say that bodies are socially constructed. She disavows what she calls "linguistic monism," where "socially constructed" means we are simply subjected by language, and agency is done away with entirely. But she is equally at pains to distance herself from a voluntarist notion of the subject, a notion some readers found in the idea of "gender performativity," so central to *Gender Trouble*. If gender is something we perform, than doesn't a "willful and instrumental subject, one who decides on its gender" (*BTM* 1993, x) do the performing? How is it possible within this framework to preserve "gender practices as sites of agency" (x), while avoiding the two extremes, of a voluntarist subject or no subject at all? Butler's answer to this question comes in the form of what she calls "constitutive constraint" (xi).

The notion of "constitutive constraint" is Butler's way of resolving the philosophical problem of necessity and freedom. In its modernist formulation, the problem of necessity and freedom was the problem of the relation between bodily existence (we are object-bodies subject to mechanistic laws of causality) and moral capacity (we are free agents in possession of a free will). In its postmodern form, extradiscursive bodily existence will play no part in the question of freedom and necessity at all. Now the problem is to explain "freedom," more often called "agency," in light of our "social construction," that is, in light of the fact that we are, along with our bodies, discursively constituted in "the chain of signification."

Butler is indebted for her theory of subject formation to Foucault and Althusser, as I've already noted. To reiterate: Foucault's notion of *assujetissement* "is not only a subordination but a securing and maintaining, a putting into place of a subject, a subjectivation" (*BTM* 1993, 34). Social construction is the process through which the subject is subjected in the double sense of bound and made, that is, the subject's very capacity for freedom emerges in and through the way that language constrains the subject. Agency is as much a product of the subject's discursive bondage as is "oppression." "To claim that the subject is itself produced in and as a gendered matrix of relations is not to do away with the subject, but only to ask after the conditions of its emergence and operation" (7). Similarly, Althusser's notion of interpellation involves the disciplinary voice of authority, which "hails" the subject, both reprimanding her and bringing her into social existence at the same time (121). Butler's example of the doctor whose announcement "It's a girl!" begins the process of "girling the girl" (7–8), brings Althusser's insight into the context of feminist concerns.

Butler's reply to the accusation that she has left out the material body is to ask, "[t]o what extent is materialization governed by principles of intelligibility that require and institute a domain of radical unintelligibility that resists materialization altogether or that remains radically dematerialized" (Butler *BTM* 1993, 35)? Her larger concern here is an important one. Motivated by an acute sense for how processes of making intelligible depend on processes of making unintelligible, and the consequences for those whose lives are lived on the "wrong" side of the barrier that separates the two, Butler's political project has to do with tracing the mechanisms through which such exclusions are effected. The reason Butler's work has been so central in the development of queer theory, and the reason it has been popularized to some extent outside of the academy (in spite of the technicality and the difficulty of her prose), is that she articulates something elusive yet fundamental about the harm of heteronormativity.

In order to understand this contribution in more concrete terms than are generally offered by Butler herself, we can consider the example of intersexed infants. Interpellation works as much through what is excluded as what is included, Butler argues. Between the culturally intelligible, "It's a girl!" and "It's a boy!" is only the culturally unintelligible. What is unintelligible will not be "materialized" in that the material body of intersexed infants will be altered to conform to one or the other intelligible cultural options.[9] The terror parents feel at the possibility of raising a child whose life will not make sense or will not be able to be thought in dominant conceptual frameworks except as an abomination, often leads them to take an excessively passive position when faced with the advice of medical experts.[10] Certainly the harm here (today publicly decried by some adults who have endured the medical procedures associated with the establishment of strictly dichotomous gender assignments as infants and young children) is in part that such interventions, accompanied by a level of adult panic about the possibility of their failure, have sometimes tended to make the lives of those affected unintelligible to themselves (until the adult or adolescent discovery of early "gender reassignment"). Butler's contribution to our ability to understand the mechanisms of such harm is invaluable. But her deconstructive efforts in this regard tend to exceed themselves so that what could well be most essential to her own political convictions is foreclosed from the inquiry at the outset. Let's look at how this happens in some detail.

The unintelligible functions for Butler as a "constitutive outside" for the intelligible. Butler's whole notion of "constitutive outside" is the key to her response to the question of the material body. The criticism has been, of course, that she has neglected what is most outside discourse—the body—but Butler's response pulls the body back into discourse. "For there is an 'outside' to what is constructed by discourse, but this is not an absolute 'outside,' an ontological thereness that exceeds or counters the boundaries of discourse; as a constitutive 'outside' it is that which can only be thought—when it can—in relation to that discourse, at and as its most tenuous borders" (*BTM* 1993, 8). This "outside" will return to disrupt the coherence of the intelligible and will return internally. "A constitutive or relative outside is, of course, composed of a set of exclusions that are nevertheless internal

9. The precise nature of this intelligibility is described in Suzanne Kessler's study of the medical management of intersexed infants, "The Medical Construction of Gender" (1994). Kessler shows that the single factor determining an intersexed infant's "sex assignment" is penis size and functioning, independently of chromosomes or other anatomical factors. Here, femaleness is understood to be the absence of maleness, defined as having a decent sized, potentially sexually functional penis (225).

10. In a rare moment of philosophical risk taking, Ellen Feder actually interviewed the parents of intersexed children and with great compassion describes the pressures on parents that tend to lead to a reliance on "Doctor's Orders" (Feder 2002).

to that system as its own nonthematizable necessity. It emerges within the system as incoherence, disruption, a threat to its own systematicity" (39). The "outside" was always the abjected and unacknowledged heart of the "inside."

Butler counters the criticisms of her interlocutors by deconstructing the whole notion of "matter." Her effort is to show that "matter" operates as a constitutive outside for the social, a "pre-social" that the social requires for its own self-definition. But as such, matter is a product of discursivity rather than a precursor to it. Butler's terms are very powerful in this regard; there is "a regulatory practice that produces the bodies it governs, that is, whose regulatory force is made clear as a kind of productive power, the power to produce—demarcate, circulate, differentiate—the bodies it controls" (21). Regulatory norms of discursive practices "constitute the materiality of bodies," she tells us. "[P]ower is that which forms, maintains, sustains and regulates bodies" (34).

Butler specifically rejects the kind of idealism that claims what she calls "the psyche" constitutes the body, and she mentions Kant in this regard; and it's true that Butler's powerful discursivity does not belong to an individual subject, is not the individualized psyche. It is, rather, consciousness collectivized and "turned inside out" as discourse. The function that in modern accounts was assigned to the individual, or sometimes transcendental consciousness, is now reassigned to that collective and externalized consciousness proper to postmodernity, that is, discursivity. Another way of saying this is that the *content* of individual consciousness becomes *context* in which the individual is formed. *Yet, discourse performs the same function vis-à-vis the body as constituting consciousness did in modernist idealism.* It's not that Butler gets things wrong, exactly, because the regulatory regimes of sexual difference do act powerfully in relation to bodies. What's wrong with Butler's account is that the matter of bodies, not the concept of matter now, but the real stuff, which we can't get to explicitly in Butler's work, is again playing its part as that passive and indistinct blob of stuff that gets worked on by consciousness in the form of discursivity.

"Matter has a history" (*BTM* 1993, 29), Butler insists, and it is to the history of matter as a sign that she turns her critique. Her account of this history is convincing. She uncovers "a violation that founds the very concept of matter" (*BTM* 1993, 53) and its discursive function "as the site at which a certain drama of sexual difference plays itself out" (49). Far from being the pre-social "outside" to constructionist accounts, matter returns as the very notion that is socially constructed in the delimitation of the difference between the social and pre-social. And this delimitation is far from innocent, it is complicit in the entire story of heterosexual hegemony. "To return to matter requires that we return to matter as a sign" (49), she argues, since what we say about matter is always already caught up in the chain of signification that constructs it as a concept. After all,

> the body posited as prior to the sign, is always posited or signified as prior. This signification produces as an effect of its own procedure the very body that it nevertheless and simultaneously claims to discover as that which precedes its own action If the body signified as prior to signification is an effect of signification, then the mimetic or representational status of language, which claims that signs follow bodies as their necessary mirrors, is not mimetic at all. On the contrary it is

productive, constitutive, one might even argue performative, inasmuch as the signifying act delimits and contours the body that it then claims to find prior to any and all signification. (30)

In the beginning was the sign; on the second day, the body was born into discourse.[11]

I find Butler's deconstruction of the concept of matter convincing, moving even, and important for feminism. It is not, however, an adequate response to the question she purports to be addressing, which is not about the concept of matter at all. The question is about extradiscursive matter. To ask the question of the material body is to ask the question of the relationship between what exceeds or resists discourse and the discursive. To "return to matter as a sign" is (obstinately?) to misunderstand the question, since matter as a sign is not in question. Butler's use of the notion of "constitutive outside" serves only to defer the question of a real outside. Instead of grappling with an outside to discourse, she merely does away with the outside by showing how things that are conceptually excluded from certain notions, such as matter is to the social, are internally constitutive of such notions. Butler has essentially, and rightfully, pointed out that our concept of the social contains a repressed concept of the pre-social that is foundational for it. This is not an unimportant accomplishment because Butler also shows that the unintelligibility of the "constitutive outside" of such concepts functions politically in often heinous ways—and making the unintelligible intelligible is important political work.

If we accept this, which I certainly do, we are still left with the question of an outside that is not merely internally constitutive in Butler's terms, an outside that is not reducible to a moment of exclusion on the inside of the discursive "system." She has shown that conceptually, "matter," like every other term, can be deconstructively devoured by discourse theory. She has shown that how we think and live our bodies is discursively constrained. Butler has answered her interlocutors by brilliantly illuminating a relationship between concepts, but they have not asked after a relationship between concepts, they have asked after the relationship between a body as what precedes, exceeds, resists, or escapes discourse—and the discursive.

For the early Butler there is finally no opening to this extradiscursive body—though at one point she seems to consider where such an opening might be found, that is, in the materiality of language itself. Her assertion is that if "materiality is considered ontologically distinct from language," then "the possibility that language might be able to indicate or correspond to that domain of radical alterity" is undermined (*BTM* 1993, 68). After showing that our very notion of "matter" is caught up in discourse, she goes on to argue that it is the ontological similarity between language and "the material" that provides the ground for a possible relation—language is itself material. The "phenomenality" of the signifying process requires, after all, that language make a material appearance, whether as sound, words on a

---

11. I am playing on Catharine MacKinnon's similar wording to describe the perceived relation between dominance and difference (1989, 220).

page, or gestures. This is a promising direction, but in the next moment, a new "radical difference" between language and extradiscursive materiality is introduced. "Apart from and yet related to the materiality of the signifier is the materiality of the signified as well as the referent approached through the signified, but which remains irreducible to the signified. This radical difference between referent and signified is the site where the materiality of language and that of the world which it seeks to signify are perpetually negotiated" (69). The "radical difference" here is hard to pin down; it seems to exist in the irreducibility of the referent to the signified, that is, the material body is not reducible to what we mean when we say "material body," which is not reducible to the sign itself "material body"—though all are material. It is unclear why this "irreducibility" does not constitute an ontological difference, and it is equally unclear why, if it did, this would mean that the "referentiality of language" would be undermined.[12]

Butler seems to need to deny the ontological difference between language and materiality in order to re-collapse materiality back into language—to ultimately sidestep the very irreducibility she claims to defend. An ontological difference would demand an accounting, an inquiry into what this not-speech/not-only-speech might be. But for Butler, materiality is something that is to be "negotiated" rather than something that disrupts precisely through its frequent refusal to be negotiated. Butler's insistence on the materiality of language, on the ontological similarity of language and the material, is what enables a dissolving of the boundary between the two, which is at once an expansion of language to colonize the very space of materiality. Thus the relationship between language and materiality is dissolved as well. Materiality becomes, on the one hand, another characteristic of speech (breath, etc.), and on the other hand, another accomplishment of speech.

This second move is made in the passage in which Butler both approaches and sidesteps the question of the relationship between language and the material as follows: "To answer the question of the relation between the materiality of bodies and that of language *requires first* that we offer an account of how it is that bodies materialize" (*BTM* 1993, 69, emphasis added). Butler's "requires first" has already established a priority. From here, her account takes us back to language, which again becomes the privileged and indeed active term of the two—language materializes the body.

It remains unclear why we are bound—"required first"—to approach the question in the way Butler prescribes. Required by whom? If we must ask first after the materialization of the body (in language), then the intersexed body of the infant, to take up our earlier example, is disciplined out of our inquiry. It would be something like an original, for which there is no copy—and in the world of discourse we can attend only to the copies, for which there are no originals. Why would we not ask after the material materialization of the body—or has this materialization been rendered unintelligible by discourse theory?

12. Indeed, elsewhere Butler raises these same questions and responds to them very convincingly, as I pointed out in chapter 5. Butler's criticism of Lacan is made precisely on these terms.

In fact, when we ask how language is materialized, we find ourselves in an opening toward the extradiscursive body, and its places, *already*. Isn't it, after all, the body that materializes language—how would we speak without breath, write without any body at all? And with the barest reflection on breath, we find ourselves already in an opening toward the place of the body; because breath, water, food, light, and warmth are the gifts of the places that sustain our speech. Discursive accounts of the body discipline our attention away from these openings. The tendency Butler takes note of, the tendency of bodies to "indicate a world beyond themselves," is effectively effaced, or in her terms abjected, by the active and determinate role assigned here to language as the materializer of the body.

Butler's "resolution" of the paradox of necessity and freedom consists in this: "constitutive constraint" both constrains and constitutes, it limits, and enables. The very constraint imposed by the outside (here the notion of "matter") constitutes the inside (here "the social"), where the agent is born into discourse. What is obfuscating about this account, and what differentiates the postmodern resolution of the paradox from Kant's, is that here both necessity and freedom are conditions of discourse. Whereas in modernist idealism the subject had to emancipate himself from the bonds of necessity (that is, the mechanical causality of the natural world) in order to exercise his freedom, had to rise above his enthrallment in the realm of nature in order to see the phenomenal object world as constituted by his own rational activity, in postmodern idealism the realm of necessity is through and through constituted in language. Nature disappears altogether. The constituting powers of consciousness (now not the consciousness of the thinking subject, but the collective discursive consciousness of postmodernity) are extended to the realm of necessity itself. This account unwittingly extends the "project of mastery" over the natural world much further than Kant himself. Here the exteriority of the natural world, which has heretofore been a constant source of trouble and reproach in relation to "constituting consciousness," vanishes. Even the reduced and impoverished exteriority this world maintains in Kant's vision disappears. Here the body is no longer "of nature" at all, because there is no nature. It's materiality is a result of discursive "negotiation." Necessity itself is sprung free from the realm of "nature" and *relocated within constituting consciousness* in its postmodern form.

Of course, the political problems posed by Butler's reduction of "matter" to another product of constituting consciousness are monumental and cannot be easily brushed aside. To return again to our example of the intersexed infant, the unintelligibility of the infant's body to the doctors or parents results in a material intervention/violation of the infant's body. What Butler calls the "chain of signification" is instrumental in the "rematerialization" (to use what is certainly too neutral and innocent a term) of the infant's body as intelligibly male or female. But the intersexed body was there to begin with, and it is significant that many adults who discover that they were surgically "corrected" as infants experience a deep sense of violation at the revelation (Kessler 1994). Butler's theory leaves out this body, thrown into a world so incapable of receiving it. It gives us no way of responding to the real presence of something else, something that is neither intelligible within current discursive systems nor a repressed "notion" that works on the inside of those systems. Certainly, this goes against the liberatory spirit of

Butler's own work entirely. But it seems that making this life, this body, an intelligible life/body, requires a return to the lived body, which exceeds discourse. This body that is birthed into a world incapable of receiving it is not *a notion*, not *the concept* of a body, it is the real presence on the inside of the discursive systems of a person, an exteriority that demands an ethical response. Certainly this response will be a response in language, but not only. It is the exteriority of the infant's body that tears language open, releases it into and intertwines it with an extradiscursive presence. For the early Butler, this opening onto and into the extradiscursive is precluded — even as her work pushes toward the necessity of such an opening, and indeed will push through to such an opening after her phenomenological turn.

But even Butler's early account here becomes provocative for an environmentalist feminism, where the Euro-masculinist abjection of the realm of necessity is recognized as a paradigm that is central to the wholesale and thoughtless destruction of the natural world, as soon as necessity is returned to its extradiscursive materiality. Against the grain of patriarchal accounts, Butler articulates the relationship of necessity and freedom without opposing the two terms. One need not be liberated from necessity in order to exercise freedom; necessity is the very enabling condition that makes freedom (as agency) possible. Freedom grows up out of necessity. If there is a "negotiation" that should be spoken of in this regard, surely it is the negotiation over the myriad ways freedom might be exercised in honor of its foundation in necessity. Once necessity is returned to its materiality, of course the body is as well. Honoring the relation of freedom and necessity will mean honoring this body, which is not the discursive body, but the lived body. It will mean honoring its places as well.

Butler on Merleau-Ponty/Merleau-Ponty on the Body and Place

In an early[13] essay entitled "Sexual Ideology and Phenomenological Description: A Feminist Critique of Merleau-Ponty's Phenomenology of Perception," Butler discusses the usefulness of Merleau-Ponty's work on sexuality for feminism. Because Merleau-Ponty sees sexuality as "a mode of dramatizing and investigating a concrete historical situation, [he] appears to offer feminist theory a view of sexuality freed of naturalistic ideology" (Butler 1989, 85). Butler criticizes Merleau-Ponty, however, and correctly, for taking the masculine body to be "the body," in his account. Sexuality is for him heterosexuality, and his notion of sexuality trades on a traditional model of dominance, bound up with the masculinist and objectifying gaze of a perceiver assumed to be male. Butler shows that Schneider, the man in Merleau-Ponty's case study of abnormal sexuality, is more of a feminist than Merleau-Ponty himself, since what arouses him is the character, the corporeal consciousness of a woman, rather than an objectification of the woman as mere body. Butler rightly shows that Merleau-Ponty's view of sexuality depends on "misogyny as an intrinsic structure of perception" (92).

---

13. Originally written in 1981, published in 1989.

But in other aspects of her critique, Butler foreshadows the problems she herself will encounter in relation to the body. She opts for a "stronger version of historical situatedness" (Butler 1989, 90) than she finds in *The Phenomenology of Perception*. This "strong version" of historical situatedness, which will be the keynote of Butler's work throughout her early career, implicitly commits her to a view of "constituting consciousness" that leads her into the very philosophical problems Merleau-Ponty attempted to work his way out of. For "historical situation" is reduced to "discursivity," and discursivity constitutes every bit as strongly as the Kantian subject did. Though it does not belong to an individual subject, though it is collectivized and "turned inside out," it is still constituting consciousness that takes center stage.

Certainly Merleau-Ponty's exhortation to philosophers to resist "escaping from existence into the universe of things said" (*PhP* 1962, xv) is very pertinent to our reading of Butler. He sets out (as does Butler) to overcome the antinomies that have characterized Western philosophical inquiry: consciousness-nature, subject-object, interior-exterior.[14] But whereas for Butler this project results consistently in the collapsing of the antinomies into discourse (nature into discursive culture, exterior into discursive interior), for Merleau-Ponty, it requires that philosophy not capitulate to a temptation to see itself as mainly concerned with language. "Philosophy is not a lexicon, it is not concerned with 'word-meanings,' it does not seek a verbal substitute for the world we see, it does not transform it into something said, it does not install itself in the order of the said or of the written as does the logician in the proposition, the poet in the word, or the musician in the music. It is the things themselves, from the depths of their silence, that it wishes to bring to expression" (*V/ I* 1964, 4). When feminist postmodernism "installs itself in the universe of things said," it reduces the field of feminist inquiry, in this case from the materiality of the body to what we say about the materiality of the body. The problem with Butler's commitment to constituting consciousness as the very foundation of her philosophical work is that it obscures the prereflective realm of the body-subject that Merleau-Ponty tried to elucidate and falls into the kind of idealism he tried to refute.

It is precisely attention to this prereflective realm that is called for if we wish to reorient ourselves in relation to bodies and places. Merleau-Ponty's genius was to focus his considerable philosophical talent on the realm of existence that Western philosophy had tended to abject, explain mechanically, or ignore entirely, the bodily realm of sensibility. Before "constituting consciousness" there is a "primary consciousness" that is bodily consciousness. "The subject of sensation is neither a thinker who takes note of a quality [as in intellectualism], nor an inert setting which is affected or changed by it [as in empiricism], it is *a power* which is born into, and simultaneously with, a certain existential environment" (*PhP* 1962, 211, emphasis added). The lived body and primary consciousness are two sides of one and the same power.

---

14. See Gary Brent Madison, *The Phenomenology of Merleau-Ponty* (1981), for a good attempt to trace this effort throughout Merleau-Ponty's career.

What is important about Merleau-Ponty's work for the current feminist inquiry has to do with the insights it can offer in regard to the question of the body and place. This work is anomalous in the history of Western philosophy precisely in Merleau-Ponty's refusal of the traditional abjection of the whole realm of bodies and places, that is, of the realm with which women have been so consistently and so negatively associated. His attention to this realm allows him to countenance an opening onto what is other (than consciousness, than speech) that is obfuscated in dominant (including postmodern) accounts.

Merleau-Ponty can countenance such an opening because our bodies, rather than being merely produced in discourse, are the very living and lived reality of that opening. They are "the way a subject is present in the world and is aware of it." The body's "other side," what Merleau-Ponty calls perceptual consciousness (or primary consciousness), is not the absolute interiority of constituting consciousness, but "a bodily presence in the world, a bodily awareness of the world" (Madison 1981, 23). Prior to objective and subjective being, Merleau-Ponty finds this "third genus of being" (*PhP* 1962, 350), which is the foundation of the other two.

The challenge Merleau-Ponty presents to Butler is the challenge he presented to subjectivism sixty years ago. If the subject is in a situation, Merleau-Ponty argues, he is not in a conceived relationship, but an ontological one, and through his very thinking and experiencing he lives his faith in the reality of this situation. "We do not say that the notion of the world is inseparable from that of the subject, or that the subject thinks himself inseparable from the idea of his body and the idea of the world; for, if it were a matter of no more than a conceived relationship, it would *ipso facto* leave the absolute independence of the subject as thinker intact, and the subject would not be in a situation" (*PhP* 1962, 408). Even the "discursive situation" of Butler's postmodernism, which seems to leave the subject face-to-face with only herself since she is made of and in discourse, ends up pointing to a world beyond discourse.

To be in a situation, for Merleau-Ponty, is always to be confronted, on the very inside of our lived experience, with something that we are not. As Madison puts it: "It is indeed unthinkable, as Merleau-Ponty remarks, to conceive of a thing which would exist completely in itself apart from all relation to consciousness. But as he also observes, the thing nonetheless appears to us as if it were a thing in itself; it is opaque and indifferent to our hold on it. . . . We encounter the thing as that which withdraws from our complete possession, as that which draws along with it an entire elusive world" (Madison 1981, 32). There is always an excess, always "something transcendent standing in the wake of one's subjectivity" (*PhP* 1962, 325). For Merleau-Ponty, things are always "transcendent in relation to our life," even though we live them (326). This is because "the human body, with its habits which weave round it a human environment, has running through it a movement towards the world itself" (327). And this world is not reducible to the world we make; it includes the natural world. Indeed, for Merleau-Ponty, "the whole of nature is the setting of our own life, or our interlocutor in a kind of dialogue" (320).

As Butler recognized, Merleau-Ponty does not offer feminists a feminist philosophy of the body. But he does offer several things that are important to developing such a philosophy. If we are interested in a feminist philosophy of the body that is neither subjectivist (the object-body is constituted by consciousness or discourse) nor objectivist (the object-body is passive matter acted on causally according to the laws of nature), here is a place to start. And if we are interested in a feminist philosophy of the body that neither severs the connection between body and place, as happens when the body is taken up into discourse, nor relegates the body to the realm of "mechanical causality," then it is the lived body we are dealing with.

The body of the postmodern sublime is the virtual body, the textual body. But it is the lived body that *lives the experience* of texuality, of virtuality, and gestures to a world beyond these experiences even in the midst of them. To insist on the irreducibility of the body to language is not to oppose the material body to the textual body. It is not to assert an extratextual body in the sense of some primary, original, untainted antithesis to the social.[15] It is to attend to the very body that lives both the experience of the social and the textual, a body that can never be wholly claimed or contained by language.

This body's very speaking gestures toward an unspoken, because neither my body, nor its capacity for language, nor the total situation I find myself in were made by me. "I am given, that is, I find myself already situated and involved in a physical and social world—I am given to myself" (*PhP* 1962, 360). For Merleau-Ponty, my being given to myself happens in the multidimensionality of a situation that necessarily includes the physical world. This reality is immediately present to us because we are dependent on the physical world even for moment-to-moment sustenance. "My body is a movement towards the world, and the world is my body's point of support" (350). I am insisting on bodies that live, again in Butler's own words, in "a world beyond themselves," where "this movement beyond their own boundaries, a movement of boundary itself," is "quite central to what bodies are" (*BTM* 1993, ix).

It is certainly a cultural achievement of enormous proportions to have rendered the relation of dependence between bodies and places unintelligible, but this is precisely the circumstance we find ourselves in. Postmodern theory celebrates these circumstances uncritically, demonstrating deconstructively that our experience of being set adrift from the world and sealed into language is "true" at the same time the theorist breathes, drinks, and eats to sustain her capacity to deconstruct.

If we call for a reconnection of bodies to the places that sustain them, we also move toward prioritization of place, and a politicization of our relationships to place. We return the body to its flesh and blood, and bring it "back to earth," where the earth is understood to be in a productive and sustaining relation to the body. Here the relation of necessity to freedom that Butler discovered in the universe of words is brought down to earth as well. It is the earth that sustains us,

---

15. This should not be read to imply that the body will be lived everywhere and cross-culturally the same, only that it is lived everywhere. To speak of "the body" is already to speak in a certain cultural context that understands "body" in an individualizing framework that will not be intelligible in some different contexts.

and this very sustenance is the condition for the possibility of lived bodily experience, therefore of subjective experience in general, including the experience of freedom. "My freedom," Merleau-Ponty writes, "the fundamental power which I enjoy of being the subject of all my experiences, is not distinct from my insertion into the world" (*PhP* 1962, 360). But neither is it, as Merleau-Ponty imagined, "a fate for me to be free" (360). A feminist politics of the-body-in-place sees our capacity for freedom as integral to the relationship between bodies and places, but realizes that this freedom requires a politics of body and of place—a politics that is founded in an affirmation of our dependence on the earth. This earth is not a prison-house, and the body that returns to it is not a text.

7

Foundations for a Feminist Sublime

The independent individual is always a fictive creation of
those men sufficiently privileged to shift the concern for
dependence on to others.

—Eva Feder Kittay

Let's face it. We're undone by each other. And if we're not,
we're missing something.

—Judith Butler

There is no being except being in place. . . . To be a sentient bodily
being at all is to be place-bound, bound to be in a place, bonded and bound
therein.

—Edward S. Casey

Of what use could an aesthetic experience like that of the sublime, that has been so
entangled with masculinist commitments, be to feminists? One answer to this
question is simply to assert that we are apparently not immune to the experience of
the sublime, since feminist theorists have recently found it at work in the best of
feminist writing and in explicitly feminist art, and therefore we ought to understand
it (Meagher 2003, Freeman 1995). Another is to recognize that we find experiences
of the sublime at work in more dangerous places. Sheila Lintott argues, for example,
that considering women's relationships to culturally prescribed notions of beauty
only takes us part way toward an understanding of the most deadly and heavily
gendered of psychological disorders: anorexia—it is the aesthetic experience of the
sublime that explains why women continue to starve themselves beyond the limits
of socially prescribed slenderness (2003). But it seems to me there are other compelling reasons to think about the sublime as a component of contemporary feminist experience.

I have already argued that the sublime marks our relationship to the natural world, and to other persons, under conditions of postmodernity—but the way this experience is articulated and lived tends toward the same expansion of subjectivism as in modern accounts of the experience. The sublime served first as "an allegory of the construction of the patriarchal (not necessarily male) subject, a self that maintain[ed] its borders by subordinating difference and by appropriating rather than identifying with that which present[ed] itself as other" (Freeman 1995, 4). Today it serves as the guarantee of an expanding discursive universe, in which whatever exceeds or resists the power of language itself becomes a mere text, to be read and written against the background of the abyss of absence at its own borders. But if this is a credible description of a powerful contemporary experience of the sublime, this certainly is not to say that it is the only sort of sublime experience at work in contemporary life.

It is my conviction that the sublime is a somewhat fickle feeling. Though certain features of the experience remain constant (the admixture of displeasure/pleasure, terror that turns to exhilaration, the sense of encountering something of overwhelming magnitude or power), the meanings that emerge from such experiences may change. In this chapter, I look for the foundations of a different sort of sublime experience. If these reflections are successful, we will find that there are modes of sublime experience that depart radically from dominant accounts of the sublime and contribute to our efforts to articulate "the emancipatory aspirations of women" in epistemological and political terms.

Given the misogynist history of the sublime, it is no surprise that feminists have been slow to affirm the importance of a kind of *counter*sublime in women's lives or women's art. One of the first to do so was Barbara Claire Freeman, who finds what she calls a "feminine sublime" at work in the writings of George Eliot, Virginia Woolf, Luce Irigaray, Gloria Anzaldúa, and Toni Morrison, among others, that turns out to mean something quite different than the masculinist versions of the experience that we find in the dominant philosophical tradition. Each of these authors, Freeman claims, "makes explicit the female subject's encounter with an alterity that exceeds, limits, and defines her" (1995, 2). This encounter with alterity is terrifying because the boundaries of the subject lose their solidity in the face of Other. One not only experiences the Other in the encounter but also is changed by the experience in ways that cannot be anticipated, controlled, or easily undone. For Freeman it is the dissolution of the fantasy of individual sovereignty and autonomy that signals the experience of the sublime. Certainly a possible human response to such experiences of vulnerability is to reassert individual sovereignty, to shore up the boundaries of the subject, to "dominate," "appropriate," "colonize," "consume," or "domesticate" (all Freeman's terms) the alterity one encounters in order to "demonstrate mastery over the experience that had seemed overwhelming" (8). Freeman's "feminine sublime" refuses the consolation of this masculinist fantasy. Instead, the subject undergoes "a crisis in relation to language and representation" (3) without retreating into fantastic narratives of mastery. The subject "enters into a relation with an otherness—social, aesthetic, political, ethical, erotic—that is excessive and unrepresentable" (2). It is on the basis of *this* *relation* that the subject is able to take up "a position of respect in response to incalculable otherness" (11) rather than one of domination or appropriation.

Freeman's notion of a "feminine sublime" is, in some respects, another formulation of the postmodern sublime, focused as it is on the blurring of the boundaries of the self and the humbling of the sovereign subject. Yet it is also a radical departure from other characterizations of sublime experience that we have encountered, since in this experience, rather than a dissolution of meaning, we find a superabundance, an *excess* of meaning. The subject of this sublime experience does not encounter an abyss or a void, but *a relation* with an alterity that is unrepresentable in the sense that its meaning *overflows* the boundaries of conceptualization. The pleasure or exhilaration in Freeman's account of the sublime has to do with a sense of "rapture," "merger," or "identification" with the other that, while maintaining rather than colonizing difference, is also a source of meaning that is overwhelmingly intense and abundant.

These themes will be taken up more explicitly as we proceed, for now I would like to emphasize Freeman's affirmation of our *vulnerability* in relation to others, which is, in some fundamental sense, the basis of the superabundance of meaning we encounter in "the feminine sublime." It is of extreme importance for feminist philosophy that we notice that something very similar to Freeman's central insight is hard at work in distinct traditions in contemporary feminist thinking in ethics and politics as well. It is clearly significant that Freeman's turn to this notion in the context of feminist aesthetics in 1995 is repeated by Eva Kittay in the context of feminist ethics in 1999 and by Judith Butler in the context of her "politically informed psychoanalytic feminism" (*PL*, 45) in 2004 (to name only three examples). It is particularly remarkable how close Butler's account of vulnerability in the realm of the political is to Kittay's account of vulnerability as the primary condition of human life that grounds the ethical—even though the two thinkers come from completely different philosophical traditions and political trajectories. I admit to being rather smitten with both accounts, which is saying a great deal, since my own engagement with Butler has often been critical, and I have a longstanding and almost lethal allergy to any sort of maternalism in feminist theory, and Kittay's work certainly comes out of this school. What I find so compelling is this: if Freeman is right in characterizing the experience she describes as sublime, and I think she is, then we find the foundations for this *other* kind of sublime experience, a *counter*experience in relation to dominant narratives of the sublime, emerging in these diverse contexts, articulated by feminists with diverse concerns— which makes me suspect that we ought to be paying more attention to it than we are.

Here I take up the notion of vulnerability in the face of alterity that is the foundation for Freeman's "feminine sublime." I trace similar notions in Butler's book of post–9/11 essays, *Precarious Life,* and in Eva Kittay's ground-breaking book in feminist care ethics, *Love's Labor.* I argue that the dependence these authors find at the very heart of our intersubjective relationships is also at the heart of our relationship to the natural world—and that these relations of dependence are the irrevocable aspect of the human condition that both lends itself to and is disclosed in sublime experience. The ethical and political implications of this vulnerability

to others can be temporarily denied or thwarted by the subject who flees dependence, but they must ultimately be affirmed if we are to live these relations in
aesthetically, ethically, and politically sustainable ways.

Intersubjective Vulnerability

Butler's "phenomenological turn," if it indeed turns out to be one, occurs on the
occasion of the dramatic attacks on the World Trade Center and the Pentagon on
September 11, 2001. Her response to the attacks and their political aftermath is
precisely the kind of thoughtful and passionate response one would have hoped for,
but for the most part did not see, from the intellectuals of the U.S. American left in
general. Influenced by her recent reading of Levinas, she turns to a fundamental
and irrevocable structure of human experience, "a vulnerability to the other that is
part of bodily life" (*PL* 2004, 29), to try to make political sense, or to construct a plea
for political sense, in the face of U.S. military aggression. For the first time in
Butler's work, this vulnerability is unambiguously, emphatically, and forcefully *not*
reducible to discursive vulnerability. "One insight that injury affords," she writes,
"is that there are others out there on whom my life depends, people I do not know
and may never know. This fundamental dependency on anonymous others is not a
condition that I can will away. No security measure will foreclose this dependency;
no violent act of sovereignty will rid the world of this fact" (xii). While political and
cultural context will change the face of dependency, will distribute it unequally,
will alter it continually, nothing that humans do will eradicate it as a fundamental
condition and experience of human life. This is "a primary vulnerablity to others
that we cannot will away without ceasing to be human" (xiv).

This fundamental condition of human life is poignantly revealed in experiences of loss, in which our dependence on others is both disrupted and made
painfully visible. "Maybe when we undergo what we do, something about who we
are is revealed, something that delineates the ties we have to others, that shows us
that these ties constitute what we are" (*PL* 2004, 22). The ties that are revealed are
both absolutely particular (no one is constituted in their relation to this particular
other in the way that I am) and universal (everyone is constituted in and by their
ties to some other or others). What becomes undeniable in these experiences is
that "we are, from the start, given over to the other . . . even prior to individuation
itself and, by virtue of bodily requirements, given over to some set of primary
others" (31).

As in Freeman's account, for Butler these powerful experiences of grief undo
the boundaries of the self. "It is not as if an 'I' exists independently over here and
then simply loses a 'you' over there, especially if the attachment to 'you' is part of
what composes who 'I' am. If I lose you, under these conditions, then I not only
mourn the loss, but I become inscrutable to myself" (*PL* 2004, 22). Here, the
response to the terrifying reality of our dependence on others is not a fantasy that
shores up the boundaries of the self and reasserts the sovereignty of the autonomous subject. The fantasy of an autonomous and sovereign subject is laid to waste
by such experiences because I find that who I am is so intimately entangled with
Others that I am not the simple agent of what these relations make of me.

And the consolation of language is lost on such occasions as well. It is not that one cannot speak at all, but that the coherence of the story one tells is disrupted.

> What grief displays . . . is the thrall in which our relations with others hold us, in ways that we cannot always recount or explain, in ways that often interrupt the self-conscious account of ourselves we might try to provide, in ways that challenge the very notion of ourselves as autonomous and in control. I might try to tell a story here about what I am feeling, but it would have to be a story in which the very "I" who seeks to tell the story is stopped in the midst of the telling; the very "I" is called into question by its relation to the Other, a relation that does not precisely reduce me to speechlessness, but does nevertheless clutter my speech with signs of its undoing. (*PL* 2004, 23)

Here, grief brings the narrator of the story up against the limits of representation because it undoes the limits of the self that make the usual kinds of narratives sensible. Butler's account of grief closely parallels Freeman's account of the sublime in that the subject of the experience not only finds herself at the border of the representable but also finds that the border does not demarcate an abyss of absence but a landscape of meaning so intense and abundant that it overwhelms speech. Whatever is said about the loss one lives will be exceeded by the living of that loss.

If human vulnerability to others is disclosed in circumstances of loss, it is exposed in acts of violence. The embodied subject is always subject to injury, and injury is the way that "this primary condition is exploited and exploitable, thwarted and denied" (*PL* 2004, 81). The relational ties by which we are constituted and by virtue of which we are vulnerable to violence "have implications for theorizing fundamental dependency and ethical responsibility" (22), Butler argues. It is the irrevocable sociality of embodied existence that grounds the ethical and political. The call here is to hesitation in the face of injury and loss. The rush to defense, to shore up the boundaries of (in this case) the sovereign nation, only serves to repress and postpone the realization that injury might afford. A politics that affirms our irrevocable injurability as a starting point will be a very different politics indeed than that which developed after the 9/11 attacks.

Eva Kittay, too, looks for a normative starting point for both ethics and politics in human vulnerability. Kittay's theory of dependence strikes me as in the very best tradition of feminist common sense. Starting with a simple and common aspect of the human condition, she proceeds to carefully and systematically dismantle the fetishization of independence in the Western political tradition. She manages this without essentializing women's relationship to mothering or caring and without pretending that these relationships are gender neutral. She insists, at the same time, that relationships in which persons depend on other persons for care are *essential* and *universal* relationships and manages *this* claim without thereby de-politicizing such relations. On the contrary, Kittay is working to found feminist ethical and political claims on the bedrock of human dependency.

Kittay focuses on the most brute sorts of dependence—dependencies that are "inescapable," "inevitable," "determined neither by will nor desire," "unassailable facts," "unavoidable as birth and death," "a mark of our humanity" (Kittay 1999, 29)—because only these kinds of dependence provide "a knife sharp enough to cut through the fiction of our independence" (xiii).[1] She is concerned with intersubjective dependence, the fact that dependents require care from other persons, and no one survives or thrives to become relatively *independent* without some minimal care from another (1). Though influenced by maternalist ethics, Kittay's work cannot itself be said to be maternalist in the sense of ascribing a special epistemological vantage point or moral insight to mothers. Her vision is far broader; she argues that the epistemological and moral footing to both know and fashion just social policies is in a *relationship* of dependence/care that *all of us* experience. It is more by virtue of having been mothered (and for Kittay, following Sara Ruddick, both men and women can mother) than by virtue of mothering, that we can know and do the right thing.

Several aspects of Kittay's work on dependence will help to fill out the notion of a primary human vulnerability that Freeman finds at work in the "feminine sublime" and that Butler deploys as a normative starting point for post–9/11 politics. First, Kittay insists that relationships of dependence have a natural *priority* in relation to other kinds of human relationships. This priority has to do with the asymmetrical and nonreciprocal character of the relation, with the vulnerability of one person to another, with the inequality of power in the relation. Second, such relationships have immediate *moral* implications, including bestowing value on persons cared for, moral obligation on those in the position to care, and an equal entitlement to care on all persons. Third, the notion of dependence connects the human condition of vulnerability to political and social covenants. And fourth, there is a muted reference in Kittay's work to the *spiritual* implications of such relations.

The priority of the relationship of dependence arises from its "ubiquity" in the human condition. "This relationship is ubiquitous in the human society and is as fundamental to our humanity as any property philosophers have invoked as distinctly human" (Kittay 1999, 25). But in addition to the omnipresence of the most basic sorts of dependence in all cultures and at all times, it is also the condition for the possibility of all other human relations, since to come to a point of engaging in any relation, one must first be cared for. We can understand this priority as twofold. First, it is a *temporal* priority in the sense that everyone who achieves independence or interdependence is first dependent on another for care (and some people are always dependent). A relationship that is asymmetrical and nonreciprocal grounds more reciprocal relationships developmentally. Second, ongoing "independence," which is always a "relative independence" rather than absolute (184), is purchased at a price.

> The world we know is one fashioned by the dreams of those who, by and large, consider themselves independent. Their self-understanding as independent

---

1. Though a kind of brute dependence is pre-social, how care for dependents is organized is deeply political, and many kinds of dependence are, at the root, political, such as the traditional dependence of men on women for the preparation of food and organizing of the household, for example, or the traditional dependence of women on men for income.

> persons is generally purchased at a price—one set so low and considered so
> inevitable that few have traditionally considered it pertinent to considerations of
> social justice. The purchase price of independence is a wife, a mother, a nurse-
> maid, a nanny—a dependency worker. (183)

The self-understanding that has founded Western conceits about independence
requires the projection of necessary daily dependency work onto others. The independent political actor dissimulates; he keeps his dependency out of sight and out
of mind by foisting it onto someone else.

The very fabric of society is made up of what Kittay calls "nested dependencies." We can understand this in terms of the classic (today more mythical than
real) situation of a young child in a relation of dependence to her mother; this
relation is in turn "nested" in a relationship of dependency between these two and
a breadwinner, who is himself "dependent" in relation to an employer, and so on.
Though this classic situation is hardly in evidence anymore, dependency relations
do seem to be nested in one another as Kittay claims, more haphazardly but no less
irrevocably than in the model of the nuclear family.

Before we go any further, I would like to begin to extend the notion of
vulnerablity that I am tracing in the work of Freeman, Butler, and Kittay to our
dependence on place, including our dependence on the earth itself—in which all
such relationships are *ultimately* nested. Our dependency on the earth is not to be
equated with intersubjective dependencies, though it is comparable in a number
of ways. We are moment to moment dependent in this more primary relation,
cannot survive for more than a few minutes without the air and warmth the earth
provides, for more than a few days without its water, for more than a few weeks
without its food.[2] The subject that was born in a fantasy of independence from *this*
relationship dissimulates even more profoundly than the masculine breadwinner.
This relation is the condition for the possibility for *any* intersubjective dependency
relation, or for any experience of relative independence. Moreover, it is a condition
that follows the subject, moment by moment, place to place. It cannot be left
behind at home like a dependency worker can.

Kittay is concerned to expose the ethical implications of dependency. "The
relationship [of dependency] at its very crux, is a moral one, arising out of a claim of
vulnerability on the part of the dependent on the one hand, and of a special posi-
tioning of the dependency worker to meet the need, on the other" (Kittay 1999, 35). In
morally charged moments, the needs of the dependent are prioritized over the needs
of the dependency worker, and at such moments "this prioritization is absolute" (52).

A crucial distinction grounds Kittay's claim here: that between inequalities
of power and domination. Inequalities of power may result from domination

---

2. The nesting of dependencies is not necessarily vertical, as the present discussion would seem to
suggest. An infant, though dependent on the person who cares for her, is at the very same moment
dependent on the earth. This dual dependency at the outset of each individual life is an important
aspect of dependence that should be explored, and that certainly leads toward a philosophy of persons-
in-place.

certainly, but also from unequal capacities and from unequal situations (whether socially constructed or not). An inequality of power, the vulnerability of one person in relation to another, is precisely the morally charged situation that calls for a caring response. "Inequality of power is compatible with both justice and caring, if the relation does not become a relation of domination" (Kittay 1999, 34). This is true whether or not the dependency relation is socially constructed, since in either case we may find that the other's vulnerability makes an ethical claim on us.

There is another aspect of the "claim" that these relations make, which is even more general. Kittay uses an anecdote about her mother, who after serving food to the entire family would justify sitting down to eat herself by saying, "I too, am some mother's child." Kittay turns this phrase, which could certainly be read as a particularly apt expression of the kind of self-effacing feminine virtue feminists criticize, into a study of how *caring* bestows *value*. There is a "fundamental connection between a mothering person and the fate of the individual she has mothered" (Kittay 1999, 24), and this fundamental connection is recognized as a source of *entitlement* for the one who has received such care. In saying, "I, too, am some mother's child," one is claiming "I am due care," "I am worthy of this care," and "this worthiness is inalienable" (68). This establishes a new basis for moral claims, not in how persons are individuated or in terms of the properties they can be said to have, but in terms of the relationships of care in which they are bound (27–28). Because we are all "some mother's child," we can all claim the entitlement to care that this relation bestows.

> That nothing can fully alienate the responsibility of others to recognize us as some mother's child resides in that feature of human existence that demands connection as a fundamental condition for human survival. . . . When we respect an individual as some mother's child, we honor the efforts of that mothering person and symbolically of all mothering persons. When we do not, not only are rights belonging to the abused individual violated, but the efforts of the mothering person are dishonored. The sanctity of the relation that makes possible all human connection per se is thereby disavowed. (69)

The moral situation in which we find ourselves, in relationship to the places we inhabit, is certainly not the same moral relation in which we find ourselves in relation to one another. We would have to anthropomorphize the earth beyond all recognition to speak of the "obligations" that "she" has to us by virtue of our dependency on "her." But there are two aspects of Kittay's discussion of the moral implications of dependency that do seem relevant to a discussion of our dependence on the earth. If, as Kittay claims, "dependency relations are the paradigmatic moral relations" (Kittay 1999, 71), then the dependency relation in which all others are nested is at the very heart of our intersubjective moral relations. This relationship, too, is characterized by vulnerability. Of course in this case we are talking first about *our own* vulnerability, but it is precisely in this sort of experience that Kittay finds epistemological footing for moral claims. That we have chosen the path of "tyranny" over and against the earth in this relationship, have "failed to recognize the integrity" of the earth as separate from ourselves, have chosen to do battle with the earth to the point of suicidal destruction of the environment bespeaks an unfathomable *moral and epistemological* failure. Yet it is *possible* to know how to behave in the face of our vulnerability in relation to both other persons and to the earth; this very vulnerability is the vantage point from which we are called to right action.

This can be more clearly understood in terms of the second aspect of Kittay's discussion of the moral implications of dependency, which seems to me to be very relevant to our dependency on the earth. Kittay's insight that dependency relations bestow value on dependents has implications for our relations with one another as all equally dependent on the places we inhabit. "I, too, am given life by this earth," might be a kind of environmentalist equivalent of Kittay's, "I, too, am some mother's child." Our inability to care for one another in our intersubjective relations (and here my "we" extends, with Butler, between nations and cultures) constitutes a second moral failure — but here we do not simply fail one another, we fail one another *in relation* to our dependency on the planet. We *dishonor* that relation as much as we dishonor one another.

That these moral failures are borne out in our social and political institutions is precisely the reason they require feminist attention. "Questions of who takes on the responsibility of care, who does the hands-on care, who sees to it that the caring is done and done well, and who provides the support for the relationship of care and for both parties to the caring relationship — these are social and political questions. They are questions of social responsibility and political will" (Kittay 1999, 1). Our failure to honor dependency relations in our social and political institutions is, on Kittay's reading, a failure to fulfill "the obligation of society to attend to relationships upon which all civic relationships depend." If dependents and those who care for them, and their *relationship*, is not protected and enabled by the social and political institutions we build, we have absolved ourselves of our "most fundamental obligation," the obligation to the "founding possibility" of society itself (130–31). For Kittay, as for Butler, how we understand, how we *revere or disregard*, relations of dependency will determine a great deal about what kind of political institutions we build.

Of course in our violence toward the natural world we turn away from an equally fundamental obligation, an obligation to the earth that gives us life, moment by moment, breath by breath, while we build a world to live in. The intersubjective dependencies that are the very fabric of the world Butler and Kittay are concerned with are completely entangled with the dependency between persons and places. This is to say that, like ourselves, *our social world* is dependent on the earth for sustenance. Further, it is in this relation of dependence that "the political" becomes meaningful to begin with. In saying this, I am both supporting and extending the claims of Butler and Kittay, that relationships of dependence and vulnerability are the ground or space on which domination is built, and struggles for liberation, equality, democracy, and so on are waged. How we understand, how we *revere or disregard* our relation to the planet, will be key in every instance to how we engage political questions. This essential relationship between persons and places gives the political another sort of weight and depth, makes the political another sort of urgent matter. If we understood our world-making to entail a fundamental obligation to protect and support our relation to the earth, *which is its founding possibility*, what a different sort of world we would make!

Instead, fantasies of finally dominating the Other, whether the intersubjective Other or the earth itself, permeate our social and political life. It seems to me that these circumstances bespeak not only a moral and political depravity, but a spiritual one as well. Though Kittay never explicitly evokes "the sacred" in her dependency critique, she seems to sense a violation of the sacred at the heart of our disregard for relations of dependence. When we are forgetful that an individual is "some mother's child," Kittay argues in a passage already cited above, "not only are the rights belonging to the abused individual violated, but the efforts of the mothering person are dishonored. The *sanctity* of the relation that makes possible all human connection *per se* is thereby disavowed" (Kittay 1999, 69, emphasis added). Kittay moves here from the political (rights) to the moral (honor) to the spiritual (sanctity) in this short passage. A violation of this fundamental relationship is a violation at all three levels.

It is interesting to note that the historical moment that was marked by an extraordinary new fetishizing of independence or autonomy as the *sine qua non* of truly human life was equally marked by an exchange of the sacred for the "profane" products of human reason. If Kittay is correct in claiming that our inalienable entitlement to recognition as "some mother's child" "resides in that feature of human existence that demands connection as a fundamental condition for human survival" (Kittay 1999, 69), then perhaps our very capacities for moral action and experience of the sacred reside in that same feature of human existence, which includes our connection to the places we live.

The word "reside" is important here, of course, evocative as it is of that very relationship. We not only depend on the earth, we live in the places it provides. It strikes me that the claim, "I, too, am some mother's child," *locates* the specific person uttering the claim in a specific relation to another, it also locates her as a child among others as equally a mother's child, crossing in one breath the border between the specific and the general, the one and the many. The utterance establishes a *place* for her in a vast world so populous with indifferent strangers, but she has this place *like others* have a place, or should have. By saying "I, too, am some mother's child," one claims, along with Kittay's mother, "I, too, have a place here at the table, which is my sacred right." To be "some mother's child" is to be some *place*, to be entitled to *place*, to take one's *place*, to be *emplaced*. I am working here both to affirm the notion of intersubjective dependence and to extend the notion of dependence in order to articulate another understanding of the relations between persons and places. These are morally charged relations based in the reality that we are tied to one another, and "we are tied to place undetachably and without reprieve" (Casey 1993, xiii).

Persons and Places

> When it comes to being ethical, there is no escaping the imperative
> of place.
>
> —Edward S. Casey

> A stance of ecocentrism does not . . . signify that the only genuinely
> ecological issue is whether we can save or preserve the land, especially

wild land. We can and should and must do just this. But the more pressing question from a lococentric perspective is whether we will *let the land save us*.

—Edward S. Casey

It is the notion of "dependence" that provides "a knife sharp enough" to cut through the self-involved subjectivism that plagues us (Kittay 1999, xiii) and orients us toward a reprioritization of place. While spatiality has received a good deal of renewed attention in postmodernity, Edward Casey is one of the first to prioritize place (Casey 1993, xi),[3] to call for "an outright geocentrism—or perhaps better, an engaged ecocentrism—[as] the most efficacious antidote to centuries of unself-questioning anthropocentrism and subjectivism" (Casey 1993, 187).

Casey's *Getting Back into Place* is perhaps one of the first postmodern redemption narratives. In this it goes against the grain of the postmodern, where we are, if nothing else, beyond redemption. For Casey, the deepest question is not whether we will save the land, but "whether we will *let the land save us*" (Casey 1993, 263). This is the motivating question behind his attention to narratives of place, the kind of attention to place that may be capable of saving "those in a displaced, secular, and postmodern age who lack any sense of a perduring place of collective self-belonging" (309). Indeed, in postmodernity we seem to be reaping the whirlwind of modern disregard for nature, and nature's gift of place.

Another look at Jameson's reading of the postmodern is useful in order to understand what getting back into place might *redeem us from*. For Jameson, the postmodern is fundamentally a repudiation of depth, as characterized by "the emergence of a new kind of flatness or depthlessness, a new kind of superficiality in the most literal sense, [which is] perhaps the supreme formal feature of all the postmodernisms" (Jameson 1991, 9). This repudiation has focused on at least four separate "depth models," including "the dialectical one of essence and appearance . . . the Freudian model of latent and manifest . . . the existential model of authenticity and inauthenticity . . . and most recently, the great semiotic opposition between signifier and signified" (12). All of these amount to an exchange of depth for surface.

But what kind of place is a postmodern surface? What happens to the earth in a world of surfaces? Is the earth itself another surface? We certainly say that we live "on" the earth, perhaps envisioning ourselves as in a child's drawing, pop-up stick figures on a smooth, round, crayon-line planet. The surfaces we are left with in postmodernism are not the "sensuous surfaces" of landscape (Casey 1993, 270); such *deep* surfaces have given way to the smooth flatness of a shopping-mall planet, where "depth, the elusive basis of all dimensions, indeed the 'first dimension,' has been eliminated in favor of shallowness of affect and image, a flatness reinforced

---

3. Casey distinguishes space and place in this way: "The infinity and silence of space reflects its emptiness. They also signify the absence of place. For space as a vast vacuum does not allow for places, even though one might think that there would be plenty of room for them! In such space there are no places for particular things" (1993, x).

by glossy walls and sleek floors" (269–70). In Casey's terms, this amounts to an exchange of places for mere sites. Places, which are everywhere local and rich in their specificity are exchanged for sites, like shopping malls, everywhere alike and interchangeable. A site is certainly a kind of location, but it is a location emptied of depth, which is "a matter—perhaps even *the matter*—of place" (67). A depthless surface is devoid of both "life [and] place" (269). "A site is no place to be, much less to remain. It is not even worth a postmodern nomadic journey to get there. Once there, moreover, where are we" (208)? We are no place, displaced on the surface. We surface dwellers, it seems, live in a perpetual state of disorientation on a mere planet, which is what the earth becomes when it is no longer able to provide us with places. Even though our lack of orientation might engender postmodern excitement, terrifying and exhilarating as all sublime experience is, we are no less *mis-placed* for our giddiness.

This mis-placement is also an emptying out (individually, collectively). For Casey, placelessness gives rise to "a sense of unbearable emptiness" (Casey 1993, x). And indeed, the postmodern subject has been emptied out, has himself/herself become a mere site in the chain of signification,[4] even as signifying activity swallows up depth, both internal and external. When we are empty sites, mere occasions ourselves, the meaningfulness of our accomplishing activity, of our "world-making," collapses into mere discursive playfulness, into surface.

The point of Casey's work (and indeed Jameson's in another dimension), is to *get us back into place*, so that "we can resume the direction, and regain the depth of our individual and collective life once again—and know it for the first time" (Casey 1993, 314). For Casey, it is the "insurrectional power of place" (314) itself that can counter the massive disorientation that characterizes postmodern life. By "getting back into place itself, back into the very idea, indeed the very experience, of place," we might "reorient" ourselves in the most radical sense (309).

Perhaps this is the time to note that I have been speaking all along of "the earth," as if we really lived on/in the entire global sphere rather than in the specific places *where we actually are*. Specific places are what we inhabit, never "the earth" in some grander sense. Yet places are nested, like Kittay's dependencies, one in the other. This specific room where I write, is in this flat, which in turn is in this one-hundred-year-old house (which survived the two great earthquakes), in San Francisco, in Northern California, and so on. My invocation of dependency to name our relationship to the earth is a shortcut to the notion of our dependency on the specific places, nested in one another, for which the earth is simply the most encompassing horizon, the boundary that gives all of these places their own limit, and thus existence.

I mean to invoke "dependency" to name our relation to place at its most brutal and unforgiving, yet where we are perhaps most ungrateful and forgetful, our

---

4. As Butler writes, "The geneaology of the subject as a critical category...suggests that the subject, rather than be identified strictly with the individual, ought to be designated as a linguistic category, a *placeholder*, a structure in formation. Individuals come to *occupy the site* of the subject (the subject simultaneously *emerges as a 'site')*" (PLP 1997b, 10–11, my emphasis).

irrevocable dependence on air, heat/light, water, and food. But this relation is no mere biological imperative—certainly without these gifts we would die, and die as bodies die—but who has ever seen a *mere body* die? Who, indeed, has ever seen a *mere body* that was not already dead? Believing ourselves trapped within a prison of mortality, cursed to be bounded by flesh and blood, what we have misunderstood is this: it is not only our biological life but our mental and spiritual life that are gifts of the planet. This very "bounding" is what gives us existence in the fullest sense, is the condition for the possibility of *every aspect* of human existence, from the most primal biological functioning to the most developed spiritual practice.

Without focusing on dependency in the brute sense I am proposing here, Casey argues for the priority of place in a way that illuminates this multifaceted relation.[5] Though he speaks on occasion of "the mutual enlivening of body and landscape" (Casey 1993, 29), "the reciprocity of person and place" (307), or "the mutual determination of person and place" (308), the overwhelming focus of his work is on restoring a proper *priority* to place. "Orientation," he argues, "is given primarily by the places and not by my own body" (225). It is urgent that we "let the land take the lead" (260), "let the earth be the guiding force" (260), because *"its* power, not ours in relation to it, is what is at stake" (264).

The priority of place in relation to the activities of the subject is (at least) threefold. Places are phenomenologically prior (in the order of description), ontologically prior (in the order of being), and also "primary in the order of culture" (Casey 1993, 31). Place is phenomenologically prior in that our implacement underlies our bodily experience and perception: places are "the pre-positions of our bodily lives, underlying every determinate bodily action or position, every static posture of our corpus, every coagulation of living experience in thought or word, sensation or memory, image or gesture" (313). Our very capacity to sense, perceive, describe is rooted in place. Places are ontologically prior. To exist at all is to be bounded or limited, to be bordered by place. This bordering or limiting is part of that very existence. If "there is no being except being in place" (313), then it is because to be at all means to be limited by place, and "the limit of an existing thing is intrinsic to its being" (15). Place is primary in the order of culture, as well. "Just as every place is encultured, so every culture is implaced" (31): place is on the *inside* of culture, as well as on the outside of culture, or under and around culture, which is always built in relation to place. Of course another way of naming the priority of place in relation to us is to say *we depend on place*, phenomenologically, ontologically, and culturally. It is not difficult to see that these three aspects of the priority of place are actually *three modes of our dependence* on place.

One short passage reflects not only our multifaceted dependence on place but how this dependence might *orient* us: "To be a sentient bodily being at all is to be

---

5. In a fascinating passage on atmosphere in wild places, Casey does allude to this dependence: "As an inherent presence, atmosphere is invigorating and has as its most palpable expression the actual 'breath' of a living creature, though it is also at play as the air that penetrates and moves through inorganic substances. The overall effect is to alleviate and animate any given wildscape: to bestow upon it an *elan vital* that vivifies the whole scene and not just the literally alive being in it" (Casey 1993, 220).

place-bound, bound to be in a place, bonded and bound therein" (Casey 1993, 313). Casey's multiple senses of "bond/bound" are important here and carry us from an ontological priority, through a kind of telos, to a moral and ethical imperative and to the human condition itself. First, we are place-*bound*, that is, dependent on place to provide a *boundary*, a limit to our existence. Second, we are *bound* to be in a place. As a condition of existence, "place-being is part of an entity's own-being" (16); we are *purposively* bound to be there; we depend on place because it is part of who and what *we are* to be there. Our dependence on place means we are "bonded" by place, which for my purposes I would like to read as both "tied by affection or loyalty" and "obligated by a moral duty, a vow, or a promise." And finally, our dependence on place means we are "bound therein," embedded in place, unable to escape place without leaving ourselves behind.

Just as Butler and Kittay find in intersubjective dependency relations an orientation that can inform our ethical choices, our social and political practice, we find in our relation of dependence on place an orientation that provides normative social, political, ethical, and spiritual direction. Casey hints at this connection when he remarks parenthetically that "anomie, a lack of social norms or values, often stems from atopia" (Casey 1993, xi). In reference to built places, Casey notes that the very activity of building or cultivation "localizes caring," that is, it gives caring a place. "We care about places as well as people," he writes, "so that we can say that *caring belongs to places*" (175). But this connection is precisely what we cannot take for granted, since we live in a world where the destruction of place, of the very ability of the earth to provide us with places, seems to be on its way to becoming an absolute of the human condition. Perhaps in this case we would have to say, of the *inhuman* condition, since once places are gone certainly humans will be gone as well. But if our intersubjective dependency is the source of the moral call to care rather than to domination, then our dependency on the earth is such a source as well.

The importance of recuperating a sense of humility in the face of our dependence on the earth is nothing less than the importance of recuperating a sense of what it means to be persons in place, that is, of our very humanity. In speaking of the indigenous people who have inhabited a particular place, Casey writes that "to inhabit a place in terms of the habitat and habitus is thus to re-inhabit it by living here on *preestablished terms* laid down long before the actual advent of current homesteaders" (Casey 1993, 295, emphasis added). But the "terms" are not just the ones that the indigenous inhabitants layed down through their traditions, they are also the terms layed down by the place itself, which the indigenous inhabitants seem to have been able, at least in many cases, to live *by and with* rather than against. These are the terms that we, in what we call the "Western world," seem determined to live in rebellion against, no matter how suicidal and homicidal such a path ultimately proves to be. These are terms that are *disclosed to us* in the dependency relation, which is the condition for all other relations, and indeed for our very existence.

When Kant believed he looked into the mirror of nature only to see himself, perhaps he was right in one sense, and one sense only—nature *gives us* ourselves. But the earth gives us to ourselves first *as children*, only later and only apparently as "independent" world-making adults. Our dependence on the earth, which accompanies us through every experience, on every journey, moment by moment, is not something we make, even with our most powerful tool: language itself. When we say "earth," as enculturated and enculturating as this speech is, still on the very inside of our speech is our breathing of the earth's air, our being warmed by its heat, our drinking of its water, our eating of its food—all of which are prior to any saying of the earth. On the inside of that utterance is the very enabling and enlivening relation of dependency. This relation is not merely constructed in language, it enables language, it is the condition for the possibility of language, and thus *inhabits* language from the outset.

A more personal story might help to illustrate this point. My niece, who is now eight, suffered from a condition from infancy until the age of 4 or 5 that caused her throat to close (as if she were underwater) when she cried. Each disappointment or moment of anger, if it brought intensive tears, ended in her slumping limply into unconsciousness. With unconsciousness, breath entered her small body again and literally seemed to bring her back to life. In spite of my sister's admonitions to her still-conscious child, "Breath, Mariah, breathe!" she was unable to take in air. Yet the moment she became unconscious, air rushed in, and she awoke filled with breath and (sleepy) life. Only the external, it seems, could save her. This repeated experience was hers before she could say "air" or "breath," or as she later said, "The air wouldn't come in." This experience, so radically outside and before discourse, is all of ours in some less obvious way. What does Mariah know about breathing? About her connection to the place she is in? What might any of us know if we paid attention to the way the places we are in *produce* us, enliven us, by crossing the border of our bodies?

Is there something "sublime" about Mariah's experience? Does the terror that gives way to pleasure when the earth fills her with breath teach us something about the earth as "the very quintessence of the human condition?" (Arendt, 1958, 2). Does it teach us something about how we are tied to place? Is freedom what this realm of bare necessity *produces* as it produces *us*? Could these connections with, rather than emancipation from, the realm of bare necessity be a different sort of sublime? Mariah's experience shows us at least that both bodies and language *would be nowhere at all* without place.

We in the Euro-masculinist cultures of the West have misunderstood our dependence on the earth as a kind of coercion and have responded by doing battle. We have not wanted to be "on nature's leading strings," so what we have made of our dependence is an ethical, social, and political disaster. We have failed the moral and political challenge of our *status as children* in relation to the earth. This is, of course, a status that is not analogous to that of actual young people vis-à-vis their parents because this moral relation demands care *from us* rather than simply for us. By this I mean we have failed to respond in a situation of dependence with care, both for the earth itself and for one another. When we claim, "I, too, am given life by this earth," this claim calls for an ethics and a politics of care that is both place-focused and intersubjective. Our response has been, instead, one of domination—against one another, but ultimately also against the places that sustain us. This means that we have failed to protect the relationship that is the very founding condition of our capacities for care, and of our world-making activity.

The earth has a claim on us, and this claim is on the very inside of our existence as subjects, of our capacities for language, and of the worlds that we make. What Thoreau called "intelligence with the earth" (cited in Casey 1993, 245) is only possible on the basis of reverence for the earth. Indeed our *irreverence* toward the earth has resulted in nothing less than environmental depravity. An "ethics and politics with the earth" requires first a wonder-filled recognition of our utter and absolute dependence in relation to it.

The entire project of contemporary feminism, as for any liberatory movement, is bound up with the *question of freedom*, which is in turn bound up with the *question of necessity*—and these are both bound to a political problem of incomprehensible proportions. Today, the "problem of nature" for feminists across the globe cannot be reduced to the problem of having been ascribed "a nature" or having been relegated to the realm of nature—the urgency of redirecting our wanton destructiveness in relation to nature means that "the problem of nature" is also, and perhaps most fundamentally the problem of how to *live this relation.*

As feminists turn toward an emphatic affirmation of the sociality of human existence and call for a reorientation of ethical and political life in terms of these relations, the ecology of human existence must be affirmed as well. The sublime that Freeman describes is one that throws the subject *into a relation with the Other*, that undoes the certainties the sovereign subject tends to walk around with. Kittay finds the very foundation for ethics in relations of dependency and refuses to entertain a fantasy that these relations are ultimately *optional*. And Butler calls for a reorientation of our collective political lives based in an acute consciousness of our own and others' embodied vulnerability to injury. These relations and their vulnerabilities are all nested in an ecological relation and an ecological vulnerability that both defines the connection between persons and places and is constitutive of our relations with one another.

It is the notion of *reorientation* that is provocative in our consideration of the possibility of kinds of sublime experience that feminists might want to affirm. As much as our intellectual and political apparatuses alienate us from connections with other persons and places under conditions of postmodernity, we are also confronted with powerful experiences that lay bare these same relations, which, after all, make us what we are. In fact, contemporary life seems to *require* such experiences to tear open the sealed narratives of autonomy and sovereignty at the heart of Euro-masculinist culture. I am suggesting that certain kinds of sublime experience are both rooted in and disclosive of our relations of dependency on other persons and on places, of our vulnerability and injurability in these relations, and of the injurability of others. In this sense, then, the sublime is a source and a resource for feminists calling for a radical reorientation of our ethical and political lives.

In what follows, I describe two sorts of sublime experience that often do tear open the sealed worlds that tend to mark our contemporary life. The first I call "the liberatory sublime." It is at home in the realm of the political, and the relations that it lays bare are intersubjective relations. The liberatory sublime shows us that the notions most central to feminist practice, notions like "women" and "liberation," are indeed unmade in the tensions between women whose lives are marked by deeply significant material and symbolic differences. But this very unmaking is at the same moment a remaking that both discloses and alters our relationships to one another.

I call the second experience "the natural sublime." It is at home in the realm of necessity, and the relations that it discloses are ecological. Here the boundary between the beautiful and the sublime is undone in the face of contemporary environmental destruction so that it is often the very experience of the beautiful that throws us into a terrifying and exhilarating awareness of our dependence on the earth. I find that these experiences run against the grain of other postmodern accounts of the sublime, since what is disclosed in both cases is a superabundance of meaning that overflows the limits of our representations rather than emptying them.

8

The Liberatory Sublime

In a brilliant little essay tucked away in the midst of chapter 2 of *The Life of the Mind*, Hannah Arendt recalls Plato's telling of the story of the Thracian peasant girl "who bursts out laughing when she sees Thales fall into a well while he watches the motions of the heavenly bodies above him. The girl declared that while Thales 'was eager to know the things in the sky . . . what was . . . just at his feet escaped him'" (1971, 82). Plato warns that anyone who commits himself to a life of philosophy will be the object of such ridicule and that "the whole rabble will join the peasant girl in laughing at him" (82). Arendt, apparently identifying for a moment with both the girl and the rabble, pokes good-natured fun at Plato for being so indignant about such laughter. She points out that, in fact, what she calls the "warfare" between the philosopher's thought and the peasant girl's common sense is "intramural," meaning an internal struggle of the philosopher himself, since even philosophers possess common sense, though perhaps in a degraded form. She claims that the "traditional persecution mania of the philosopher" is a kind of paranoid projection that emanates from the inevitable tension in a philosophical life, "since surely the first to be aware of all the objections common sense could raise against philosophy must have been the philosophers themselves" (82).

I like Arendt's telling of the story of the peasant girl and the philosopher for a number of reasons. She puts on the table a gendered story of the humbling of philosophy by common sense, drawing on the canonical association of women with the world of sense and men with the world of reason, but reconfigures philosophy in the process. The philosopher is now responsible to and for *both* thought and common sense. What is powerful in Arendt's account is that the peasant girl's laughter is affirmed as essential to the practice of philosophy, as central to the life of the philosopher himself, and certainly, as we see in the example of Arendt's own life, to the philosopher *herself*, as well. I want to suggest that the movement between thought and common sense is at the heart of the experience of the liberatory sublime, which is at work in feminist thinking and practice. This sublime experience is a *counter*sublime in the sense that the subject of this experience, far from retreating into a fantasy of autonomy and mastery, or into the consoling idea of a random play of signifiers that leaves an abyss between the subject and the other, is thrown *into relation* with the other through the experience. The relation that is laid bare does not defy representation by emptying language of meaning, but by overflowing its boundaries.

Thinking set free from common sense is, Arendt notes, "somehow self-destructive." "The business of thinking is like Penelope's web," she writes, "it undoes every morning what it has finished the night before" (1971, 88). Common sense, by contrast, is more stubborn. Arendt refers to common sense as a "sixth sense that fits our five senses into a common world," which is to say that common sense is, for Arendt, a faculty of perception. Common sense is, then, a *kind of sense*, that is, it belongs to the prereflective realm of the body-subject. Arendt is so taken with Kant's *Critique of Judgment* because Kant has discovered "something nonsubjective in what seems to be the most private and subjective sense" (1992, 67). Judgments of taste are always about the presence of others, never merely egotistical, which means that they bring us down to earth since "I judge as a member of a community, never as a member of a supersensible world" (67). Arendt's common sense world is the spatiotemporal particularity of the everyday in which we are immersed when not engaged in speculative thinking. In fact even as thinking's striving after universals "annihilates temporal as well as spatial distances," in Arendt's words (1971, 85), common sense restores them. "While thinking I am not where I actually am," Arendt writes, "I am surrounded not by sense objects but by images that are invisible to everybody else. It is as if I had withdrawn into some never-never land, the land of invisibles" (85). Common sense, by contrast, is embedded in the particularities of place.

Which leads me to emphasize that Thales doesn't fall into just any hole, but this particular one, and he falls into the drinking water as well. The well belongs to place, it is a feature of a landscape, and of a community. Common sense is the capacity that engages us immediately in the particularities of *this* place, in which this well provides water for *these* people, who are, no doubt, not so happy about Thales swimming around in it. For Arendt, "the nonsubjective element in the nonobjective senses is intersubjectivity" (1992, 67), which means, in this case, that a tumble into the well throws one immediately into relation with one's neighbors, who are sure to have something to say about it.

Nature and the social meet at places like wells, where depth, gravity, and water provide for people, who also tend to congregate there to talk. Thales's fall into the well reminds him of the spatiality of the place that sustains him, but also of the social world he inhabits; this is his drinking water too. It relocates him from the never-never land of invisibles, as a person among others, with a common interest in keeping the well clean, and himself out of it. And it reminds him of the sometimes playful resistance of the particularities of the material world to a philosophical life focused on the stars.

Here in Arendt's essay, we find a tension and a relation between the particularity of place and the universalizing propensity of thought, between the commonsense anchoring of a life in space and time and the speculative annihilation of space and time, and between the realm of necessity in which bodies are subject to gravity and fall into wells and the realm of freedom in which minds fantasize themselves as independent. These three: particularity and universality, spatiotemporal specificity and its annihilation, and necessity and freedom are really three names for the same relation, or three dimensions of the same problem. What is important about Arendt's essay is that she binds these usually dichotomous terms together in a relation and a movement. *The prereflective spatiotemporal moorings that common sense provides are not only a challenge to thought but also an opening for thought, an opening onto the immediate lived situation of a body-subject.* The girl's laughter is the philosopher's chance to think that situation.

The girl's laughter is also, particularly after the linguistic turn in feminist theory, the *feminist* philosopher's chance to think the immediate lived situations *of women.* For the association of women with things like water and wells, and men with the heavens and the stars, however old and still pervasive, provides no protection once women claim the title of philosopher and enter into the mainstream philosophical debates of our day. It is perhaps a misfortune of our success that along with this claiming and this participation we inherit the philosopher's tendency to fall into wells while gazing at the stars, which is to say we inherit the Western philosopher's propensity for a kind of idealism that has historically assigned the world of sense to those not capable of philosophy, that is, women. Now that women are doing what we are not capable of, the world of sense, the material and the natural, threatens to vanish altogether.

Epistemology: Feminist Thinking and Feminist Common Sense

The tendency to tumble into the drinking water becomes epidemic after the linguistic turn. And this even though after, as before, the majority of the world's women live strikingly material lives, lives that neither lend themselves to flights of textual *jouissance* nor find easy expression in a cynical postmodern pastiche. This is only to say that many women continue to live under conditions of grinding poverty and/or epidemic levels of gender-based violence and/or environmental destruction so profound that access to clean air, safe water, decent food, and nontoxic fuel is becoming a problem for *all* of us (unequally). (It might overburden an academic text like this one to connect Arendt's metaphor of the woman at the well with the mundane statistics about how far many of the world's women must carry water everyday, especially after structural adjustment programs that privatize local water sources.) Feminism in all its local manifestations is about the women who are living these lives. And if feminist thinking/speaking/writing does not speak *of* or *to* the emancipatory aspirations of some women somewhere, living in the face of some circumstance of drudgery or domination, we hardly need bother to call it feminist at all. An initially discursive endeavor, like the deconstruction of metanarratives, is feminist only to the extent that it exceeds itself as a project in discourse and spills over into the entire project of women's liberation. When it becomes a project-in-itself, it becomes mere know-how, a showing off rather than *showing up* for the emancipation of women. When our skill in unraveling language takes precedence over any sense of what that unraveling might be for, when the unraveling of thought becomes the point of thinking, then thinking is uprooted from living and becomes a mere technology.

And here I am indebted again to Hannah Arendt, for part of what I am calling for is simply that we "think what we are doing" (Arendt 1958, 5) when we deconstruct metanarratives. Arendt's dual insights—that Cartesianism moved the Archimedean point "into man himself" (284) and left his mind playing with itself (284) and that the rise of modern science is marked at the same time by the ascendancy of technical capacity *to do*, which has completely overrun our understanding of what we are doing (thinking has become a mere "handmaiden of doing" [292])—are helpful in understanding our fascination with the technologies of postmodern theory. If the claim that postmodernity is marked by a kind of inwardness turned outward, a kind of mentalism become context, has any efficacy, then the postmodern Archimedean point itself agitates over the abyss. The unraveling of thought becomes the point of thinking, conducted from an "Archimedean point" that takes these moments of unraveling themselves to be the central point of reference.

Which is not to say, of course, that philosophical thought can or should be jettisoned from the feminist project simply because it tends to undo everything it has just done. The movement of unraveling at the heart of philosophical thought is at the very heart, as well, of all feminist epistemology worthy of the name. There is, then, *an aesthetic experience of the sublime* that is and should be at the very center of feminist philosophy. There is an aesthetic that disrupts and defies the conceptual, the juridical, in feminist thinking.

This becomes clear when we note, as postmodern thinkers have done, that when feminist thinkers approach such notions as "woman," "nature," or "liberation," we are never able to finally grasp them or pin them down. But whereas current trends would have us conclude that these terms are therefore *empty*, masking a perfect *absence* of content, within the context of feminist practice these notions behave much more like inexhaustible wells of meaning than like empty concepts. Each of our efforts to turn them into concepts, useful in a particular situation, necessary in a local context, fails at another level because their meaning in the material world *overflows* the boundaries we have set in the process of definition. "Women," for example, always ends up meaning something more than we have imagined. When Wittig wrote, "Lesbians are not women," she did not expose the emptiness of the category "women." The violence of this sentence is that it bursts the boundaries of the category because, of course, lesbians *are* women, and the sentence would have no power at all if we weren't. The meaning of "women" overflows the (shattered) category "women." Similarly, critiques by women of color about white-race- and middle-class-bound uses of the term "women" don't empty it of meaning, but expose the concept-as-it-is-used as incapable of containing the lived meaning of "women."

There is an aesthetics to this experience. The failure takes the form of the sublime, of an approach to a limit, a glimpse or a feeling of what is beyond the limit, the intense displeasure of the failure of thought to conceptualize feminism's central notions, and the intense pleasure of a meaning that emerges at crucial moments, in spite of (or through?) thought's failure, that can be experienced, and even *practiced*, but not grasped, not *exhausted*. If a certain understanding of the sublime has emerged after the linguistic turn as a new "good" for feminism, as I have argued, and dis-placed the *feminism* in feminist intellectual practice, it is not, despite its masculinist history, simply as an external, hostile, masculinist notion that has invaded feminist thinking from the outside. It has emerged on the very inside of feminist thinking, as a key experience at the very heart of the practice of feminism itself. The trouble is, we have taken up this experience within an *inherited masculinist framework* that habitually and obsessively elevates thinking at the expense of the material. All the more urgent then, to take up the notion and the experience explicitly, to trace its masculinist genealogy. But it is even more urgent to begin to think the experience *on feminist terms*.

Because the sublime emerges in feminism in the course of feminist thinkers thinking the central notions of feminism (and not initially as an issue in art, for example) we take up the question of a feminist sublime, first, as a question of feminist epistemology. The question of the sublime in feminism is a question of a complex aesthetics of knowing that we live and experience in feminist intellectual and political practice, particularly when that practice spans "differences," that is, becomes cross-cultural or transnational or crosses classes or sexualities.

Consciousness Raising/Razing: Thinking and Common Sense

It was Catharine MacKinnon who most explicitly and exquisitely claimed consciousness raising as feminist method (MacKinnon 1989, 106–25). What is this term "consciousness raising" that, at least in English (as opposed to the Portuguese *concientizacao*, for example, or the Spanish, *"tomar conciencia"*), has been so central to the development of feminism in English? What does it mean for a consciousness to be "raised"? Raised above what? The body? The lived situation? Why raised rather than, say, "animated," or some less spatial term? Why raised rather than "razed" since the development of feminist consciousness certainly involves the "razing" of whole systems of thinking, of the entire *commonsense world* that has grown up around masculinist domination and women's subordination.

And isn't this the reason that Simone de Beauvoir's earth-shattering sentence, "One is not born, but rather becomes a woman," has become such a legendary one? Here an entire commonsense world clustered around the natural category "woman" is unmade. "Woman" is deconstructed as a natural category and reconstructed as a social category all in one blow. There is an extraordinary movement in the sentence, a movement from necessity to freedom that historically spills from the page into women's lives in country after country, language after language, where discursive acuity points immediately to lived possibility.

A commonsense world is *razed*. If Arendt's Thracian peasant girl is at home in a kind of everyday common sense, feminists philosophers, by contrast, have been at home in its unraveling. Judith Butler uses the term "common sense" in a single passage in *Contingency, Hegemony, Universality*; she writes, "[p]ower is not stable or static, but is remade at various junctures within everyday life; it constitutes our tenuous sense *of common sense*, and is ensconced as the prevailing epistemes of a culture" (2000, 14, emphasis added). Certainly, it is these prevailing epistemes that feminist thinking is in the business of deconstructing and disrupting; it is power ensconced in common sense that is at stake.

So if feminist consciousness is "raised" above something, it is raised above the commonsense world it has just "razed" to the ground. It is "raised" above an everyday experience of the naturalness of certain relations of power, certain forms of authority, certain curtailments of expectations, certain corporeal habits. Feminist consciousness is raised then, above certain aspects of everydayness, certain kinds of spatiotemporal immersion in an immediate lived situation.

The aesthetics of this experience are sublime every bit as much as more classic experiences of terror-exhilaration, of necessity giving way to freedom, of an approach to a limit and a feeling for something beyond it. It is the experience of "consciousness raising" that suddenly breaks open and reorganizes an epistemic system, on feminist terms.

But if this feminist sublime disrupts, unravels, fragments, unlike the masculinist sublime, it is not exhausted in the lightning strike that razes the common sense of masculinist privilege. Another common sense emerges even before the ashes have cooled. Beauvoir deconstructed woman as a natural category, but a commonsense notion of "woman" emerges *within the very same sentence*, as a social category. Wittig's bold claim that "Lesbians are not women" forces a new sense of the word "women" and the word "lesbian" into the language we share. The criticisms of feminists of color about the falsely universalist deployment of "women" immediately reconstructs the term as a not-seamless, not-simple term that *we are all then called on to recognize, to share, or to contest.* The efficacy of the critiques is only evidenced in their ability to immediately become a kind of common sense, at least as a ground of contestation, at times as a genuine shared political commitment. It is this second common sense, a common sense that emerges between us, a sense that "fits us" (however uncomfortably) into a common world that is just emerging, that deeply fascinated Arendt, whereas Butler's common sense is clearly the one we are in the business of undoing. The sublime in feminist consciousness raising is the movement between Butler's common sense and Arendt's.

It is the second moment of this movement that is resisted in postmodernist accounts that are giddy with the *technology* of thinking. The conceptual impossibility of pinning down, of mastering the notions that are central to feminist practice ("women," "liberation," etc.), is taken to indicate the emptiness of the terms themselves, which can then be invested with multiple meanings at will. When thought fantasizes its complete liberation from common sense, this is, as Arendt reminds us, precisely what tends to happen.

But feminist common sense emerges in feminist practice and feminist thinking, even as it also unravels. Indeed, what is *feminist* about feminist thinking is (in large part) its resistance to the abjection of the material, of the spatiotemporal, the specific—or to put it more accurately, its resistance to *what is done to women*, specific women, living specific lives in the context of forms of domination that build themselves on the abjection of the life-world itself. The notions that are central to feminist practice *do* keep reinventing themselves, in a sense, but not in a purely contingent discursive universe. They reinvent themselves in the constant movement and relation between necessity and freedom *in life*, between thought and common sense *in life*. They reinvent themselves in feminist practice and become both the dividing lines and the unifying common orientations that make feminist practice meaningful.

From Epistemology to Politics

This means, then, that the experience of the sublime that I am calling "feminist," which I am acknowledging at the heart of feminist thinking, is not an experience that is bound by thinking, contained by thinking. What makes feminist thinking feminist, in part, is its spilling over into life, into the realm of the practical. And part of what spills thinking over into practice is sublime experience itself, an experience that, in its feminist version, may be said not only to approach the limits of conceptual thought but also to flow, to move, against them; even, eventually, to wear them out.

What is startling about the linguistic turn, to a feminist sensibility, is the degree to which theorists and theory have become forgetful of women, not the term "women," but living women. What grates against a feminist sensibility is the degree to which living women have become irrelevant to theories about "women" absorbed in the world of signs. Yet this "gap" between theory and life is not without its structural determinants *in life*. I have argued that the turn toward what we now recognize to be a masculinist version of sublime experience in postmodernity is a symptom of the way we, in the so-called developed world, live now—of a fragmented, technologized existence, carried out at a dizzying pace across impossible distances. It is a symptom of a loss of place, an apparently final mastery of distance, a paradoxical mastery of and enslavement by time. It is also, in feminist thinking, a symptom of the structural constraints of academic life, in which the production of theory seems to become an end in itself but is actually a way for some of us to keep our jobs. These "symptoms," like all good symptoms, make sense on a certain level. The masculinist version of the sublime really does describe a key aesthetic experience of terror and exhilaration that characterizes our material predicament. It is expressive of an ineffable postmodern "freedom" gained at the historical moment of the apparent completion of the Euro-masculinist project of domination over the natural, of the apparent success of the effort to "free" the human from the bounds of the natural, of the earth, of the *necessary*. It is at the same time expressive of a repressed relation to that very realm, most concretely in the way that the production of theory and academic employment, which, let's not kid ourselves, is a kind of livelihood, are connected.

As Fredric Jameson reminds us in passages already cited, this "freedom," and its electronic accoutrement, mask the relationships *between persons* that are its condition of necessity. It is a Marxist point that seems out of place and, precisely for that reason, merits our close attention. To cite the key passage again: "Indeed, the point of having your own object world and walls and muffled distance or relative silence all around you, is to forget about all those innumerable others for a while" (Jameson 1991, 315). The fixed camera view cultivated by the owners of the *maquiladoras* on the Mexican/U.S. border keeps the relationships of women there to the consumers of their products out of view, keeps the focus on daily wages and bathroom privileges and working faster. The key components of a postmodern life—the cell phones, the computers that store the fragments of lives lived on the model of collage at an impossibly accelerated pace, the palm pilots, the TVs with hundreds of stations to choose from and infallible remote control, the automobiles, the microchips implanted in the family dog—conceal *relationships*. Someone made them. (Someone who is not likely to own them.) They are the dead evidence of living relationships of the most base sort of exploitation.

And they are the evidence of such relationships between women, to make the feminist point, who also live the disjuncture Jameson describes between the phenomenology of daily life experience and the structural truth of that experience. The "fixed camera view" of an academic in the United States keeps the relationships that she is entangled in out of view, relationships, after all, that are with women in Mexico and Singapore and Indonesia and other impossibly distant places. Those of us in the North, feminists included of course, live in a kind of perpetual ignorance about the most basic structural "truths" of our daily lives. It would be a research project of enormous proportions to discover where the food that we eat, over the course of one day, comes from and what chemicals are used to grow it and who produced them at what profit, what the source of pollutants are in the air that we breath, how the water that we drink gets to us, and what political and economic circumstances made a particular tank of gas available to us at the price that we paid for it—and who *suffers* for all of this. But each object in our "object" world is teeming with relationships with other people in other places around the globe (and with other people locally who are almost as profoundly "absent" as those more distant).

The "disjuncture" that keeps these relationships invisible, however, is not the final truth of the matter either. What is the point of the massive demonstrations and international resistance to globalization, after all, if not precisely to force into visibility the interrelatedness of profit and suffering, abundance and scarcity, privilege and privation, across the globe? What is the point of studying the paths traveled by food, water, air, and fuel, as many have begun to do, if it is not to refuse the "fixed camera view" that we are bound by? Why not remain, as most do, enthralled by the speed of a life endlessly mediated by electronic gadgets, big screens, and the minute-to-minute conquest of distance? Why not settle for the more or less exhilarating experience of the electronically magnified individual subject? Why care at all about the relationships that are evidenced in the object worlds we inhabit? Which is to say, why care at all, *about the persons* who are on the other end of those relationships? After the linguistic turn, this question is not so much ignored, it simply becomes unintelligible.

The Liberatory Sublime

If postmodern theory is expressive of postmodern experience, is a kind of refracted reflection of a structural truth, then breaking out of Jameson's "fixed camera view" is a formidable task. If our very experiences of space and time tend toward fragmenting and obscuring the relationships with others that enable those experiences, then the "unintelligibility" of our myriad and complex relationships to others is not merely a kind of moral mistake that we each make individually, over and over again. We are sealed within our own view by the moment-to-moment patterns and habits, movements and practices, that make up daily life. (For a feminist academic in the North, for example, I turn on the computer, I check my email, I pick up my cell phone, I board the plane to the conference where others who turn on their computers, check their email, and pick up their cell phones will also arrive by plane and take taxis driven by undocumented workers from El Salvador; we will eat Thai food together between sessions and order coffee produced in Nicaragua.) There is a *common sense* about such a life that sediments and hardens, that stiffens into "the real," that reflects and explains itself to itself endlessly, minutely. Others are functionalized in this commonsense world (the ones who made the gadgets, who prepared the food); they don't enter my world as persons, but as *functions*. This is a commonsense world that lacks an opening onto *an outside*, that is a continual self-referring and self-reflecting. This world is impermeable by other *persons*, by other *women*.

This is what Enrique Dussel must have meant by his powerful criticism of phenomenology. "What are phenomenology and existentialism," he asks, "if not the description of an 'I' as a *Dasein* which opens a world, *always one's own*" (1985, 8, emphasis added). For Dussel, an exiled Argentinian-born, European-trained philosopher of the Latin American liberation tradition, the confrontation with phenomenology and existentialism goes to the very heart of history and geopolitics, the very heart of the meaning of the colonization/exploitation of Latin America by Europe and the United States. Dussel's problem is precisely how to reanimate the "person to person relation" across *worlds*, that is, across the frontiers of power that mark geopolitics. If phenomenology always opens *one's own* world for the European, then the presence of an other in that world will always be a functionalized presence (some worker made this computer, *for me*; some worker built my car, *for me*.) The world opened by a particular person is not a simple world, it has its own complex ontology, but it is a sealed world, admitting of no genuine, irreducible exteriority. For Dussel, reanimating the person-to-person relation requires an opening onto the *trans-ontological*, that is, requires that one world break open in relation to another, that the "I" at the center of the Euro-masculine self-experience (which has never been exclusively the province of men) be radically decentered in an encounter with a person who is genuinely outside of that world *as a person*, though she may well be very much on the inside of that world *as a function*.

Dussel believes that phenomenology, opening as it does the "my-worlds" that philosophers of the North find so compelling, is incapable of opening a transontological space in which a person-to-person relationship can thrive across geopolitical boundaries. The only thing strong enough to break open the sealed worlds of the North is "epiphany." Dussel draws the term "epiphany" self-consciously out of the Christian tradition. If the sealed worlds of the North are to be opened, something like an overwhelming religious experience is called for. We in the North experience other persons so habitually as functions that a bolt of lightning or a burning bush will be required to create an opening toward other persons *as persons*.

Dussel's criticism of phenomenology is compelling in this context for a number of reasons. His understanding of the phenomenological "opening" as an opening onto a world centered on the privileged "I" echoes some of the deepest insights of Western feminism regarding masculinist theology, philosophy, and science. Irigaray's claim that the male philosophers (to give what is perhaps the most obvious example), even when writing explicitly about women, are actually writing about themselves projected onto a screen of "difference" that always reduces to the same is very much in keeping with Dussel's work here.[1] For Dussel, the totalizing systems of Eurocentric philosophy engage, temporally and spatially, in an "insatiable cannibalism" (Dussel 1985, 49). "Face to face proximity with another person disappears," he writes, "because the fetish eats its mother, its children, its siblings" (49). An "ontology" is, for Dussel, the result of the inwardness, in the case of Europe the cannibalistic inwardness, that constitutes my-world. What makes Dussel's particular approach important for the current inquiry is his concern with geopolitics, that is, his concern *for place* in the most literal, most political sense.

In a feminist context, the intractability of men's self-involvement, particularly in the cultural and historical works of great "wisdom" we study in the West/North, but also in politics and life, has been a constant source of feminist frustration and analysis. The experience of coming up against the sealed boundary of these worlds is perhaps one of the most basic experiences that contributes to feminist consciousness raising and feminist militancy. It seems that an act of (symbolic? political?) violence is needed to tear open the boundary of an entire world, of an entire *ontology*, lived and (re)constructed with the masculine "I" at the center. Decentering the masculine I, opening this sealed world to difference in any genuine sense, requires the radical unraveling of its epistemes, but also a moment of shocking, awe-inspiring *epiphany*—an epiphany that shifts the center so completely as to bring the whole edifice down.

But for feminists of the North, this early insight was complicated by our position vis-à-vis one another locally; the worlds that opened in consciousness raising were generally "always our own," that is, closed to the irreducible differences of race, sexuality, ability, and so on. It was also complicated by our position *geopolitically* as we lived the daily structures, the habits and patterns, produced in an international context of exploitation. Those of us who existed on the outside, in one way or another, of the world that sealed itself around what was taken to be "mainstream feminism" came crashing against that same sealed boundary, a still-circumscribed world opened with the emergent "I" of feminist thinking and practice at the center. What was required to tear open *that* sealed world, what is still required, is at the level of Dussel's "epiphany." And criticism of the closed world of mainstream feminist thinking has been a burning bush, and sometimes a lightning bolt, has razed the prevailing epistemes that kept the experience of certain women at the center.

There is, of course, an aesthetics to this experience. A *liberatory sublime*, in the context of feminist politics, is the experience that pushes one to the limit of a closed

---

1. This insight runs through Irigaray's work to such an extent that it hardly seems necessary to cite a specific text here. The first text in which this insight was developed fully was *Speculum of the Other Woman*.

"I-centered" world, an assault on the boundary that seals it, or a glimpse (from the inside) over that boundary to an exteriority that will not be reduced to the same. It is the feminist assault on masculinist politics and policies that insists on a woman's standing *as a person* rather than *as a function* in a masculinist system (of law, of government). And it is the opening of a transontological space between women, the refusal of the "gap" between phenomenological experience and its structural truths, the refusal of a reality sealed off to the other by the intervention of clever gadgets. It is the ability to push against the boundary of one's own "I-centered" world, to tear the lining, to spill the contents of that world out into a transontological space where other women appear *as women* rather than as mere functions. If there is a liberatory sublime experience, it is in the moment when we are, in Butler's words, undone by each other. Others break open our worlds from the inside (where they exist as functions, but functions that haunt us) and give us a pathway to what is outside of not only our "worlds" as individual subjects but our cultural, social, and political worlds as well. The liberatory sublime is the unconceptualizable *living* of this space between.

A Common Place

After the linguistic turn, the burning bushes are taken as signs of the emptiness of the category of "women" but also as signs of the emptiness of the feminist political project in general, which like it or not depends on those categories. The *burning itself* is celebrated as the one worthwhile thing, as the proof that *there is no transontological space/place* in which a new common sense might emerge. There is a proliferation of sealed interiorities (Lyotard's language games, Kipnis's private languages, Butler's chains of signification) without exteriority.

Dussel's philosophy of liberation is hopeful, even utopian, because it insists on the viability of the transontological. "Others reveal themselves as others in all the acuteness of their exteriority," Dussel writes, "when they burst in upon us as something extremely distinct" (1985, 43). Freedom is the opening of an ontology that misunderstood itself to be closed and complete. In Dussel's epiphany—and this is what distinguishes it from the postmodern—I recuperate a sense of reality in regard to the other.

The sense of reality I recuperate in this epiphany is very much a *common sense*, as it fits my five independent senses into a "transontological" meaningfulness. If we understand "ontology" in Dussel's sense, as the inwardness of a world that has no place for the *ontology* of the other, what is "common" in the "common sense" of epiphany is that it *transverses* the boundary between my ontology and the ontology of the other. The common sense internal to a world is thus unraveled and rebuilt *politically*, as a political space *between* worlds.[2]

Feminist politics has to do most fundamentally with an insistence on the reality of women as persons that breaks open the other's world and spills them into

---

2. The resonance with Hannah Arendt's work on political "spaces of appearance" should be apparent here, though I would want to expand that notion to include all kinds of political practice that are not necessarily focused on speech, as Arendt's notion is.

this political space between. It has to do with a sense of the reality of the other's world breaking in upon my world, breaking open that world and spilling me out into the space between. Out of an experience of what we describe aesthetically as the liberatory sublime emerges this between, *which is also the common*, this space, which is an open space, where men and women, and women and women, face one another *as persons rather than functions.*

Feminist practice then, is not reducible to the sum of a set of localized concerns about women. It is not reducible to a haphazard list of women's experiences here and there (as in so many feminist anthologies of the 1990s!). Feminism manifests itself in particular times and places but cannot be contained in them because it contributes to the continual emergence of the space or ground *between women*, between persons. And this space between calls us to account not for some clever ideas about gender but for how we live in relation to one another. Feminism is nothing more or less than an impulse to justice in this lived relation.

The liberatory sublime is the aesthetic experience of the opening of worlds onto a space between, in which the claims of one woman on another, of one person on another, can be heard and lived. It is the aesthetic experience of the other's presence as a person that interrupts the comfort of a world organized to reduce other persons (women in relation to men, women in relation to one another) to mere functions. Sublime experience is *orienting* for feminism because it breaks open a space for feminist practice across all kinds of differences. And if that space is a ground of fierce contestation, then it is also a common ground, a ground on which we are called to give an account of how we live, think, and work in relation to one another.

The liberatory sublime orients us toward our own but also the other's freedom in the realm of the political. It is the other's freedom, in fact, that is disclosed to me in the sublime experience that shatters the borders of my circumscribed world. It is my own freedom that is disclosed to me in the epiphany of feminist consciousness raising. Feminists need an account of sublime experience in the realm of the political because we need an account of *what orients us toward freedom from domination*, of what orients feminist practice toward liberation. If "Women's Liberation" became an anachronism after the linguistic turn, it is simply because *we gave up on one another*. We accepted the sealed boundaries of the worlds we inhabit and made those boundaries into the very terms and conditions of feminist thinking. Within those boundaries we were, indeed, already free: free to imagine any meaning at all, any content at all, as feminist. And we were free from one another, free from the space between worlds that both calls us to account for how we live in relation to one another and makes a project like "Women's Liberation" meaningful. But the sealed worlds break open, over and over again, the space between reasserts itself, and feminism, if it is to be a viable movement at all, will (re)orient itself, again and again, in place after place and time after time.

9

The Natural Sublime

As I labored over the final revisions of this book, Hurricane Katrina made land on the Gulf Coast of the United States. Along with the rest of you, I watched hours of television coverage, horrified at the loss of life and place, but even more horrified at the willingness of the federal government to abandon the stranded (pre-dominantly African American) residents of New Orleans to the flood waters. The latest news is that folks who simply tried to walk away were met at the borders of the ruined city by armed guards ordering them back into the flood.[1] The entire complex of events has finally dispelled any remaining fantasies we might have entertained about progress on questions of racial justice in the United States. Scene after scene of black Americans without food or water for days, of bodies left to decompose in the watery streets, of the interminable wait for relief that took too long to come exposed the fact that many died of the waiting rather than of Katrina herself. Which is to say that many died, and many more are suffering, not so much from the ravages of wind and water as from the ravages of the federal government's failure to *care*, or to care *enough*. It is only public outrage and the threat of political disaster that have finally mobilized the resources of the richest nation on earth so that the most basic necessities—water, food, shelter, and physical safety—get to those who were first abandoned, then imprisoned at gunpoint, and finally evacuated from the places that Katrina took with her.

It is not unusual for an event in nature to expose political injustice, of course. When humans are displaced by earthquakes, tsunamis, volcanoes, or hurricanes, when we find ourselves literally at the mercy of the earth, we also find ourselves at the mercy of one another. I have already argued that we can trace political urgency back to the realm of necessity, in the sense that it is our embodied lives that both

---

1. "Hurricane Katrina: Our Experiences," by Larry Bradshaw and Lorrie Beth Slonsky at www .notinourname.net/war/Katrina-exp; Sept. 5, 2005.

make us vulnerable to want and suffering and make us capable of freedom, and it is our capacity for freedom that makes it possible to build a world in which we can meet "our collective responsibility for the physical lives of one another" (*PL* 2004, 30). The dominant traditions of the Euro-masculinist West have understood the realm of necessity and the realm of freedom to be radically distinct, in fact they have understood the very possibility of freedom to emerge only when the human is decisively set apart from the natural. Events like Katrina bring home to us the impossibility of that fantasy.

Events like Katrina also seem to give the lie to accounts of the natural world that see "nature" as one more linguistic convention or cultural formation. Who could argue, in the face of a hurricane, that nature is what we make of it? Here, when we refer to nature, we refer much more to what it makes of us. The extra-discursivity of nature keeps pushing back against the contemporary tendency to reduce it to an accomplishment of language. Indeed, as Kate Soper has noted, "it is not language that has a hole in its ozone layer" (1995, 151), and perhaps we should add, it is not language that flooded New Orleans, not this time.

But in saying this, I have not said nearly enough, because of course there is a sense in which even the nature that produced Katrina *is* a cultural formation. In other words, the fantasy of nature as a human construction is not *mere* fantasy. Our creations have changed our relationship to the natural world and are changing nature itself, in often terrifying ways. As scientists have long warned, the increased intensity of today's weather phenomena is yet another effect of global warming. If claims that Katrina got her power (transforming from a category 1 hurricane into a category 5, then receding back to a 4) from the too-warm waters of the Gulf are correct, then nature is, even at its most violent, in some sense *also* what we are making of it. "In our own time," Soper cautions, "the human impact on the environment has been so extensive that there is an important sense in which it is correct to speak of 'nature' as itself a cultural product or construction" (152). The horror of an event like Katrina throws us into the tension between the reality that we have, in very significant respects, re-created nature and the reality that this re-creation has never, in spite of our fantasies to the contrary, been under our control.

Yet every aspect of our dependence on the natural world is plagued by the Euro-masculinist project of sovereignty. A more mundane example than that of Katrina illustrates this point as well: we can understand the invention and prolif-eration of the automobile as an effort to master distance and save time. Yet the centrality of the automobile in postmodern life has fouled the air that we breathe to such an extent that children in every major metropolitan area of the United States suffer epidemic levels of asthma and other kinds of respiratory distress. We might point to example after example of ways in which the *project of mastery* over the natural world has spun out of control and turned back not only on the masters but on everyone else as well. Of course when this "return" happens in the form of a hurricane like Katrina, it is, or should be, terrifying to all of us.

While I don't want to imply that Hurricane Katrina was primarily an aesthetic experience, either for those in it or for those of us watching the scenes on TV, there is a sense in which such events can evoke the sublime. When Kant said that the sublime is occasioned by "bold, overhanging, . . . threatening thunderclouds piled up in the vault of heaven, borne along with flashes and peals, volcanoes in all their violence of destruction, hurricanes leaving desolation in their track, the boundless ocean rising with rebellious force, the high waterfall of some mighty river" (*CJ* 1928, 261), he also said that safety from the power of such events was essential to the experience. Such occurrences are never reducible to this or that aspect of the event: the personal and the aesthetic will emerge along with the economic and political meanings. Yet this hurricane did something that the experience of what I will call "the natural sublime" also does. If those of us watching the events from a safe distance were paying attention at all, it threw us into an acute and terrifying awareness of our dependence on the natural world, and on one another.

What I am calling the natural sublime is a powerful experience that lays bare our relation to the natural world, and it lays bare the deep entanglements of natural and intersubjective dependencies. There is no clear way, then, to assign our relations to nature to the realm of necessity, and our relations to one another to the realm of freedom. These two realms can and must be distinguished, but they can never be disentangled to the point of separation. If there is an experience of the sublime in relation to nature that feminists might want to recuperate and affirm, it is an experience, again, that exposes rather than severs relations: between persons and places, between this place and that, and between people here and people there.

The natural sublime under conditions of contemporary life is not a unitary experience, though the meanings that are given in the experience are cohesive in an important sense. We might say that it is a manifold rather than a simple experience, occasioned differently at different times and places, with different features of the experience taking precedence at different moments. In what follows, I take up various themes that seem important to a feminist understanding of sublime experience in relation to nature. If feminist thinkers wish to give an account of the sublime on other than masculinist terms, we will find ourselves recuperating the very aspects of sublime experience that are most foreclosed, repressed, denied, or triumphantly "superseded" in the masculinist stories that are told about the sublime in the dominant tradition.

Place

At the very heart of the natural sublime is place. Aesthetic experience *is* spatiotemporal experience in the sense that it is a radical experience of one's immersion in and/or displacement from the spatiotemporal. The natural sublime discloses a kind of foundation and a kind of validity in our experience of place that is not at bottom an intersubjective validity (as in the realm of the political). In fact, the natural sublime gives the lie to the fantasy of two subjects facing each other in abstract space. It discloses the "real" of subjects *enlivened* by place and teaches that the intersubjective is always in relation to place.

The natural sublime in contemporary life retains several important features of the Kantian sublime. Most important, it retains the moment of the Kantian sublime when we know ourselves to be at the mercy of the natural world. Kant described sublime experience as a confrontation with nature at its most wild and formless, its most terrifying. His descriptions of hurricanes and volcanoes, wild oceans and thundering waterfalls, towering rocks and thunderstorms evoke a nature that seemed to defy our human capacity to domesticate and control. No pastoral images here of grazing livestock, fruit trees, or fields planted in neat rows! Here we have nature terrifying to humans, terrifying to humans *in need of* nature, terrifying to humans *dependent on* nature. Yet for Kant, in the midst of an age that did indeed bring the natural world under technical control in multiple ways, the sublime was the experience of *the rupture in this relationship of dependence*, the undoing of this terror and the triumph of reason. The natural sublime in contemporary life is different in that it does not have recourse to the comfort of Kant's flight into the sanctuary of a self-aggrandizing constituting consciousness. This is a kind of sublime experience that does not disclose "man's infinite superiority" over nature, man's "destiny" to be free of nature, as the Kantian sublime did. Ironically, our very projects of mastery in relation to nature have put the consoling belief in such mastery out of reach.

From our perspective more than two centuries later, terror still has its place in our encounter with the natural world, but a place much changed, as our place vis-à-vis nature has changed. In fact, I would suggest that nature has become more terrifying to us, not less. On the one hand, the ghost of Kant's sort of terror lingers today in news stories of tsunamis and earthquakes, hurricanes and floods. We engage in a technological shoring up against the power of nature. In New Orleans, the levees will be rebuilt, and stronger this time (if funding priorities don't win out again). In California, all public employees are trained, buildings are retrofitted, and bridges are strengthened against the major earthquake that is sure to come. Active volcanoes are monitored minute by minute across the globe. Yet our projects of mastery have in many cases undercut our ability to survive the kinds of events in nature that are most threatening, as hurricane Katrina so clearly pointed out.

On the other hand, our more mundane creations are still more likely to kill us. Our intervention in nature is *producing a nature* that terrifies in much more daily and much more insidious ways. There is lead in the water coming out of the drinking fountains at our schools. Our food is poisoning us, depositing pesticides in fat tissue that later becomes cancerous or clogging our blood vessels to the point of bringing beating hearts to rest. And the fuel that we use in our daily conquest of distance and time fouls the air and the water and the earth that grows our food. A terror of what we are eating, drinking, and breathing, of the *lethality of the places* in which we live, and on which we depend, is now the mundane, daily terror that we feel in relation to nature.

Indeed, we are at the mercy of the land, and the air, and the water—and what we've made of them. We are at the mercy of the earth, and its answers to our interventions. What kind of sublime experience speaks to this contemporary terror? I would like to suggest that it is an entirely different sort of sublime than the liberatory (intersubjective) sublime, for here, it is not freedom that we experience, but the contrary. This sublime experience does not unravel our dependence on the planet but weaves it tighter, until we choke on our own mistakes. What I call here the "natural sublime" is not only, then, an experience of *terror*, of the suspense over what's to become of us. We cannot look upon waterfall or mountain, raging river or vast forest, without the *grief* associated with the question, what have we done? combining with our terror. The natural sublime orients our terror and our grief, our responsibility and our hope—our one hope, that if we save the land, the land will save us.

Here we find an admixture of terror and grief in relation to place that undoes the boundaries of the self, and undoes the fantasy of triumph over nature that has prevailed in the Euro-masculinist West for so many generations. A possible response to this experience is certainly the shoring up of the self, the reassertion of the fantasy. But if we find the courage to linger in and with both the grief and the terror, then the fantasy of sovereignty becomes empty in the face of the relations that bind us. It is the meaning of these relations, a meaning we are always discovering and making, that has the power to reorient our individual, cultural, and collective political practices.

This power of orientation is concentrated in our relation to place because it is this relation that phenomenologically and materially links the particular to the general in a way that is capable of moving us out of our sealed inwardness, our closed "my worlds." An ecological approach recognizes the sublime as an experience of a *particular* place but immediately lays bare the relation between this place and others. Places are materially particular *and* general, which is, of course, the very meaning of ecology. They are phenomenologically particular for the subjects who live in them but can link these very subjects to the general, phenomenologically, through, among other things, powerful aesthetic experiences such as the sublime.

On a very early morning hike through an oak forested state park in Northern California, I once saw a wild turkey, his tail fully fanned, step slowly through the morning mist. My breath was quite taken away by the sight, which was so exquisitely beautiful I felt a kind of pain pass through me. My mind flashed forward immediately, to a time when there would almost certainly be no such turkey, no such forest, no such soft morning mist. Every experience of nature is plagued by the terror of nonexistence, the fear that natural beauty will be forever stamped out, that our own existence, as a species, will end. We are suspended over the abyss of the impending *absence* of nature. But this suspense, in turn, gives way to exhilaration and movement. We are exhilarated: "Such beauty still exists!" "Such places are still here!" "I am here!" And we are moved, pushed beyond the particularity of place, pushed to an ecology of place, the ultimate horizon of which is the earth itself.

The play of terror and exhilaration moves us beyond this specific place to ask, How might this place be saved? For places, like persons, depend on one another. What might a Brazilian rain forest have to do with this California state park? What might the Arctic tundra contribute to the survival of oak trees and wild turkeys? The natural sublime orients us toward the open horizon of the earth itself. Places are particular, but ultimately unbounded, because always connected to a beyond. The earth is there, on the inside of our experience of *this* place, as the horizon, the threshold, that the sublime allows us to approach.[2] In the natural sublime, we experience the relation of a particular place to the whole earth. Understanding and preserving this relation is the project of ecology.

Beauty

The wild turkey I saw that morning was extraordinarily beautiful, stepping through the forest grass in what seemed to be an utterly self-conscious way, mist rising from the ground in the cool dawn air. But the experience was remarkably different from the experience of beauty as it is discussed in the dominant philosophical tradition in aesthetics. In this tradition, especially Kant's version of it, beauty does not involve either pain or terror—in my experience, beauty, especially in nature, often involves both. And we need not stay with my example of the wild turkey, which will certainly come under the charge of romanticism. We see beauty, after all, in less obvious places, a compost pile might be one example (and surely there is nothing more beautiful than the life of a well-maintained compost bin!).

My point here is that the beautiful has a role to play in relation to the natural sublime that defies its separation from the sublime in the philosophical tradition. The role of the beautiful in the experience of the natural sublime is extremely powerful, in fact. In contemporary life, beauty itself is capable of evoking in us the experience of the sublime, since a very particular experience of natural beauty is, in today's world, likely to be painful—and as likely to give rise to terror as to a sensation of harmony and belonging.

This mixing of the beautiful and the sublime in our experience of nature calls for an explanation. The beautiful and the sublime are distinct experiences for Kant. Beauty certainly cannot occasion the sublime. In fact, in Kant's account, experiences of beauty and of the sublime involve distinct events within the inner life of the subject. Beauty is "the feeling of the internal sense of the concert in the play of mental powers" (*CJ* 1928, 71) experienced in the harmonious relation between the imagination and the understanding, whereas the sublime is experienced in a relation of conflict and domination between the imagination and reason. Beauty is a wholly pleasurable aesthetic experience; the sublime requires displeasure. Beauty is disinterested, meaning independent of any interest in the actual existence of the object that occasions it. It is universal, but in a "special sense"—it "exacts agreement from every one" (82).

In the context of the current discussion, where our intimate relation to the natural world is affirmed rather than denied, we will neither desire nor be able to stay true to the Kantian notion of beauty. Yet aspects of this notion are provocative in the current context.

---

2. Certainly, this limit is itself one that opens out to a further limit, to space, the galaxy, the universe, etc. I stop at the threshold we call earth because it is the ecology of the earth that is most clearly revealed in such experiences. Even our experience of sky, planets, stars is at first, before scientific investigation, utterly earthly, i.e., earthbound.

I have already noted that experiences of beauty in contemporary life lose, at least on some occasions, the quality of simple harmony and pleasure that is associated with them in the dominant tradition. The sudden perception of natural beauty, particularly if it takes us by surprise, carries with it an immediate and deeply wrenching displeasure—an almost physical pain that is associated with a temporally dislocated grief. Grief in association with the natural sublime will be discussed in detail below, but for now it is important to note that far from being exclusively an experience of harmony and belonging, this encounter with beauty occasions a profound disharmony. I encounter the scene as if, on the one hand, I were to suddenly come face-to-face with someone against whom I had done wanton and grievous injury. Meeting the eyes of the injured party with no time to shore up my defenses, the look of the other both sentences and condemns me. On the other hand, in the same moment, forgiveness and reprieve are offered freely, generously, yet almost indifferently, by the injured party. I am not met with malice but permitted, if not invited, to linger in the presence of the beauty that is there in spite of me. I am Barabas lowered from the cross while Jesus continues to bleed and wish me well.

Such an event, if lived well, gives rise to a certain passion. Kant claimed that judgments of taste were independent of all interest, that is, had no interest in the real existence of the beautiful object (since what is, in the end, beautiful, is a formal factor that induces the play of faculties). In the experience I am describing here, beauty will no longer be disinterested. In fact, natural beauty exhorts us to an interest in existence. It is not, however, primarily or even significantly *self-interest*. After all, I live at a time when the wild turkey is still there, at least *somewhere*. The pain and the terror are in relation to future generations as much or more than in relation to my own. Yet beyond this, the pain and terror are in relation to the natural world itself. When we experience nature in what Dussel would call an "epiphany," nature is defunctionalized, is not primarily encountered as nature-for-our-use—whether immediately or in the future.

And here we come to an important distinction within the realm of necessity. For insofar as we are dependent on nature, we are, and should be, interested in preserving it *in order to be preserved by it*. We are aware of the destructive power we wield in relation to nature, as well as the ultimate threat of destroying ourselves. The natural sublime discloses the radical dependence of persons in relation to nature. But insofar as we experience beauty in nature, we are interested in preserving it in order that it should *continue to be*—whether or not we survive to bear witness to it. The natural sublime in this instance is both occasioned by and disclosive of the *intrinsic* beauty of the natural world.

When beauty evokes the experience of the sublime, it pries open the sealed closedness of "my world" and awakens a passion for the wild turkey and the oak forest, for the morning mist itself. If we are reoriented in our relation to the natural world by experiences of beauty that evoke the sublime, then we are oriented toward the preservation of the beauty of nature quite apart from human interest. Here the ecology of place becomes a global ecology, which is meaningful whether or not I benefit directly by meeting the demands it places on me, and whether or not people in general benefit by it. This is not to say that the preservation of the beauty of nature will trump human interest at every turn, only that my very experience of beauty immediately places an ethical demand on me in relation to nature, not in relation to myself. I am claimed by such experiences in ways that, while not canceling out other ethical considerations, do become part of the manifold of meaning that grips me and demands a response. Kant's insistence that judgments of taste exact agreement will be echoed here. I cannot help but assume that anyone, if they are paying attention, will be or should be similarly claimed by experiences of beauty in nature. The claim that nature makes on us is not in the form of a mandate, it is not an encoded message that we can decode and live by. It is, rather, the kind of claim that emerges in the context of a relation: complex, ambiguous, wrenching, relentless, impossible — in short, it is the kind of claim by which we are undone, even as we are irrevocably obligated to live by it.

Grief

The natural sublime is intimately bound up with place, often occasioned by a beauty that is painful, and entangled with the grief we experience at the overwhelming losses we have inflicted on the natural world and one another in relation to it. If the beauty of a wild turkey in an oak forest is capable of occasioning the sublime, it is because there are, indeed, elements of the experience that are overwhelmingly powerful and of incomprehensible proportions. One of these elements is grief (the other is terror). Such experiences are so unsettling because the harmony and sense of belonging that accompany encounters with beautiful nature are immediately disrupted by the presence of loss, the magnitude of which exceeds human comprehension.

Though Butler's discussion of grief and mourning in *Precarious Life* is rooted entirely in the realm of the intersubjective, it is useful to extend her discussion to experiences of the natural world. To review, for Butler, we are "constituted politically in part by virtue of the social vulnerability of our bodies" (PL 2004, 20). This social vulnerability is also a physical vulnerability to injury and a psychic vulnerability to loss. Bodies are necessarily public, in that they manifest an external surface to others, which is to say that they are irrevocably exposed to the possibilities of care, abandonment, or violence. We begin our bodily life thrown into passionate relations with primary others, relations by which we are necessarily "enthralled," even though we don't choose them. Even before there is the constitution of an "I" who speaks and acts for itself, we are at the mercy of a primary sociality, which means that we can and do experience the loss of ties to others as also a loss of what constitutes the very "I" of the experience. This irrevocable vulnerability implies that mourning is central feature of social life. "One mourns when one accepts that by the loss one undergoes one will be changed, possibly forever" (21). The scope and direction of this change will be unchartable.

There are several features of Butler's description of grief in the context of intersubjective relations that lend themselves to a discussion of grief in our encounters with the natural world. First, Butler describes the experience itself as having a power and magnitude that overwhelm our sense of control. Second, grief contains something hidden, unknowable, we might call it an ineffable element at the heart of the experience of loss. Finally, grief, far from being a privatizing emotion, actually throws us into relations with others that are capable of "furnishing a sense of political community of a complex order" (*PL* 2004, 22).

Butler claims that grief interrupts our sense of personal sovereignty. "I think one is hit by waves, and that one starts out the day with an aim, a project, a plan, and finds oneself foiled. One finds oneself fallen. . . . Something is larger than one's own deliberate plan, one's own project, one's own knowing and choosing" (*PL* 2004, 21). One is confronted by an ocean of loss, a depth of feeling that is overwhelming to any sense of individual control. One becomes small in the presence of one's own grief. Our experiences of grief in relation to nature are similarly overwhelming. When we try to comprehend not only the loss that confronts us again and again but also our complicity in it, the enormity of the grief that is unleashed threatens to submerge us. Part of what ties experiences of beauty in nature to the sublime is this sense of being lost in a sea of horror and sadness at what we ourselves, collectively, have done.

There is, of course, no way of enumerating or cataloging this loss, which is part of what makes it so overwhelming. The lists of extinct species, the recording of climate changes, the tracking of ecological devastation only serve as a preliminary accounting. As necessary as this accounting is, the *meaning* of the loss is lost in such efforts. We are, in Butler's words, "losing what we cannot fathom" (23) because there is no way to record the meaning or value of a species or an ecosystem that no longer exists or is close to losing its footing in existence. Of course, we might articulate the loss or possible loss in terms of its value *to humans*: this plant would have been the cure to cancer, this animal kept the pests that are devouring our crops under control—but even if we understand value in this impoverished sense, we fail to grasp the meaning of the loss because the future is radically open, and we can never imagine all of the possible ties that would have brought us into relation with the lost species. But much more important, the inconceivably complex network of ecological relations that already held us in some unfathomable bond with this or that creature is simply ineffable. The loss we have inflicted in relation to the natural world is beyond the limits of comprehension, of representation, because we don't and cannot comprehend the magnitude of what we've done in conceptual terms. Yet at certain moments our grief brings us up against these limits in ways that throw us into a renewed, if overwhelming, awareness of the loss itself.

Butler wonders whether and in what ways grief is or can be politically meaningful. "Is there something to be gained from grieving, from tarrying with grief, from remaining exposed to its unbearability and not endeavoring to seek a resolution for grief through violence" (*PL* 2004, 30)? Loss and grief can "fortify a sense of political community" (22), Butler believes, because they "tear us from ourselves, bind us to others, transport us, and implicate us in lives that are not our own irreversibly" (25). What is to be gained by "tarrying with grief" for Butler is the intersubjective itself. "You are what I gain through this disorientation and loss" (49), she concludes. Grief allows us to recuperate the meaningfulness of the intersubjective even as it undoes the autonomous and sovereign self. It orients us ethically in relation to others, in relation to the vulnerability and injurability of others, by placing a claim on us that may well bind us to a politics of nonviolence.

Our grief in relation to the natural world is certainly a repressed grief. While our public life does include scientific accounts of the losses associated with nature, it is not replete with eulogies or laments. We have a strong sense of the battle being waged between humans over the wanton use or preservation of the natural world, but we don't have a public culture of mourning. Is there something to be gained, then, from tarrying with the grief that sets us adrift in our encounters with the natural world? Could "remaining exposed to its unbearability" be important to the ties that bind us in relation to the natural world? What kind of ethical claim do we find ourselves subject to in the midst of this grief?

Drudgery

If beauty occasions the natural sublime in a way that orients us toward the intrinsic value of nature, other kinds of experience occasion the natural sublime in a way that orients us toward one another in relation to place. Here, we are not so much claimed by nature (although also this) as we are claimed by one another in terms of our relation to nature. Another way of putting this is that our dependency on place is the site for the discovery of and living of our relations to one another.

Even here, Kant will be of some help. "Only when men have got all they want," Kant writes in relation to hunger, "can we tell who among the crowd has taste or not" (*CJ* 1928, 49–50). Kant supposed, as has been typical of the Euro-masculinist tradition since Aristotle (who saw leisure as the precondition for phi-losophizing), that it was *freedom from want* that would enable all of the finer pursuits of philosophers and scholars, including the experience of the beautiful. Yet in this passage he says something quite different. It is not when persons are *free of want* but when their wants *are satisfied* that the beautiful might be experienced. Of course, a feminist reader immediately detects here an irony, for it is the drudgery associated with the satisfaction of want that has been projected onto wives and house servants, farm laborers and slaves. One wishes to be free of the drudgery associated with want rather than the want itself. In regard to want itself, one wishes simply to be satisfied. It is the satisfaction of want, Kant tells us, that frees us for beauty.

If the natural sublime discloses the irrevocable nature of our dependence on place, feminists might well worry whether its affirmation would tie women, again, to the realm of necessity. But this is a strange way of thinking about it, given that we, like all living creatures, are already irrevocably bound to this realm. Feminist thinking based on transcending the realm of necessity will always be a lifeless fantasy. What we need is to speak more precisely about the problem. The injustice in the persistent relegation of women to the realm of necessity stems more specifi-cally from the relegation of women to the drudgery associated with the satisfaction of want. Feminists still confront the problem, cross-culturally and transnationally, that the drudgery associated with satisfying the demands of embodied human existence is assigned to women culturally and economically. It is ultimately the unequal distribution of this drudgery that is justified by more abstract claims about the closeness of women and nature, that is, by traditional essentialist accounts of women. Yet an abjection of the realm of necessity must be rejected, even as the drudgery associated with this realm must be a central concern in feminist politics, including feminist environmentalist politics. The impossible project that a feminist politics will need to insist on is freedom from drudgery in relation to the satisfaction of want.

Just as the liberatory sublime enables an orientation of feminist practice in the realm of the political, the natural sublime will enable an orientation of feminist practice in the realm of necessity. Feminists have a particularly important role to play in the complete reorientation of our lives in regard to the realm of necessity, not because women are biologically or mystically bound to this realm in some special way—all living beings are equally and absolutely bound to the earth. Neither is it because our ascribed role in bearing and raising children gives us an epistemological advantage in seeing what's to be done; all of us are born into dependence and may claim that as an epistemological vantage point. It is because the justification of the unjust distribution of drudgery by the relegation of women to the realm of necessity across and within (many) cultures and epochs infuses these politics with a particular urgency for women. This history means that women, wherever we are on the planet, have an especially strong political stake in *how we organize the satisfaction of want*.

This organization, of course, happens politically and culturally, not naturally. In fact, the example of drudgery provides a particularly acute illustration of the relation between the two realms. *Drudgery* is the name for what political domination in the intersubjective realm relegates women to in the realm of necessity[3]; it is what necessity-work becomes under conditions of injustice.

What I am calling "drudgery" is absolutely necessary, repetitious, and thankless work: the cleaning of houses, the carrying of water, the diapering of babies, the washing of clothes, the preparation of food. Its necessity is the very essence of the human condition; its repetitiousness is a quality of the activities themselves; but its thanklessness is an effect of the context of domination in which the work is unfairly distributed, organized in ecologically debased ways, and uncelebrated.

Hannah Arendt called necessity-work "labor," to distinguish it from the kind of work that produces a durable product. Her discussion of labor in *The Human Condition* goes to the heart of my concerns here. For the Greeks, Arendt tells us, "to labor meant to be enslaved by necessity" (1958, 83), and so labor was considered to be a degraded, slavish activity. The products of this labor, life and freedom for those in charge, are not the tangible products of work. "It is indeed the mark of all laboring that it leaves nothing behind, that the result of its effort is almost as quickly consumed as the effort is spent. And yet this effort, despite its futility, is

---

3. Even in the most developed Western countries, women still do the vast majority of necessity-work. The trend of the last decades, to make women available for the workplace by reducing the amount of necessity-work to be done, most particularly by the introduction of fast food as a mainstay of the diet (especially in the United States) has had devastating health consequences. This is another example where freeing persons from necessity-work rather than *attending* to the work and organizing it fairly, or collectivizing it, has been a profound mistake. Of course the trend is not driven by an interest in women's liberation, it is driven by the market.

born of a great urgency and motivated by a more powerful drive than anything else, because life itself depends on it" (87). This is a kind of human activity that, while absolutely necessary, "never 'produces' anything but life" (88).

But while it produces life, the necessity of labor is also the incontrovertible evidence that we are a part of nature. Most important, it is through this necessity that nature forces human beings into the cyclical structure of time that the human world, marked as it is by events that lend themselves to stories which have a beginning and an end, always denies. Unlike the rest of human life, "all human activities which arise out of the necessity to cope with [the biological process in man and the process of growth and decay in the world] are bound to the recurring cycles of nature and have in themselves no beginning and end" (Arendt 1958, 98). This is why "laboring always moves in the same circle" (98), that is, it is always and necessarily repetitious.

Arendt's account is somewhat ambiguous, but at moments she interjects a very different view of laboring activity than the dominant account she has been at pains to describe. She argues that labor "still partakes of the superabundance we see everywhere in nature's household" (Arendt 1958, 106) and is, therefore, "the human way to experience the sheer bliss of being alive which we share with all living creatures" (106). This sets laboring activity apart from all others, since "the blessing of life as a whole" is "inherent in labor" (107). The political import of Arendt's claim is alluded to when she argues that "whatever throws this cycle out of balance . . . ruins the elemental happiness that comes from being alive" (108). The implications of this ruin are extremely profound in Arendt's view. The notion that labor could or should be eliminated from the human condition, or foisted from some onto others, is rejected since "the perfect elimination of the pain and effort of labor would not only rob biological life of its most natural pleasures but deprive the specifically human life of its very liveliness and vitality" (120). Laboring activity and the pain and effort associated with it are, in fact, "the modes in which life itself, together with the necessity to which it is bound, makes itself felt" (120). Without the intensities associated with labor, we lose our very sense of the reality of life.

If Arendt is right, then a feminist response to the drudgery associated with the satisfaction of want should not be to challenge the necessity of necessity-work nor its repetitiousness (though it may be mediated by ecologically sound technological interventions). What we should be challenging is the thanklessness of the work, which can only be remedied by bringing it out of the context of domination and distributing it fairly. In short, since it is neither possible nor desirable to do away with drudgery, we'll have to turn it into something else—I'll call this something else "beautiful work." But the process through which this transformation occurs cannot be imaginary, cannot be mere wishful thinking. To change drudgery into beautiful work is, in fact, to change everything.

Let me say a bit more about all this. First, it is refusing the fantasy of freedom from the *necessity* of such work that provides footing for attending to it politically and socially. There is no technological fix that will free us from the realm of necessity. We are bound to such work by the very structures of our existence, as living beings, not as a gender or a class. The work of satisfying want, and want itself, is such an integral part of the human condition that we engage in mere delusion when we imagine such work disappearing. While leisure is certainly important to a good life, a life lived only in leisure would, if Arendt is correct, be a life without an intense sense of its own living.

Second, the repetitiousness of such work is an inevitable aspect of the work itself. Appropriate technological intervention is one way of mediating this aspect of the work. Here we must always balance ecology and simplicity. What feminist could seriously decry the invention of the washing machine or the vacuum cleaner? Yet these are ecologically noxious inventions. Because clothes are easy to wash, we throw them in the laundry long before they are actually dirty, much more water is wasted, and much more polluting detergent is flushed into our water systems. Vacuum cleaners have invited the carpeting of houses. Carpeting materials are toxic and clog the landfills. When "emancipation" for women and men is no longer understood to be "emancipation from necessity" but rather the just and ecological organization of necessity-work, it becomes possible, as a feminist, to question (though perhaps not to decry) these inventions.

The thanklessness of necessity-work is the most amenable to political intervention. How the work is experienced varies extraordinarily, even in one individual life, across contexts. Housecleaning might be meditative, joyous, or sheer misery, depending on the political, physical, and intersubjective context, mood, and individual predilection. The preparation of food might be high art or grudging compliance with the expectations of one's role. Laundry might be a social event or an unbearable burden. It is certainly safe to say that contexts of domination or exploitation tend to turn such work into the worst kind of drudgery.

What ameliorates the thanklessness of necessity-work? Certainly, with some thought, we could begin to understand what tends to make such work more or less joyous, more or less unbearable. I would like to suggest two points for feminist consideration. The first is that the intersubjective context, if the work is shared with others, fairly distributed, and valued, can and does make the work more bearable. The second is that doing such work in a physically pleasant, even beautiful, setting helps to moderate the burden of it. Political and social attention to such questions are, I would argue, as essential to human life, and to feminism, as is the work itself. A feminist political agenda would strive not to eliminate this work, nor to foist it from the shoulders of some women onto others, but to make it "beautiful work" by prioritizing and celebrating it in culture and politics, by distributing it fairly and by attending seriously to the beauty of the places in which the work is done.

Instead, in our flight from the drudgery associated with the satisfaction of want, we have built and rebuilt inequalities, between women and men, between peoples, between nations—but very important for feminists, between women. It has been a mistake for feminists to abject the realm of necessity in the project of women's liberation. If we consider that freedom from necessity-work is necessary to the project of political freedom, then we will land (and have landed) in strange contradictions, since such a perspective virtually assures that some women will be relegated to the realm of necessity while others fantasize an escape. Increasingly, necessity-work is contracted out by women in a position to do so, so that other women are hired to do the care work and the cleaning. Of course, the burden on those performing this work is extraordinary indeed, since these women must do virtually the same work at home, they take on a double burden of caring, cooking, and cleaning. This is to say that the gendered division of labor in dominant countries is not so much overcome as redistributed. It is redistributed among women so that those women who are in the most economically and socially precarious positions increasingly take on the traditionally feminine tasks of necessity-work, while others enter the professions on (apparently) equal footing with economically privileged men (Schutte 2002).

Of course these sorts of arrangements are by no means new; some women have always shouldered a good deal of drudgery for others. What is new is the structuring of such arrangements into the economic framework of postmodern life, where the compression of time means that the pace of the demands for professional success have increased to such an extent that many more women find themselves in the position of needing to hire someone to do the caring and cleaning for them. What we too often fail to notice is that our newfound gender equality in the professions (in some nations) is only guaranteed by the individual arrangements women in these professions are able to make to take care of the necessity-work—which doesn't sound much like equality when you think about it. What's new is also the extraordinary vulnerability of women workers displaced from their own homeplaces by global capital to such an extent that feminists have begun to speak of a "care deficit" in nonglobally dominant countries (Schutte 2002, 153). That these inequalities of class generally fall out along predictable lines of race and nation should come as no surprise. It is fair to say then, that when public and visible forms of gender equality rest on private or invisible forms of inequality, this is not the kind of gender equality that feminists should embrace.

Neither should we neglect to attend to the places in which we work, especially to the aesthetics of the places in which necessity-work is done. In the United States most egregiously, we have nearly achieved the complete quarantining of beauty to a few select places: the art museum, the park, the bodies of women (and, more and more often, men) marketed by various parts of the entertainment and advertising industry. Beauty is something we visit, or consume in the way we consume an object (if only imaginatively), but not what we live in. Freeways, the fast-food/hotel/gas strip, the shopping mall, the screen (computer, TV, Palm Pilot), the ugly office building, the devastatingly ugly parking structure: these are the surroundings of public life that predominate. Enormous areas of nearly every U.S. American town or city become virtually interchangeable, and interchangeably unpleasant. Having long-since given up on any pretence of according importance to beauty in our collective surroundings in the interest of saving time and making money, beauty lives increasingly under a kind of house arrest, where it occupies the limited space of the private home or garden at the whim of those who can afford either the time or the money to attend to it.

When feminists have taken up the problem of beauty, we have often done so in relation to the politics of the image and the body, engaging or criticizing the terms of the relation between women and beauty established in the dominant tradition. I am not aware of feminist thinking that connects beauty to work, in the sense of a political demand that our workplaces be places of aesthetic delight that neither dull the senses nor blunt the mind. This is to say that we have tended to discuss the problem of beauty as a problem of women being treated as beautiful objects, or in more recent formulations to defend the activities that women engage in to make ourselves more beautiful as sites of agency. What we have neglected is an affirmation of *the senses*, in relation to place. Think of the hospital laundry, the megafarm, the fast-food kitchen, the canning factory, the state-funded day-care center. All of these places are places where basic human needs are at issue in very basic ways, yet they are the sorts of places that distress the senses.

If Arendt is right to claim that necessity-work is a primary way that life "makes itself felt," then affirming this aspect of the work will mean a political mandate to please the senses (of the workers), especially in places where such work is centered. Such a mandate would mean, of course, the total reorganization of the work itself—but if we acknowledge that, under some circumstances, a deep pleasure is often associated with necessity-work and affirm the possibility of organizing the work so that it lends itself to such pleasure, then I think we have the beginnings of a feminist political philosophy of work. This philosophy would absolutely affirm practices of economic justice and fair distribution, the cultural work that goes into convincing folks that necessity-work is for men too, but it would insist on the aesthetic meaning and the aesthetic dimensions of the work as well.

What the natural sublime shows is that while the two realms of necessity and freedom are distinct, they are not separate. Either eliding the distinction between them or treating them as quite separate results in the misunderstanding of both realms. It was the fascists who collapsed the political into the necessary, making of all politics something destined. (But then again the colonialist movements of Europe did precisely the same thing. What is the idea of manifest destiny if it is not the collapse of political will and political choice into an end viewed as necessary?) On the other hand, if we collapse the necessary into the political, then every decision becomes "free" in an odd sense. This is the logic that invents "pollution credits" so that dirty air becomes an economic value that circulates on the free market. This is the logic that believes each farmer can and should, independently, decide which poisons to use on a given crop—even though the air itself defies the individuality of such individual choices and carries the herbicide over to the neighbors organic farm. The sustenance provided in the relation of persons to place is a condition for the possibility of the intersubjective, the political, because it is the condition for the possibility of our constitution as subjects at all. Yet it is only our freedom as subjects in the political realm that allows us to organize our relationships to place, that allows us to work toward beauty in relationship to place.

Of course the relation between these two realms is not so simple since the *necessity* in the relation of persons to place *conditions* the intersubjective realm. We are bound by place to a shared interest in organizing our relationships of dependence on place beautifully. The realm of necessity binds us, or conditions us, *politically* to act with common sense vis-à-vis one another. At the same time, our orientation toward freedom in the intersubjective realm must orient us away from intersubjective domination in the realm of necessity. It requires that no one person or people *dictate* in any determinate way the relations of other persons to place. The particularity of relations to place is to be worked out in each instance between the persons that live those relations. The natural sublime calls us to build common sense rather than relations of domination in both the realm of the political and in the realm of necessity.

Conclusion

This book began with terror, and it will, it seems, have to end the same way. I first began thinking about the experience of the sublime exactly at the turn of the century, and in the ensuing five years, occasions for the kind of terror that motivated the project in the first place have been far too abundant. Events that have accompanied this research include the dramatic attacks of 9/11; two wars launched in a rush to shore up a fiction of U.S. invulnerability, which instead have decimated the places and lives of others; a tsunami that destroyed communities and lives in eleven countries; the exposure (still under way) of the regular and systematic torture of prisoners held by the United States in Abu Ghraib, Guantánamo Bay, Camp Mercury; two hurricanes, Katrina and Rita, that destroyed not only homes and lives but finally the political credibility of the president; and all of these events are, of course, entirely outdone by the grinding reality of poverty and disease that not only underwrite the politics of the events already listed but have themselves taken far more lives, far more quietly, than any single event could.

These events seem extraordinary, perhaps because they push those of us in the dominant countries of the globe into an awareness of our own vulnerability, to other persons and to our own places. At the same time, the response in the United States has mostly taken the form of an effort to "man-up," to clothe the sovereign state in a spectacle of violence and power that will "shock and awe"[1] our "enemies" into a renewed subservience. The America that suffered a devastating humiliation at the hands of a few angry men with box cutters engages in the construction of a new national identity built on the fantasy of a power so spectacular that it

---

1. This phrase itself comes from a National Defense University document written in 1996 with the intention of bringing U.S. combat strategy into the postmodern age (Ullman and Wade 1996). This document is itself of considerable interest; see Mann 2006.

eliminates the threat of injury at the hands of Others altogether. As Butler so succinctly put it:

> In the initial campaign of the war against Iraq, the US government advertised its military feats as an overwhelming visual phenomenon. That the US government and military called this a "shock and awe" strategy suggests that they were producing a visual spectacle that numbs the senses and, like the sublime itself, puts out of play the very capacity to think. This production takes place not only for the Iraqi population on the ground, whose senses are supposed to be done in by this spectacle, but also for the consumers of war who rely on CNN or Fox. (*PL* 2004, 148)

This is to say, the United States launches a project of self-making after 9/11 on a model of hypermasculine invulnerability, and invites its citizens to experience this identity through a sublime media spectacle.

The wars in Afghanistan and Iraq are both fought in defense of the manliness of "America." Prisoners are tortured in ways that extend the spectacle of U.S. power, inscribing it on the bodies of the "enemies" themselves. President Bush is reelected on a platform of never changing his mind, never reconsidering a decision once taken, and never worrying about what others might think or feel in relation to U.S. actions globally. Since this model of national sovereignty in the face of a foreign threat leaves little room for worrying about individual lives at home, victims of natural disasters are subjected to an unimaginably callous carelessness. And the events in nature that shock and awe the senses are used as excuses for doing away with those minimal environmental protections that still constrain the fossil fuel industry.

But in the face of this massive effort to reaffirm or remake U.S. national identity—this outpouring of resources, actions, images, and words—the events themselves keep pushing back. They keep bringing home to us the impossibility of securing our freedom from the relationships that make us irrevocably vulnerable, both to other persons and to the natural world. The Iraqi resistance, the courage of a man like Captain Fishback,[2] the power of Katrina testify to the impossibility of either assimilating or crushing the Other once and for all. Our own actions, in fact, bind us more and more tightly into relation, both with other persons and with the places we (and they) live. Given that these relations are irrevocable, how we live them is the only political question.

The events of the last few years arrive like clarion calls, announcing the centrality of the sublime in contemporary life. A feminist account of the experience is important now because the dominant framework for encountering the sublime is one that leads precisely to the fated efforts toward sovereignty and invulnerability we see all around us. But as we have seen, other responses are possible. The sublime might also be an occasion for the affirmation of relations that are both inevitable and ethically binding.

---

2. Captain Fishback is the officer who tried for months to report regular torture of prisoners to his superiors, who threatened him with his career, and then went directly to the Senate, where John McCain finally listened to him and brought the reports of torture to light.

These other sublimes will require a different kind of courage, one that is able to linger with grief when it swells to unmanageable proportions, when it overtakes and overthrows pretensions to a power so grand that it borders on omnipotence. They will require the courage to face the pain that we must live in our encounters with beautiful nature, and with powerful nature, in spite of the fact that this pain takes the punch out of the spectacles of invulnerability we create with ourselves at the center. They require, as well, the courage to face Others to whom we have done great harm (also those who may have harmed us) and admit that we are stuck with one another—if for no other reason than that we share this planet and its places. These experiences of the sublime will be marked by a persistent refusal of escape fantasies, of the fictions of sovereignty and power that have been so central to the narratives of the Euro-masculinist West.

The feminist movement in the United States has been remarkably silent in regard to the remaking of America. This is not to say that individual feminists have not often taken courageous stands vis-à-vis U.S. foreign policy, nor that Iraqi and Afghan feminists have not been at the forefront of challenging U.S. interventions. Yet there has been no massive public outcry in a feminist voice at home, in spite of the fact that the reconstruction of U.S. national identity is so blatantly masculinist in form. There are certainly many reasons for this, not the least of which are that the feminist movement itself has been undermined by a dramatic shift to the right in U.S. politics, that American youth seem largely convinced that feminism is out of date, and that the Bush administration itself has taken up the banner of feminism in a cynical move to justify its Rambo-on-steroids foreign policy.

It is also the case that, after the linguistic turn, it is extraordinarily difficult for feminists to imagine a common place or a common politics from which a powerful response to these developments might be launched. Yet, if ever there was an un-ethical silence, this is the time. Wars and floods and hurricanes alike call on us to speak, because they lay bare the relations that bind us to other persons and to place. This call comes to us uninvited, demanding a response without consideration for whether or not an adequate response is actually possible, without consideration for the theoretical difficulties that make it impossible to speak. These events bring our sojourn in the world of signs to an unceremonious end and call us back to the common sense that both demands action and is reconstituted through it.

If life has become art under conditions of postmodernity, then a committed feminist engagement with and in the region of human experience we call "the aesthetic" has the impossible task of bringing art back to life. This "bringing back" must itself work *through* the aesthetic. Dominant narratives of the sublime tell a story of triumph and rupture, and these stories are only undone through a return to the experience itself, a return to the relations of vulnerability that structure the experience from the outset. The forgetfulness of women and of nature, which plagues us in the world of signs, is undone to the extent that the events that overtake us spill us out into a world that resists and exceeds the products of human making. Our own worlds are torn open at certain moments of disruption, in which the powerful presence of some Other breaks into the sealed complacency that tends so thoroughly to enthrall us. The projects of women's liberation are built in the space between worlds that open at such moments, in spite of the fact that the meanings that are disclosed in and through these openings (though they must always be conceptualized) can never *finally* be conceptualized. These are meanings that ultimately have to be lived and struggled over and remade, and the very struggling and living and remaking is all the evidence that we have ever needed of the common place that makes an impossible common sense both possible and necessary.

References

Ahmed, Sara. 1998. *Differences that Matter: Feminist Theory and Postmodernism*. Cambridge: Cambridge University Press.

Alcoff, Linda. 1988. "Cultural Feminism versus Post-Structuralism: The Identity Crisis in Feminist Theory." *Signs: Journal of Women in Culture and Society* 13, no. 3.

———. 2005. *Visible Identities: Race, Gender, and the Self*. New York: Oxford University Press.

Alcoff, Linda, and Elizabeth Potter. 1993. *Feminist Epistemologies*. New York: Routledge.

Anzaldúa, Gloria. 1990. "La Conciencia de la mestiza: Towards a New Consciousness." In *Making Face, Making Soul: Haciendo Caras; Creative and Critical Perspectives by Feminists of Color*. San Francisco: Aunt Lute Books.

Anzaldúa, Gloria, and Cherie Moraga, eds. 1981. *This Bridge Called My Back: Writings by Radical Women of Color*. New York: Kitchen Table Press.

Arendt, Hannah. 1958. *The Human Condition*. Chicago: University of Chicago Press.

———. 1961. *Between Past and Future: Eight Exercises in Political Thought*. New York: Penguin Books.

———. 1963. *On Revolution*. New York: Penguin Books.

———. 1971. *The Life of the Mind*. New York: Harcourt Brace Jovanovich.

———. 1992. *Lectures on Kant's Political Philosophy*. Chicago: University of Chicago Press.

Bar On, Bat-Ami. 1993. "Marginality and Epistemic Privilege." In *Feminist Epistemologies*, edited by Linda Alcoff and Elizabeth Potter. New York and London: Routledge.

Battersby, Christine. 1990. *Gender and Genius: Towards a Feminist Aesthetics*. Bloomington and Indianapolis: Indiana University Press.

———. 1995. "Stages on Kant's Way: Aesthetics, Morality, and the Gendered Sublime." In *Feminism and Tradition in Aesthetics*, edited by Peggy Zeglin Brand and Carolyn Korsmeyer. University Park: Pennsylvania State University Press.

Baudrillard, Jean. 1983. "The Ecstasy of Communication." In *The Anti-Aesthetic: Essays on Postmodern Culture*, edited by Hal Foster. Port Townsend, Wash.: Bay Press.

Beauvoir, Simone de. 1952. *The Second Sex*. New York: Random House.

Bell, Diane and Renate Klein. 1996. *Radically Speaking: Feminism Reclaimed*. North Melbourne, Australia: Spinifex Press.

Benhabib, Seyla, Judith Butler, Drucilla Cornell, and Nancy Fraser. 1995. *Feminist Contentions: A Philosophical Exchange*. New York: Routledge.

Berman, Morris. 1981. *The Reenchantment of the World*. Ithaca, N.Y.: Cornell University Press.

Böhme, Hartmut, and Gernot Böhme. 1983. *Das Andere der Vernunft: Zur Entwicklung von Rationalitätsstrukturen am Beispiel Kants*. Frankfurt am Main: Suhrkamp Verlag.

Bordo, Susan. 1987. *The Flight to Objectivity: Essays on Cartesianism and Culture*. Albany: State University of New York Press.

———. 1993. *Unbearable Weight: Feminism, Western Culture, and the Body*. Berkeley: University of California Press.

———. 1999. *Feminist Interpretations of Rene Descartes*. University Park: Pennsylvania State University Press.

Brand, Peggy Zeglin and Carolyn Korsmeyer, eds. 1995. *Feminism and Tradition in Aesthetics*. University Park: Pennsylvania State University Press.

Brodribb, Somer. 1992. *Nothing Mat(t)ers: A Feminist Critique of Postmodernism*. North Melbourne, Australia: Spinifex Press.

———. 1996. "Nothing Mat(t)ers." In *Radically Speaking: Feminism Reclaimed*, edited by Diane Bell and Renate Klein. North Melbourne, Australia: Spinifex Press.

Burke, Edmund. 1970. *A Philosophical Enquiry into the Origin of Our Ideas of the Sublime and Beautiful*. Meston, England: Scolar Press.

Butler, Judith. 1989. "Sexual Ideology and Phenomenological Description: A Feminist Critique of Merleau-Ponty's Phenomenology of Perception." In *The Thinking Muse: Feminism and Modern French Philosophy*, edited by Jeffner Allen and Iris Marion Young. Bloomington: Indiana University Press.

———. 1990a. "Feminism and the Question of Postmodernism." Presented at *The Greater Philadelphia Philosophy Consortium*.

———. 1990b. *Gender Trouble: Feminism and the Subversion of Identity*. New York: Routledge.

———. 1991. "Imitation and Gender Insubordination." In *Inside/Out: Lesbian Theories, Gay Theories*, edited by Diana Fuss. New York and London: Routledge.

———. 1992. "Contingent Foundations: Feminism and the Question of 'Postmodernism.'" In *Feminists Theorize the Political*, edited by Judith Butler and Joan W. Scott. New York. Routledge.

———. 1993. *Bodies That Matter: On the Discursive Limits of "Sex."* New York: Routledge.

———. 1997a. *Excitable Speech*. New York and London: Routledge.

———. 1997b. *The Psychic Life of Power*. Stanford, Calif.: Stanford University Press.

———. 2000. *Antigone's Claim: Kinship Between Life and Death*. New York: Columbia University Press.

———. 2004. *Precarious Life: The Powers of Mourning and Violence*. London and New York: Verso.

Butler, Judith, and Joan W. Scott. 1992. "Introduction." In *Feminists Theorize the Political*, edited by Judith Butler and Joan W. Scott. New York: Routledge.

Butler, Judith, Ernesto Laclau, and Slavoj Žižek. 2000. *Contingency, Hegemony, Universality: Contemporary Dialogues on the Left*. London and New York: Verso.

Casey, Edward S. 1993. *Getting Back into Place: Toward a Renewed Understanding of the Place World*. Bloomington: Indiana University Press.

———. 1997. *The Fate of Place: A Philosophical History*. Berkeley: University of California Press.

Cassirer, Ernst. 1951. *The Philosophy of the Enlightenment*. Translated by Fritz C. A. Kölln and James P. Pettegrove. Princeton, N.J.: Princeton University Press.

Cheah, Pheng, and Elizabeth Grosz. 1998. "The Future of Sexual Difference: An Interview with Judith Butler and Drucilla Cornell." *Diacritics* 28, 1 (spring): 19–42.

Chicago, Judy. 1975. *Through the Flower: My Struggle as a Woman Artist.* New York: Doubleday.

Christian, Barbara. 1996. "The Race for Theory." In *Radically Speaking: Feminism Reclaimed,* edited by Diane Bell and Renate Klein. North Melbourne, Australia: Spinifex Press.

Churchill, Ward. 1997. *A Little Matter of Genocide: Holocaust and Denial in the Americas 1492 to the Present.* San Francisco: City Lights Books.

———. 1998. "In the Service of Empire: A Critical Assessment of Arnold Krupat's *The Turn to the Native.*" In *Fantasies of the Master Race: Literature, Cinema and the Colonization of American Indians.* San Francisco: City Lights Books.

Daly, Mary. 1978. *Gyn/Ecology: The Metaethics of Radical Feminism.* Boston: Beacon Press.

———. 1984. *Pure Lust: Elemental Feminist Philosophy.* Boston: Beacon Press.

———. 1998. *Quintessence . . . Realizing the Archaic Future: A Radical Elemental Feminist Manifesto.* Boston: Beacon Press.

Davis, Angela. 1983. *Women, Race, and Class.* New York: Vintage Books.

Degérando, Joseph-Marie. [1800] 1969. *The Observation of Savage Peoples.* Edited by F.C.T. Moore. Berkeley: University of California Press. Quoted in Fabian 1983, 7.

de Lauretis, Teresa. 1994. "The Essence of the Triangle or, Taking the Risk of Essentialism Seriously: Feminist Theory in Italy, the U.S., and Britain." In *The Essential Difference,* edited by Naomi Schor and Elizabeth Weed. Bloomington: Indiana University Press.

Deleuze, Gilles, and Félix Guattari. 1983. *Anti-Oedipus: Capitalism and Schizophrenia.* Minneapolis: University of Minnesota Press. Originally published in 1972.

Delgado, Richard, and Jean Stefancic, eds. 1997. *Critical White Studies: Looking Behind the Mirror.* Philadelphia: Temple University Press.

Devereaux, Mary. 2003. "Feminist Aesthetics." In *The Oxford Handbook of Aesthetics,* edited by Jerrold Levinson. Oxford and New York: Oxford University Press.

Dines, Gail, Robert Jensen, and Ann Russo. 1998. *Pornography: The Production and Consumption of Inequality.* New York: Routledge.

Donovan, Josephine. 1993. "Everyday Use and Moments of Being: Toward a Nondominative Aesthetic." In *Aesthetics in Feminist Perspective,* edited by Carolyn Korsmeyer and Hilde Hein. Bloomington and Indianapolis: Indiana University Press.

Dussel, Enrique. 1985. *Philosophy of Liberation.* Translated by Aquilina Martinez and Christine Morkovsky. Maryknoll, N.Y.: Orbis Books.

———. 1998. *The Invention of the Americas: Eclipse of "the Other" and the Myth of Modernity.* Translated by Michael D. Barber. New York: Continuum Press.

Eagleton, Terry. 1996. *The Illusion of Postmodernism.* Oxford: Blackwell Publishers.

Ebert, Teresa L. 1996. *Ludic Feminism and After: Postmodernism, Desire, and Labor in Late Capitalism.* Ann Arbor: University of Michigan Press.

Echols, Alice. 1983. "The New Feminism of Yin and Yang." In *Powers of Desire: The Politics of Sexuality,* edited by Ann Snitow, Christine Stansell, and Sharon Thompson. New York: Monthly Review Press.

———. 1984. "The Taming of the Id: Feminist Sexual Politics." In *Pleasure and Danger: Exploring Female Sexuality,* edited by Carole S.Vance. Boston: Routledge and Kegan Paul.

Eze, Emmanuel Chukwudi, ed. 1997. *Race and The Enlightenment: A Reader.* Oxford: Blackwell Publishers.

Fabian, Johannes. 1983. *Time and the Other: How Anthropology Makes its Object.* New York: Columbia University Press.

Feder, Ellen. 2002. "'Doctor's Orders': Parents and Intersexed Children." In *The Subject of Care: Feminist Perspectives on Dependency*, edited by Eva Feder Kittay and Ellen Feder. Lanham, Md.: Rowman and Littlefield.

Felski, Rita. 2000. *Doing Time: Feminist Theory and Postmodern Culture*. New York and London: New York University Press.

Flax, Jane. 1990. *Thinking Fragments: Psychoanalysis, Feminism and Postmodernism in the Contemporary West*. Berkeley: University of California Press.

———. 1992. "The End of Innocence." In *Feminists Theorize the Political*, edited by Judith Butler and Joan W. Scott. New York: Routledge.

Foster, Hal, ed. 1983. *The Anti-Aesthetic: Essays on Postmodern Culture*. Port Townsend, Wash.: Bay Press.

Freeman, Barbara Claire. 1995. *The Feminine Sublime: Gender and Excess in Women's Fiction*. Berkeley: University of California Press.

Frye, Marilyn. 1983. *The Politics of Reality: Essays in Feminist Theory*. Trumansburg, N.Y.: Crossing Press.

———. 2001. "Categories in Distress." Paper given at the *Western Division of the American Philosophical Association Conference*. San Francisco.

Fuss, Diana. 1989. *Essentially Speaking: Feminism, Nature, and Difference*. New York: Routledge.

Galeano, Eduardo. 1973. *Open Veins of Latin America: Five Centuries of the Pillage of a Continent*. New York: Monthly Review Press.

Gilbert-Rolfe, Jeremy. 2000. "Kant's Ghost Among Others." In *Differential Aesthetics: Art Practices, Philosophy and Feminist Understandings*, edited by Penny Florence and Nicola Foster. Burlington, Vt.: Ashgate Publishing.

Gould, Carol. 1974. "The Woman question: Philosophy of Liberation and the Liberation of Philosophy." In *Women and Philosophy: Toward a Theory of Liberation*, edited by Carol Gould and Marx Wartofsky. New York: Capricorn Books.

Gould, Timothy. 1995. "Intensity and its Audiences: Toward a Feminist Perspective on the Kantian Sublime." In *Feminism and Tradition in Aesthetics*, edited by Peggy Zeglin Brand and Carolyn Korsmeyer. University Park: Pennsylvania State University Press.

Greer, Germaine. 1979. *The Obstacle Race: The Fortunes of Women Painters and Their Work*. New York: Farrar, Straus and Giroux.

Grosz, Elizabeth. 1994. "Sexual Difference and the Problem of Essentialism." In *The Essential Difference*, edited by Naomi Schor and Elizabeth Weed. Bloomington: Indiana University Press.

———. 1995. "Sexual Difference and the Problem of Essentialism." In *Space Time and Perversion*. New York and London: Routledge.

Hall, Kim. 1997. "*Sensus Communis* and Violence: A Feminist Reading of Kant's *Critique of Judgement*." In *Feminist Interpretations of Immanuel Kant*, edited by Robin May Schott. University Park: Pennsylvania State University Press.

Harding, Sandra. 1993. "Rethinking Standpoint Epistemology: 'What is Strong Objectivity?'" In *Feminist Epistemologies*, edited by Linda Alcoff and Elizabeth Potter. New York: Routledge.

Hartmann, Heidi. 1979. "The Unhappy Marriage of Marxism and Feminism: Towards a More Progressive Union." *Capital and Class* 8: 1–33.

Harvey, David. 1990. *The Condition of Postmodernity: An Inquiry into the Nature of Cultural Change*. Cambridge: Blackwell Publishers.

Hegel, G.W.F. 1977. *Phenomenology of Spirit*. Translated by A. V. Miller. Oxford: Oxford University Press.

Hein, Hilde, and Carolyn Korsmeyer. 1993. *Aesthetics in Feminist Perspective*. Bloomington and Indianapolis: Indiana University Press.

Hess, Thomas B., and Linda Nochlin, eds. 1972. *Woman as Sex Object: Studies in Erotic Art, 1730–1970*. New York: Newsweek.

Hess, Thomas B., and Elizabeth C. Baker. 1973. *Art and Sexual Politics: Women's Liberation, Women Artists, and Art History*. New York: Collier.

Heyes, Cressida. 2000. *Line Drawings: Defining Women through Feminist Practice*. Ithaca, N.Y.: Cornell University Press.

Honig Fine, Elsa. 1978. *Women and Art*. Montclair, New Jersey: Abner Schram.

Husserl, Edmund. 1970. *The Crisis of European Sciences and Transcendental Phenomenology*. Evanston, Ill.: Northwestern University Press.

Ignatiev, Noel, and John Garvey, eds. 1996. *Race Traitor*. New York: Routledge.

Irigaray, Luce. 1985. "Paradox a Priori." In *Speculum of the Other Woman*. Translated by Gillian C. Gill. Ithaca, N.Y.: Cornell University Press.

Jameson, Fredric. 1981. *The Political Unconscious*. Ithaca, N.Y.: Cornell University Press.

———. 1988. "Cognitive Mapping." In *Marxism and the Interpretation of Culture*, edited by C. Nelson and L. Grossberg. Urbana and Chicago: University of Illinois Press.

———. 1991. *Postmodernism or the Cultural Logic of Late Capitalism*. Durham, N.C.: Duke University Press.

Jeffreys, Sheila. 1996. "Return to Gender: Postmodernism and Lesbianandgay Theory." In *Radically Speaking: Feminism Reclaimed*, edited by Diane Bell and Renate Klein. North Melbourne, Australia: Spinifex Press.

Kant, Immanuel. 1928. *The Critique of Judgement*. Translated by James Creed Meredith. Oxford: Clarendon Press.

———. [1775] 1950. "On the Different Races of Man." In *This Is Race*, edited by E. W. Count. New York: Henry Schuman.

———. 1959. "Metaphysische Anfangsgründe der Rechtslehre." In *Metaphysik der Sitten*. Hers. Von Karl Vorländer. Hamburg: Verlag Von Felix Meiner.

———. 1960. *Observations on the Feeling of the Beautiful and Sublime*. Translated by John T. Goldthwait. Berkeley: University of California Press.

———. 1965. *Critique of Pure Reason*. Translated by Norman Kemp Smith. New York: St. Martin's Press. German Edition: *Kritik der reinen Vernunft*, vol. 1 & 2, herausgegeben von Wilhelm Weischedel. Frankfurt am Main: Suhrkamp Verlag.

———. 1978. *Anthropology from a Pragmatic Point of View*. Translated by Victor Lyle Dowdell. Carbondale: Southern Illinois University Press.

Kelly, Kathy. 2005. *Other Lands Have Dreams: From Baghdad to Pekin Prison*. Oakland, Calif.: AK Press.

Kessler, Suzanne J. 1994. "The Medical Construction of Gender: Case Management of Intersexed Infants." In *Theorizing Feminism: Parallel Trends in the Humanities and Social Sciences*, edited by Anne C. Herrmann and Abigail J. Stewart. Boulder: Westview Press.

Kipnis, Laura. 1999. *Bound and Gagged: Pornography and the Politics of Fantasy in America*. Durham, N.C.: Duke University Press.

Kittay, Eva Feder. 1999. *Love's Labor: Essays on Women, Equality, and Dependency*. New York: Routledge.

Klein, Renate. 1996. "(Dead) Bodies Floating in Cyberspace: Post-modernism and the Dismemberment of Women." In *Radically Speaking: Feminism Reclaimed*, edited by Diane Bell and Renate Klein. North Melbourne, Australia: Spinifex Press.

Klinger, Cornelia. 1997. "The Concepts of the Sublime and Beautiful in Kant and Lyotard." In *Feminist Interpretations of Immanuel Kant*, edited by Robin May Schott. University Park: Pennsylvania State University Press.

Kneller, Jane. 1993. "Discipline and Silence: Women and Imagination in Kant's Theory of Taste." In *Aesthetics in Feminist Perspective*, edited by Carolyn Korsmeyer and Hilde Hein. Bloomington and Indianapolis: Indiana University Press.

———. 1994. "Kant's Immature Imagination." In *Modern Engenderings: Critical Feminist Readings in Modern Western Philosophy*, edited by Bat-Ami Bar On. Albany: State University of New York Press.

Korsmeyer, Carolyn, and Hilde Hein, eds. 1993. *Aesthetics in Feminist Perspective*. Bloomington and Indianapolis: Indiana University Press.

———. 1995. "Gendered Concepts and Hume's Standard of Taste." In *Feminism and Tradition in Aesthetics*, edited by Peggy Zeglin Brand and Carolyn Korsmeyer. University Park: Pennsylvania State University Press.

———. 2004. *Gender and Aesthetics: An Introduction*. New York and London: Routledge.

Lauter, Estella. 1990. "Re-enfranchising Art: Feminist Interventions in the Theory of Art." *Hypatia* 5, no. 2 (Summer). Reprinted in *Aesthetics in Feminist Perspective*, edited by Hilde Hein and Carolyn Korsmeyer. Bloomington and Indianapolis: Indiana University Press, 1993.

Lintott, Sheila. 2003. "Sublime Hunger: A consideration of Eating Disorders Beyond Beauty." In *Hypatia: Special Issue on Women, Art and Aesthetics* 18, no. 4 (Fall/Winter).

Lippard, Lucy. 1976. *From the Center: Feminist Essays on Women's Art*. New York: Dutton.

Loomba, Ania. 1998. *Colonialism-Postcolonialism*. New York and London: Routledge.

Lugones, Maria. 1990. "Playfulness, 'World'-Traveling, and Loving Perception." In *Making Face, Making Soul: Haciendo Caras: Creative and Critical Perspectives by Feminists of Color*. San Francisco: Aunt Lute Books.

Lugones, Maria, and Elizabeth Spelman. 1999. "Have We Got a Theory for You! Feminist Theory, Cultural Imperialism and the Demand for 'The Woman's Voice.'" In *Feminist Philosophies*, 2nd ed, edited by Janet Kournay, James Sterba, Rosemarie Tong. Upper Saddle River, N.J.: Prentice Hall.

Lyotard, Jean-Francois. 1974. *Libidinal Economy*. Translated by Iain Hamilton Grant. Bloomington: Indiana University Press.

———. 1984. *The Postmodern Condition: A Report on Knowledge*. Translated Geoff Bennington and Brian Massumi. Minneapolis: University of Minnesota Press.

———. 1988. *The Differend: Phrases in Dispute*. Translated by Georges Van Den Abbeele. Minneapolis: University of Minnesota Press.

———. 1989a. "Das Interesse des Erhabene." In *Das Erhabene: Zwischen Grenzerfahrung und Grossenwahn*, edited by Christine Pries. Weinheim, Germany: VCH.

———. 1989b. *The Lyotard Reader*. Edited by Andrew Benjamin. Oxford and Cambridge: Blackwell Publishers.

———. 1989c. "One of the Things at Stake in Women's Struggles." In *The Lyotard Reader*, edited by Andrew Benjamin. Oxford and Cambridge: Blackwell Publishers.

———. 1989d. "The Sublime and the Avant-Garde." In *The Lyotard Reader*, edited by Andrew Benjamin. Oxford and Cambridge: Blackwell Publishers.

———. 1991. *Lessons on the Analytic of the Sublime: Kant's Critique of Judgement*. Stanford, Calif.: Stanford University Press.

MacKinnon, Catharine A. 1987. *Feminism Unmodified: Discourses on Life and Law*. Cambridge, Mass.: Harvard University Press.

———. 1988. "Desire and Power: A Feminist Perspective." In *Marxism and the Interpretation of Culture*, edited by C. Nelson and L. Grossberg. Urbana and Chicago: University of Illinois Press.

———. 1989. *Toward a Feminist Theory of the State*. Cambridge, Mass.: Harvard University Press.

————. 1993. *Only Words*. Cambridge, Mass.: Harvard University Press.

Madison, Gary Brent. 1981. *The Phenomenology of Merleau-Ponty*. Athens: Ohio University Press.

Mann, Bonnie. 2002. "Dependence on Place, Dependence in Place." In *Theoretical Perspectives on Women and Dependency*, edited by Eva Feder Kittay and Ellen Feder. Feminist Constructions Series. Lanham, Md.: Rowman and Littlefield.

————. 2003. "Talking Back to Feminist Postmodernism: Toward a New Radical Feminist Interpretation of the Body." In *Recognition, Responsibility and Rights: Feminist Ethics and Social Theory*, edited by Robin Fiore and Hilde Nelson. Feminist Constructions Series. Lanham, Md.: Rowman and Littlefield.

————. 2005. "World-Alienation in Feminist Thought: The Sublime Epistemology of Emphatic Anti-Essentialism." In *The Epistemic Significance of Place*, edited by Christopher Preston. Special issue. *Ethics and the Environment*, (Winter).

————. 2006. "Justifying America's War: A Modern/Postmodern Aesthetics of War and Sovereignty." *Hypatia* 21, no. 4 (Fall).

Mattick, Paul, Jr. 1995. "Beautiful and Sublime: 'Gender Totemism' in the Constitution of Art." In *Feminism and Tradition in Aesthetics*, edited by Peggy Zeglin Brand and Carolyn Korsmeyer. University Park: Pennsylvania State University Press.

Meagher, Michelle. 2003. "Jenny Saville and a Feminist Aesthetics of Disgust." *Hypatia: Special Issue on Women, Art, and Aesthetics* 18, no. 4 (fall/winter): 23–41.

Merleau-Ponty, Maurice. 1962. *The Phenomenology of Perception*. Translated by Colin Smith. Atlantic Highlands, N.J.: Humanities Press.

————. 1964. *The Visible and the Invisible*. Evanston, Ill.: Northwestern University Press.

Mies, Maria. 1986. *Patriarchy and Accumulation on a World Scale: Women in the International Division of Labour*. London: Zed Books.

Mies, Maria, and Vandana Shiva. 1993. *Ecofeminism*. London: Zed Books.

Miriam, Kathy. 1998. "Disciplining Feminism: On the (Im)possibility of Feminist Academic as Public Intellectual." Presented at the Radical Philosophy Association Third International Conference, San Francisco State University.

————. 2000. "Wither Feminist Praxis? From the Normative to the Performative or the Expressivist Turn in Feminism." Presented at The Fourth Biannual Conference of the Radical Philosophy Association, Chicago.

Munro, Eleanor. 1979. *Originals: American Women Artists*. New York: Simon and Schuster.

Newman, Amy. 1990. "Aestheticism, Feminism, and the Dynamics of Reversal." *Hypatia* 5, no. 2 (Summer). Reprinted in *Aesthetics in Feminist Perspective*, edited by Hilde Hein and Carolyn Korsmeyer. Bloomington and Indianapolis: Indiana University Press, 1993.

Nicholson, Linda, ed. 1990. *Feminism/Postmodernism*. New York: Routledge.

Nochlin, Linda. 1971. "Why Have There Been No Great Women Artists?" *Art News* 69. Reprinted in her *Women, Art, and Power and Other Essays*. New York: Harper and Row, 1988.

Nussbaum, Martha C. 1992. "Human Functioning and Social Justice: In Defense of Aristotelian Essentialism." *Political Theory* 20, no. 2 (May): 202–46.

Owens, Craig. 1983. "The Discourse of Others: Feminists and Postmodernism." In *The Anti-Aesthetic: Essays on Postmodern Culture*, edited by Hal Foster. Port Townsend, Wash.: Bay Press.

Patchesky, Rosalind. 1979. "Dissolving the Hyphen: A Report on Marxist-Feminist Groups 1–5." In *Capitalist Patriarchy and the Case for Socialist Feminism*, edited by Zillah R. Eisenstein. New York and London: Monthly Review Press.

Petersen, Karen, and J. J. Wilson. 1976. *Women Artists: Recognition and Reappraisal*. New York: Harper and Row.

Pillow, Kirk. 2000. *Sublime Understanding: Aesthetic Reflection in Kant and Hegel.* Cambridge, Mass., and London: MIT Press.

Pries, Christine, ed. 1989. *Das Erhabene: Zwischen Grenzerfahrung und Grossenwahn.* Weinheim, Germany: VCH.

Raven, Arlene, Cassandra L. Langer, and Joanna Frueh. 1988. *Feminist Art Criticism: An Anthology.* Ann Arbor and London: University of Michigan Research Press.

Roland Martin, Jane. 1994. "Methodological Essentialism, False Difference, and Other Dangerous Traps." *Signs* 19, no 3: 630–57.

Said, Edward. 1978. *Orientalism.* New York: Vintage Books.

Sargent, Lydia, ed. 1981. *Women and Revolution: A Discussion of the Unhappy Marriage of Marxism and Feminism.* Boston: South End Press.

Sawicki, Jana. 1988. "Identity Politics and Sexual Freedom: Foucault and Feminism." In *Feminism and Foucault: Reflections on Resistance,* edited by Irene Diamond and Lee Quinby. Boston: Northeastern University Press.

Schor, Naomi. 1987. *Reading in Detail: Aesthetics and the Feminine.* New York: Methuen Publishing.

Schor, Naomi, and Elizabeth Weed. 1994. *The Essential Difference.* Bloomington: Indiana University Press.

Schott, Robin May, 1988. *Cognition and Eros: A Critique of the Kantian Paradigm.* Boston: Beacon Press.

———, ed. 1997. *Feminist Interpretations of Immanuel Kant.* University Park: Pennsylvania State University Press.

Schröder, Hannelore. 1997. "Kant's Patriarchal Order," translated by Rita Gircour. In *Feminist Interpretations of Immanuel Kant,* edited by Robin May Schott. University Park: Pennsylvania State University Press.

Schutte, Ofelia. 2002. "Dependency Work, Women, and the Global Economy." In *The Subject of Care: Feminist Perspectives on Dependency,* edited by Eva Feder Kittay and Ellen Feder. Lanham, Md.: Rowman and Littlefield.

Simpson, Lorenzo. 1995. *Technology, Time, and the Conversations of Modernity.* New York: Routledge.

Soja, Edward W. 1989. *Postmodern Geographies: The Reassertion of Space in Critical Social Theory.* London: Verso.

Soper, Kate. 1995. *What is Nature?* Oxford and Cambridge: Blackwell Publishers.

Spelman, Elizabeth. 1988. *Inessential Woman: Problems of Exclusion in Feminist Thought.* Boston: Beacon Press.

Spivak, Gayatri. 1994. "In a Word: Interview." In *The Essential Difference,* edited by Naomi Schor and Elizabeth Weed. Bloomington: Indiana University Press.

Stannard, David. 1992. *American Holocaust: The Conquest of the New World.* New York: Oxford University Press.

Sullivan, Maureen. 1998. "Who's Zoomin' Who? Feminism, Pedagogic Porn, and Auto-Essentialism." Presented at Locating Feminism: The Education of a Generation Conference, Duke University Women's Studies Program Lecture Series.

Sutherland, Ann Harris and Linda Nochlin. 1976. *Women Artists: 1550–1950.* New York: Knopf.

Thompson, Denise. 1996. "The Self-contradiction of 'Post-modernist' Feminism." In *Radically Speaking: Feminism Reclaimed,* edited by Diane Bell and Renate Klein. North Melbourne, Australia: Spinifex Press.

Todorov, Tzvetan. 1984. *The Conquest of America: The Question of the Other.* Translated by Richard Howard. New York: Harper and Row.

Tufts, Eleanor. 1974. *Our Hidden Heritage: Five Centuries of Women Artists*. New York and London: Paddington Press.

Turner, Fredrick. 1980. *Beyond Geography: The Western Spirit Against the Wilderness*. New York: Viking Press.

Ullman, Harlan K., and James P. Wade. 1996. *Shock and Awe: Achieving Rapid Dominance*. Washington, D.C.: National Defense University Press.

Warren, Karen J., ed. *Ecofeminism: Women, Culture, Nature*. Bloomington and Indianapolis: Indiana University Press.

Waters, Kristin. 1996. "(Re)turning to the Modern: Radical Feminism and the Post-modern Turn." In *Radically Speaking: Feminism Reclaimed*, edited by Diane Bell and Renate Klein. North Melbourne, Australia: Spinifex Press.

Weedon, Chris. 1987. *Feminist Practice and Poststructuralist Theory*. Oxford: Blackwell Publishers.

Weinbaum, Batya. 1978. *The Curious Courtship of Women's Liberation and Socialism*. Boston: South End Press.

Williams, Linda. 1989. *Hard Core: Power, Pleasure, and the "Frenzy of the Visible."* Berkeley: University of California Press.

Wiseman, Mary Bittner. 1993. "Beautiful Exiles." In *Aesthetics in Feminist Perspective*, edited by Carolyn Korsmeyer and Hilde Hein. Bloomington and Indianapolis: Indiana University Press.

Wittig, Monique. 1975. *The Lesbian Body*. Translated by David Le Vay. New York: Avon Books.

———. 1988. "One is not Born a Woman." In *For Lesbians Only: A Separatist Anthology*, edited by Sarah Lucia Hoagland and Julia Penelope. London: Onlywoman Press.

———. 1992. *The Straight Mind and Other Essays*. Boston: Beacon Press.

Wollstonecraft, Mary. 1986. *A Vindication of the Rights of Woman*. New York: Penguin Books.

Zack, Naomi. 2005. *Inclusive Feminism: A Third Wave Theory of Women's Commonality*. Lanham, Md.: Rowman and Littlefield.

Zammito, John H. 1992. *The Genesis of Kant's Critique of Judgment*. Chicago and London: University of Chicago Press.

Žižek, Slavoj. 1989. *The Sublime Object of Ideology*. London: Verson.

Index

3714 025